Simple & Free

Simple & Free

7 Experiments Against Excess

PREVIOUS EDITION PUBLISHED AS 7

JEN HATMAKER

CONVERGENT
NEW YORK

Published in the United States by Convergent Books, an imprint of Random House, a division of Penguin Random House LLC, New York.

CONVERGENT BOOKS is a registered trademark and its C colophon is a trademark of Penguin Random House LLC.

Originally published in significantly different form under the title *7: An Experimental Mutiny Against Excess* in the United States by LifeWay Press, Nashville, in 2012, and subsequently self-published in 2017.

Hardback ISBN 978-0-593-23676-5
Ebook ISBN 978-0-593-23677-2

PRINTED IN THE UNITED STATES OF AMERICA ON ACID-FREE PAPER

crownpublishing.com

2 4 6 8 9 7 5 3 1

2021 Convergent Books Edition

Design by Elizabeth Rendfleisch

For Jesus, who lived so lightly on this earth,
He didn't even have a place to lay His head.
I want so deeply to be like You.

SIMPLE & FREE . . . SEVEN YEARS LATER

Welcome! Welcome to this story, Risk Takers, Trouble Makers, Rule Breakers, Status Quo Upenders, World Changers, Question Askers, Rabble Rousers. I'm guessing you fit in at least one of those categories or you wouldn't be interested in a story like this one. Something is under your skin. Something feels . . . off—about how much you have, how much you spend, how much you waste. Maybe it is all completely undefined, as it was for me when I first began this adventure seven years ago. Or maybe you are just munching popcorn and here for the free show.

Either way, I couldn't be happier to welcome you into a little social experiment that changed our lives for good. I can say that now, because although this specific season is in my rearview mirror, as I read back through every word recorded during Simple & Free (formerly 7), I was surprised how many ideas were new to me then, because they are the air we breathe today. Let that be good news to you: No matter if anything you read here seems too hard or too crazy or *too overwhelming, maybe it will just be Step One into a new idea. And in seven years, you'll discover an assimilation so deeply embedded in your life, you won't even remember not thinking that way.*

Also, you may say in seven years: I'm glad that part is over. Let's just be honest. *Eating the same seven foods for four weeks is bananas (a food item I sadly did not partake of during that month). What we learned during and since* Simple & Free *was that the mechanics of it all were temporary but the lessons were permanent. And that is exactly why I am glad you are here.*

Let me tell you what is different now from when I first wrote Simple & Free. *This will be obvious if you've followed along with me since, but we had only three kids at the onset of this experiment. During the last month of* Simple & Free, *"Stress," we were matched with Ben and Remy, our two youngest, adopted children from Ethiopia. We brought them home the year after* Simple & Free *was over. So now we have five kids, and they are such a normal, treasured part of our family now, I can't even remember before. In fact, I felt something close to sadness going back through* Simple & Free *because Ben and Remy weren't here for it. Shared memories before they joined our family are bittersweet, yet still precious, because those years count too, but with the reverse knowledge that our little crew was incomplete. (But I'll tell you right now that Ben Hatmaker would have had exactly none of Food Month. He'd have moved in with my parents. That boy loves food.)*

Life has also gotten a bit bigger and more public, which has made it a touch lonelier than I like. And there are certainly way more of you now, but that has been a joy, not a burden. I've seen more of the world since, too; I got my very first passport during the writing of Simple & Free. We've been to Africa a dozen times now, and even though I mentioned in the Intro that I'd never been to Italy, I literally returned from there two days ago, after taking the trip of a lifetime with Council Members Jenny and Shonna and their husbands. I've fallen hard for the world, you guys. It is beautiful and marvelous, and it has much to teach us on living simply, living well, living smaller, slowing down. There is nothing like trying to visit a store in Spain around 1:00 P.M. and finding it closed for a siesta until 3:00, the owner having coffee with friends or a nap, lost profits be damned. The world has been my best teacher since the completion of Simple & Free, a continuing education program that awes me.

Other than that, we are still at our beloved Austin New Church. I still have the same friends you'll read about. We still retreat at my mom and dad's ranch every Thanksgiving. (Oh! One other new development: Dad put a double-wide trailer on the ranch so we are no longer sleeping on forty-year-old sofas in the barn. See Day 26 in the last section. We're fancy now.) We still eat pretty clean except when we don't. We still protect the Sabbath pretty fiercely, although we observe it on Sundays, the only true day of rest in our weird life with our weird schedule. I still live in Buda, Texas, just south of Austin, although we moved into a 1908 farmhouse four minutes away that we remodeled on HGTV, which I don't have time to explain here because what in the world.

I still love Jesus so much and believe in this life He asked us to live. I think He knew what He was talking about when He told us to not store up too many treasures on this earth *but to live well and love well, because as it turns out, that is what matters more than anything. And listen, Jesus has seen us through some suffering in the last seven years— real, desperate, unexpected pain—so I believe Him more than ever. He is exactly who He said He is, and when liter- ally everything you hold dear falls away, Jesus remains. So yeah, I'm still all in here.*

On Day 15 of Month Four, I wrote: "I giggle to imagine what 2017 Jen would come back to teach me; I don't even know what I don't know." I love that I wrote that. I love that I decided to be a lifelong learner who is less attached to cer- tainty and being right and more interested in paying atten- tion and developing. One thing the 2017 Jen would say to the 2010 Jen who originally experienced Simple & Free *is this: Number one, use sunscreen. I'm serious. You are in your final days of irresponsible sunning with no consequences. But number two, this weirdo little life you are constructing where you follow Jesus to strange places doing bizarre things and taking risks is all worth it. Every day of it. It only gets more exciting and meaningful. When God asks you to do something, do it. He is such a trustworthy leader. Don't be afraid. You've put all your chips on the right number.*

I am delighted you are here, reader. As I've said a thou- sand times since, Simple & Free *is not a template. It is not a list of rules. It is not a program. It is simply an imperfect social experiment to help us find God in an overcrowded, overindulged, overscheduled life. And it did. If any word, any sentence, any section you read helps you cut through the chaos and simplify down to something meaningful, I will count it nothing but a privilege that I was able to walk alongside you in some small way. This has absolutely noth-*

ing to do with rules or guilt and everything to do with free-dom.

> *Much, much love to you, dear reader.*
> *Welcome to the* Simple & Free *experiment.*
>   *Jen*

SIMPLE & FREE . . . TEN YEARS LATER

I was at Tray and Jenny's last night along with Shonna and Trace, and we decided at 10:30 P.M. that we needed suste-nance in the form of thin-crust pepperoni and jalapeño Domino's pizza. If I could paint my feelings about this exact pizza, well, it would look like a middle-aged lady stuffing her mouth hole with forty of its exquisite little squares. The crunchy cracker crust, the spicy jalapeños and pepperonis, the dousing of red pepper flakes and Parmesan . . . this is possibly my favorite food. I loaded up my plate with chain-store pizza at nearly midnight, a bastion of good choices, and without really meaning to, my inside voice looked at my pizza and whispered out loud accidentally: "I just can't quit you." (This was met with mockery from my friends, which is a very fair response. I'll allow it.)

Of all my writing projects, Simple & Free *is my thin-crust Domino's pizza. I just can't quit it. I keep going back to it, learning from it, revisiting it, reworking it. It keeps having more to say. It keeps meaning something. Shockingly, it keeps serving my community. Evidently, there is more to evaluate when it comes to excess and consumerism, care-lessness, and an unchecked plunder of the earth. I'm also learning, ten years later, that there are seasons of restraint, layers and levels of growth that unfold over time. What I understood in 2010 is a fraction of what I know now, a fraction of what I've experienced since. There is nothing wrong with this. I feel tender toward 2010 me. She was learning.*

Like Teddy Roosevelt famously said: "It is not the critic who counts; not the man who points out how the strong man stumbles, or where the doer of deeds could have done them better. The credit belongs to the man who is actually in the arena, whose face is marred by dust and sweat and blood; who strives valiantly; who errs, who comes short again and again, because there is no effort without error and shortcoming; but who does actually strive to do the deeds."[1]

So, a very brief word to the new Simple & Free *readers here, specifically those for whom these ideas are incredibly stretching or fairly new: You are in the arena! As I mentioned,* Simple & Free *changed my life, but it was a wobbly hot mess in real time, which you will shortly discover. I am no longer interested in opinions from the cheap seats. This is how we learn. This is how we grow. We start . . . somewhere. Are there people far, far ahead of us already? Um, yes. Will we be cringey or awkward or clueless? Also, yes. Will we look back ten years later and be shocked at what shocked us then? Probably. But the alternative is looking back and realizing we never moved at all; we are still standing in the exact same spot. The arena was too daunting. We lost a decade.*

Could the doer of deeds have done better here? Of course, she could have. I was learning literally as I was writing. Additionally, my life has changed in irreversible ways since

2010, and thus, I look back on Simple & Free *now and see tons of places where I was indeed cringey, awkward, and clueless. Instead of editing it all out, I decided to leave it in and rather [insert bracketed updates] when I want to go back and teach 2010 Jen something about what she wrote; something she didn't understand or hadn't learned or needlessly offended by writing. This is a better approach to take as a leader than just deleting the words that didn't hold up as if I never wrote them. I'll show you what I've learned, and I ask for your grace.* Simple & Free *was the beginning of my education, not the end.*

Finally, I wish I could bundle up all your Simple & Free *stories I've collected over the last decade. This little book created some monumental changes in its readers' lives. Mega-movements. God did stuff with this message that completely transcended the capacity of its content. You moved to other countries. You fostered and adopted. You started churches. You started nonprofits. You overhauled your financials and gave stuff away. You downsized. You served your communities in fantastical ways. I mean, let's be honest, I wrote one whole entry on missing Starbucks coffee. Let's not imagine I was some muse here. The* Simple & Free *community turned out to be pretty spectacular. I will treasure your stories for the rest of my life.*

New readers, welcome. Who knows what Simple & Free *will look like in your little corner of the world? I look forward to finding out right alongside of you. I am delighted you are here. Welcome to the arena.*

With such love,

Jen

CONTENTS

INTRODUCTION

This is all Susana's fault. She had to trot out her little social experiment, Pick Five, right when God was confronting me with my greed, excess, materialism, consumerism, envy, pride, comfort, insatiability, irresponsibility, and well, there was other stuff, but I want you to like me, so I'll shelve the rest for later. (Did I mention "need for approval"?) Let me back up. My family has undergone profound transformation in the last three years. Let me sum it up: God really messed us up. We were happy-go-lucky; Brandon was a pastor at a big ol' church making excellent scratch, and we spent our money however we wanted (on ourselves). We were climbing the ladder, baby. Fortunately, we didn't have to worry with the poor because we were paid pros serving the saved. We spent so much time blessing blessed people, there was nothing left over. Besides, that wasn't really "our thing."

Then, let's see, a bunch of stuff happened, the Holy Spirit leveled us and laid our motives bare, we turned into crazy people, yada yada yada . . . we started a new church centered on justice. Sorry for the gaps, but it's too much (but my book

Interrupted will walk you through the thrilling account of God turning our world upside down).

Our adventure in relearning the essentials of faith, Austin New Church, has been on the ground for two years. It's a little faith community that has, quite simply, changed my life. Our mantra is "Love your neighbor, serve your city." Taking a cue from Francis Chan, we take the Scripture "love your neighbor as yourself" seriously, and we give away half of all we receive. We won't spend more on ourselves than on our poor neighbor. *[ANC just passed its twelve-year mark, and it has transcended even our wildest dreams. It has become a home base and refuge for so many orphaned evangelicals, misfit toys, and outcasted rabble rousers. It feels like the Statue of Liberty in south Austin: "Bring us your tired, your poor, your huddled masses yearning to breathe free."]*

A poor church plant operating on half of its intake means we rent a worship space with dancing frogs painted on the back wall and carpet that saw the Nixon administration. Our front door won't open properly, which resulted in one guy leaving during church to get something, not being able to get back in, and sitting on the curb until service was over. Our parking lot looks like it was hit by an earthquake—and then patched up by drunken monkeys. We have no support staff, no secretaries, no copy machine. Our band is almost entirely homegrown. When we needed a drummer, one of our guys reported playing "a few times in college." The next week he was onstage, where he kicked over a cymbal and accidentally launched a drumstick into the crowd. These are deficiencies most pastors (or most churchgoers) would never stand for, but we won't buy carpet at the expense of orphans. Ten thousand dollars for a new parking lot could fund a hundred thousand tree seedlings to reforest Africa's decimated land and stimulate their local economy. It's kind of a no-brainer. *[I won't update you constantly, I promise, but I am tickled to see that we are still operating on a shoestring budget. Ten years later, we have two (as in one, two) full-time staff. Not a single assistant. We do have a copy machine, but we are still running the leanest machine in town. This church, man. I love it. My dear Church of Christ friend was visiting last Sunday, and one of the announcements at the end was a meetup for "Pipes and Porters." And as I heard him chuckle, I said, "You knew what you were getting into here today."]*

But before you launch a parade, let's revisit my description in the first paragraph. Granted, we descended many rungs in the last three years, and transformation did not come cheaply or without pain. We suffered loss—relationships, reputation, position, security, approval, acknowledgment—all the stuff I used to crave. But here is what I gave up the least:

Comfort.

I might have disagreed two years ago, when having a conversation with a homeless man was the most uncomfortable situation I could envision. When God first sent us to serve the poor, every moment was awkward. Each confrontation was fraught with anxiety. In *Interrupted,* I made this statement: "I thought I'd never be happy again."

However, God changed me and grafted genuine love for the least into my heart. *[2010 Jen, you mean so well here and I honor your intention. But this is a catchy evangelical phrase that is kind of gross. Are they "the least"? Would you like to be called "the least" by a rich white girl? I know it comes from Matthew 25, your favorite, but Jesus can say that . . . you shouldn't. You'll learn to be less condescending. It will help to imagine saying something to a person's face instead of about them.]* I looked forward to every encounter, rejected service that was labor-intensive rather than relationally focused. I became a girl who loved the marginalized. I couldn't get enough of them in my personal space.

So, what used to be comfortable (being a big fat consumer

Christian) became uncomfortable; then what was uncomfortable (engaging the poor) became comfortable. Follow? Perhaps I gave up emotional comfort for a while, but then God affirmed Himself as our provider, established the vision He gave us, and taught me how to love. The uncomfortable turned into our life's mission, and we would never go back.

That said, a new tension began lurking. The catalyst was the week we housed twelve evacuees from Hurricane Ike. Our little church, four months old at the time, took in eighty strangers from the coast who had nowhere to go. We moved our three kids into our bedroom, washed sheets, blew up mattresses, rolled out sleeping bags, and readied the house for an onslaught. As carloads arrived and we welcomed them in, one ten-year-old boy walked into our home, looked around with huge eyes, and hollered:

"Dad! This white dude is *rich*!"

We are.

For years I didn't realize this because so many others had more. We were surrounded by extreme affluence, which tricks you into thinking you're in the middle of the pack. I mean, sure, we have twenty-four hundred square feet for only five humans to live in, but our kids have never been on an airplane, so how rich could we be? We haven't traveled to Italy, my kids are in public schools, and we don't even own a time-share. (Roll eyes here.)

But it gets fuzzy once you spend time with people below your rung. I started seeing my stuff with fresh eyes, realizing we had everything. I mean *everything*. We've never missed a meal or even skimped on one. We have a beautiful home in a great neighborhood. Our kids are in a Texas exemplary school. We drive two cars under warranty. We've never gone a day without health insurance. Our closets are overflowing. We throw away food we didn't eat, clothes we barely wore, trash that will never disintegrate, stuff that fell out of fashion.

And I was so blinded I didn't even know we were rich.

How can I be socially responsible if unaware that I reside in the top percentage of wealth in the world? (You probably do too: Make $35,000 a year? Top 4 percent. $50,000? Top 1 percent.) Excess has impaired perspective in America; we are the richest people on earth, praying to get richer. We're tangled in unmanageable debt while feeding the machine, because we feel entitled to more. What does it communicate when *half the global population* lives on less than two dollars a day, and we can't manage a fulfilling life on twenty-five thousand times that amount? Fifty thousand times that amount?

It says we have too much, and it is ruining us.

It was certainly ruining me. The day I am unaware of my privileges and unmoved by my greed is the day something has to change. I couldn't escape the excess or see beyond my comforts though. I wrung my hands and commiserated with Brandon but couldn't fathom an avenue out. We'd done some first-tier reductions, freeing up excess to share, but still . . . the white dude *was* really rich.

Which brings me back to Susana. About this time, she announced her Pick Five project: only five foods for forty days, subtitled "Simplified Life, Amplified God." My first reaction was "She's so crazy." (I really love food, and that will become apparent in the next section.) But as the experiment unfolded and I heard what she was learning, I became a teeny bit enamored.

See, I am an extremist. I don't learn lessons easily, subtly, or delicately. I can't be trusted with loose boundaries. If God gives me an inch, I will take a marathon. Dipping one toe in doesn't work for me; it simply hastens my return to the couch, where I can go back to my regularly scheduled program. I am a difficult student who is extremely bullheaded. Total immersion is the only medium that can tame me.

I was where all my best ideas happen (the shower), and in forty minutes—I apologized to God for the egregious waste of water—Pick Five turned into *Simple & Free*. It had sloppy edges and "undeveloped" is too kind a description, but I realized this extreme social experiment was my ticket out of nauseating consumerism. Or at least it would start the engine.

I ruminated for six months, letting it marinate, forcing my friends to discuss it with me. I started praying about what God wanted; what would move me closer to His agenda and further from mine. How could this be meaningful, not just narcissistic and futile? What areas needed the most renovation? How am I blind and why? Where have I substituted the American Dream for God's kingdom? What in my life, in the lives of most westerners, is just *too stinking much*?

- Food
- Clothes
- Possessions
- Media
- Waste
- Spending
- Stress

Seven months, seven areas, reduced to seven simple choices. I'm embarking on a journey of less. It's time to purge the junk and pare down to what is necessary, what is noble. *Simple & Free* will be an exercise in simplicity with one goal: to create space for God's kingdom to break through.

I approach this project in the spirit of a fast: an intentional reduction, a deliberate abstinence to summon God's movement in my life. A fast creates margin for God to move. Temporarily changing our routine of comfort jars us off high center. A fast is not necessarily something we offer God, but it assists us in offering ourselves. As Bill Bright, founder of Campus Crusade for Christ, said, "It is exchanging the needs of the physical body for those of the spirit."[1]

" 'Even now,' declares the Lord, 'return to me with all your heart, with fasting and weeping and mourning.' Rend your hearts and not your garments. Return to the Lord your God, for he is gracious and compassionate, slow to anger and abounding in love" (Joel 2:12–13). According to Scripture, fasting was commanded or initiated during one of six extreme circumstances:

- Mourning
- Inquiry
- Repentance
- Preparation
- Crisis
- Worship

As I write this, I enter the next seven months for (at least) two of these extreme reasons. First and foremost, repentance. *Simple & Free* will be a tangible way to bow low and repent of greed, ungratefulness, ruined opportunities, and irresponsibility. It's time to admit I'm trapped in the machine, held by my own selfishness. It's time to face our spending and call it what it is: a travesty. I'm weary of justifying it. So many areas out of control, so much need for transformation. What have we been eating? What are we doing? What have we been buying? What are we wasting? *What are we missing?* These questions grieve me, as well they should. I'm ready for the deconstruction.

My second reason is preparation. Most of my life is in front of me yet. I'm thirty-five and only six years into my assignment as a writer and Bible teacher. The bulk of my work lies ahead. My children are young—still entirely impressionable. It is not too late to untether them from the lie of "more." Our church vision is new, and our mission is really just beginning. I'm hungry for the reconstruction.

I'm ready to adopt Jesus' version of *rich, blessed,* and *generous.* He had plenty to say on the subject. I look forward to what God will accomplish in the next seven months. He will meet me, I'm certain. I'm anxious about turning the soil, but I'm so eager for liberation that I'm still willing to become weird and eccentric for the next seven months. It's the means to the harvest.

Jesus, may there be less of me and my junk and more of You and Your kingdom.

Here we go.

THE COUNCIL

I have a personality that would land me in prison without a steady influx of wise intervention. I'm something of a loose cannon. Left to my own devices, I'd be a recurring character on *Dog the Bounty Hunter*. Luckily, I married Mr. Responsible, who has rescued me from disaster more times than I'd like to admit. Brandon senses when I am about to self-destruct:

"Take your fingers off the keyboard and back away from that e-mail."

"You have that look in your eyes. Go for a nice drive in the country."

"Now is a good time to stop allowing words to flow out of your mouth."

"Once that picture goes on the Internet, it's there forever."

So, a project like *Simple & Free* sounds straightforward to you, but to me it sounds like a wealth of opportunities to hedge. I've already polished up the phrase "extenuating circumstance" to use regularly for the next seven months. What about a wedding? What about the airport? What about a season finale? What about a *series finale*? For the love of the land.

I will clearly need help to keep me on the straight and narrow.

Enter The Council. Six friends, six personalities, six chances to keep this thing from derailing. The seven of us will confer on all things *Simple & Free* for the duration of the project. They are advisers, cheerleaders, decision makers, counselors, collaborators, and brainstormers. They are my personal think tank.

When I encounter a weird situation or roadblock, these girls are the Supreme Court. They helped develop the framework for *Simple & Free* already and hinted at probable participation. Their creative ideas go straight into the *Simple & Free* bucket, although Trina insists that her angle on Month One could become a bestseller and net her millions, which she won't share. (Jenny argued that she was codeveloper of the angle and is entitled to half. I'm going to let them fight this out in the courts, knowing they will not land on the Oprah Network and instead will just advise some random author for seven months for no pay.)

MEET THE COUNCIL

Becky earned a clear spot on my Friend List with her dry-as-dry-can-be humor and self-deprecating wit, two qualities I rank above honor and integrity. Out of sheer will she just dropped eighty-five pounds and is so smokin', we worry she might go for friend upgrades. She's a massage therapist, which seems so exotic, like being a belly dancer or geisha girl.

Becky brainstormed three brilliant topics for my last book when my brain turned to cornmeal and I couldn't remember how to spell J-E-S-U-S.

Jenny became my first friend in Texas twelve years ago, when she asked me over fajitas if I'd had a nose job. Jenny and Tray packed up their life in Corpus Christi, home for eighteen years and forever respectively, and moved to Austin to start our church with us. We bought houses on the same street and started our campaign for neighborhood domination. The only Council member more likely to land in jail than me is Jenny. She uses hot glue for everything, including custom curtains and Girl Scout badges.

Molly laid down a string of sarcasm during our first conversation in our 'hood, and I vowed to make her mine. Appealing to the nerd in me, she brought notes on a legal pad to our first *Simple & Free* brainstorming session; words failed me. She has three DVRs because there is not enough recording space on one (or two) for all her shows. Molly executed a perfect herkie jump during a recent football party, which we captured on film and still marvel at with regularity.

Shonna adopted me as a friend through Jenny, and now we spend a piece of nearly every day together. When I was talking about my girlfriends recently, a woman asked, "You and your friends have so much fun. Do you have any time left to parent?" Shonna and I are both adopting, and we are raging bleeding hearts; pass the Kleenex to the girls crying over sermons and orphans. At the abovementioned football party, Shonna completed a toe touch that was so stunning it generated forty-three responses on Facebook. She's still got it, folks.

Susana has long red hair that defies comprehension; she's like Samson. She is an excellent banter partner and loyal disciple of the Texas Longhorns, so if you don't get why we became fast friends, you clearly don't know me. Susana's Pick

Five project was the inspiration behind *Simple & Free,* so in the future I will either copy everything she does or absolutely nothing. Let's see how it plays out. She bakes gourmet cakes and sews and creates handmade cards, and *I still like her.* She's that cool.

Trina was my first friend in Austin ten years ago, even though she forced me into women's ministry, which terrified me (it all worked out). She pretends to be a hard-nosed, tough-as-nails broad, but she cries over refugees and volunteers as a horse therapist with special-needs adults. Whatever, Treen. We're all onto you. If you're ever around her without a conversation topic, just ask her about dogs, beaches, or how to transition from boxed wine. She's an expert, I tell you.

This is The Council, who will keep the wheels on *Simple & Free.* You'll notice their input throughout. A social experiment of this scope requires good friends, and I have the best. Should you have any questions about food limitations or green living, feel free to call them because I'm sure they'd be happy to boss you around too.

SOME STUFF I THOUGHT TO TELL YOU AFTER I WAS ALREADY FINISHED WITH *SIMPLE & FREE*

Guess what I'm doing? Trolling Twitter while watching a Texas basketball game with a bowl of salsa on my lap. I'm wearing whatever I want, and ten minutes ago I ordered Melissa Fay Greene's new book, *No Biking in the House without a Helmet,* on my Kindle. I am clearly liberated from the confines of *Simple & Free,* which I finished two months ago. (Wish you knew what happened? Sorry. You'll have to read the actual book to find out the goods. No spoilers here.)

I started this project with some vague boundaries and a fuzzy notion of how this would all go down. Now, on the other side of it, I've collected the FAQs lobbed my way for the last year, and I'm going to preemptively answer your questions, because there is a 100 percent chance they are the exact same ones every person in the universe has asked me over the course of this zany thing.

1. **How are you organizing this book?** I wrote *Simple & Free* sort of like a blog, sort of like a diary. I decided to write it in real time rather than retro-report on each month. I didn't give myself time to sanitize an experience or gloss over it with pretty words or a hazy memory. It went like this: experience it ➜ feel it ➜ write it. So at the end of a day, I sat down with my laptop and typed, "Day 13: If I eat one more bite of spinach, I am going to start stabbing people." Or some such. I didn't follow exact calendar months, but each "month" of *Simple & Free* was four weeks long. The book is organized by month, then by day, with a conclusion at the end of each month. I took about two weeks off after each new month of *Simple & Free*. This was to fine-tune the writing, elaborate on any sections I had truncated for time, and take a blasted break before wrapping my head around the next collection of reductions. *Simple & Free* started in mid-January and ended the week of Thanksgiving. Much like my husband crammed four years of college into five, I squeezed seven months of *Simple & Free* into ten.

2. **Are your kids doing this?** Yes and no. If my children were reduced to eating avocados, spinach, and eggs, they would've starved to death before we ever reached the second month. Some months of this project were simply not kid friendly. I did not feel like answering to their therapists one day for why I made them wear the same

seven pieces of clothing for a month of fourth grade. The kids bowed out of the first two months: seven foods and seven clothes. The rest of the months were whole-family endeavors. They gave up their Wii and Game-boys, they gave away a ton of clothes and toys, they took eighty trips out to the compost bin, and they observed the Sabbath, among a bunch of other *Simple & Free* stuff. Sometimes they were delightful and sometimes they were hostile. So pretty much exactly like normal.

3. **Are you going to be bossy and make us feel guilty?** I don't think so, but I can't be sure. Sometimes conviction is mistaken for guilt, and I can't promise you won't traverse that gray area a bit. And I feel my feelings really strongly, so my fanaticism could sound like bossiness. I don't know. But I'll tell you this: *Simple & Free* was most assuredly written from a place of repentance, not arrogance. You'll find I included a smorgasbord of my own personal failures and bad attitudes, so don't imagine I'm writing from the cardboard house I chose to live in next to the homeless refugees I feed with money diverted from our health insurance. I'm so not here to boss you or make you feel guilty. I don't have an agenda with you other than sharing our little journey of reduction, and if you find a point of connection meaningful to *your* story, marvelous. If not, well, this book cost you around the price of an entrée at P.F. Chang's, and it is fat-free. No big loss. Carry on.

4. **Are you weird?** Because *Simple & Free* is weird, and I'm not sure if this is for normal people. Well, obviously. But here's the lowdown on my vanilla existence: I married my college sweetheart, and we had three kids who look just like us. We live in the suburbs and we're into church. My house is painted pretty colors, and I wear cute shoes

sometimes. I spend twenty minutes straightening my hair with a Chi I bought off an infomercial for $115, which I hid for a month after FedEx delivered it. I like my toenails painted. My kids are in public school. I love trips. I have a book collection that is embarrassing. We go on date nights. I love to cook and eat and laugh and watch movies. I go on every class field trip and bring cupcakes to school on Teacher Appreciation Day. I really, really like to have fun with my friends. I'm kind of normal. So is my family. And that's the problem. More likely, *Simple & Free* would sound weird to a *real* radical living in the Congo or sharing all his worldly possessions; that person would read all this and deadpan, "Wow, everyone. Stop the presses. Jen turned off the Internet for a month. Let's throw a party and give her a book contract." I wrote this from the middle of the American pack, nauseated by the normalcy. So did I answer your question? I kind of dodged it. But then again, weird people never really know they're weird.

5. **I need to know something else, and you didn't answer it in this cute little section.** Come ask me. You can find me on Twitter at @jenhatmaker, on Facebook (how many Jen Hatmakers can there be?), or through my website at www.jenhatmaker.com.

Simple & Free

FOOD

Picking seven foods is like trying to pick my favorite kid. Some people eat to live, but I live to eat. I come from a long line of eaters; my sister is in culinary school in New York City as I write this. We long-distance foodie talk once a week until the family gives me the "I just can't take it anymore" look. I would positively get rid of cable tomorrow if it weren't for the Food Network. I read cookbooks like they are Jodi Picoult novels.

Food is the centrifugal force that draws together my people. According to me, a party needs no activity other than eating. I shoo the kids out of my space around 5:00 every day, put on some music, pour a glass of Cabernet, and enter cooking heaven. I love to chop. I love to sauté. I love to deglaze. I can't live without shallots. Sauces, spices, herbs, marinades, slicing, julienning, rough chopping, butterflying, searing, slow roasting, whipping, braising—these put a tear in my happy little eye.

So I've thought hard about my seven foods, perhaps more than any other month in the project. I've consulted experts and websites and less-skilled advisers, like my girlfriends.

I've gone on some trustworthy nutrition sites[1] to determine healthy ratios of vitamins and minerals. I've researched superfoods and organic produce. I've prayed over my choices, and here they are:

- Cheeseburgers
- Tortilla chips
- Fresh salsa
- Mozzarella sticks
- Veggie lovers pizza
- Dark chocolate
- Coffee

I'm kidding, people. These are some of my favorite foods, and I will miss them sorely. Farewell, *mis amores*. I love you, but you have given me a situation with my pants. I'll be back to enjoy you all in moderation, but for now this good-bye hurts me worse than it hurts you. Find someone else to make fat and happy for a month. Here is my real cast of characters:

- Chicken
- Eggs
- Whole-wheat bread
- Sweet potatoes
- Spinach
- Avocados
- Apples

This healthy roll call will be washed down with water, and that's that. Don't get me started on "no coffee"; I'll begin wailing and gnashing my teeth. The Council approved salt and pepper and olive oil in modest increments. That's it. No rosemary. No onions. No oregano. No Salt Lick barbecue sauce. These foods are a good balance of protein, calcium, fiber, vitamins and minerals, and good fat. There are some decent mixy-matchy options in there, and since The Council gifted me with salt, I might stay sane.

Because Michael Pollan and Barbara Kingsolver and Eric Schlosser and all their little "eat real food" friends are in my head (more on this later), I'm going with organic produce and free-range, cage-free chickens and eggs. I realize calling eggs and chickens "free-range" can be as misleading as labeling Lucky Charms "heart healthy," but it's a baby step toward healthier food and more humane farming practices. I'm deviating from my giant grocery store for the first time, so let me imagine my birds roamed the countryside in chicken bliss eating grass and frolicking with their fowl pals while the farmer petted their wee chicken heads and gave them all names.

Four members of The Council are adopting a version of seven foods: They chose seven of the most impoverished countries, and for three days each, they are eating like that nation's poorest. During those three days, we will pray for that country and its people, learn about its struggles, and in some small way identify with those who suffer there. They will eat the humblest of food from Haiti, Ethiopia, Uganda, Afghanistan, Bolivia, Cambodia, and Sudan.

So with that I begin Month One with excitement, anxiety, and a little trepidation. As you read the first few pages, kindly take note of these findings by researchers from the University of Vermont College of Medicine and Johns Hopkins University School of Medicine: "The team demonstrated that stopping daily caffeine consumption produces changes in cerebral blood flow velocity and quantitative EEG that are likely related to the classic caffeine withdrawal symptoms of headache, drowsiness and decreased alertness."[2] All right? So nothing is my fault for the next five days, including bad writing and/or aimless ranting. If you encounter either, just attribute it to my *condition*.

DAY 1

Lemon cheesecake, spinach and artichoke dip, salsa, crab dip, White Russian cupcakes, pimento cheese sandwiches (from Central Market and can't be disrespected with inadequate words), a plethora of tortilla chips/crackers/Wheat Thins/bread chunks to shovel all this goodness into my mouth: This was the buffet last night at my girlfriend's baby shower. I kept telling my girlfriends it was the Last Supper. They pretended to still care after the ninth time I'd referenced it. I took my last bite at 11:28 P.M.

Let *Simple & Free* commence.

However, the experiment started today in the most unnormal way. My kids are out of school, and I scattered them around so we could sleep in. Thus, Brandon woke me up at 10:15 (don't hate—I did my time in baby prison and can now enjoy the occasional leisurely morning) and said, "We have lunch with that couple at eleven, remember?"

If by "remember" he meant write it down or put it in my calendar, then no. So I found myself in a bloody restaurant for my first meal of *Simple & Free*. The menu caused an instant panic attack. I'm still operating by the letter of the law here. I don't know if I'm going to be flexible in social settings or eat something with parsley. I'm just not sure. I'm a total legalist at this point. I haven't even had a chance to follow the rules, much less break them.

I see spinach salad with chicken, but it's covered in honey roasted walnuts, goat cheese, baby tomatoes, and red onions and tossed in homemade vinaigrette. This description alone could send me into the fetal position. How will I endure this kind of temptation?

You don't understand how much I love food. *Good food.* I adore innovative ingredients with fresh produce and perfectly cooked meat, especially the kind that is doused in condiments. I believe food is simply a vehicle to devour sauces. I am a flavor junkie, and my happiest moments take place with a fork in my mouth.

Perhaps I am being dramatic because my head is pounding out of my skull. Council Member Susana advised me to step down my caffeine intake for a few days before I started. And then some other words came out of her mouth that sounded like blah, blah, blah. So I weaned myself off coffee, meaning I had only two cups yesterday instead of four. Why would I deprive myself of coffee before I had to? I said I'd rather suffer through withdrawal, which is precisely what I am enjoying right now. Awesome.

But back to lunch. If I followed my food rules, I'd have to ask the chef to make something that didn't exist on his menu. Or the instructions would be so annoying that I would probably regret whatever the chef sent out to the impossible granola weirdo girl at Table 12: "Can you hold everything on that spinach salad? Can you not flavor the chicken? And can you not use the onions and seasonings and eggs in my sweet potato cakes? Is the bread prebuttered? Are the apples cinnamoned?"

Then I saw it: à la carte. This was my answer, and by divine intervention, breakfast was served at Galaxy Cafe until 1:00 P.M. Plain scrambled eggs (yes, I asked), dry wheat toast, and a side of sliced avocado. And water. I was in business. The Council approved salt and pepper, so my first meal fell nicely within the boundaries of *Simple & Free*.

I tried not to look at my friend's heaping pile of French toast smothered in fresh strawberries, maple syrup, and powdered sugar. I certainly didn't concentrate on his side of bacon. (If you think there is a better combination than bacon and syrup, drive to Austin and I'll fight you.) I chose gratitude that neither of these two fresh faces ordered coffee, and thus I didn't have to resort to violence or hate. *[Fun fact: This unknown young couple was Lamar and Jill Stockton, and this was his first "interview" to be the worship pastor at ANC, where he still leads to this day. He and I have been all around the world together with Help One Now, where he also serves on staff. I tell them all the time, "You guys are in Day One of* Simple & Free!" *and they are like, "How enthusiastic do we have to act about this every time you mention it?"]*

I also had a love surge for Brandon, who is doing this month with me, even though he asked if he could substitute cheeseburgers for spinach. I held my tongue when he ordered a tortilla wrap with eggs, spinach, and avocados, because everyone knows *a tortilla doesn't count as bread.* I tried not to be judgmental. He didn't eat the salsa, which demonstrated such unfathomable heroics, I can hardly fuss about the tortilla. It's bread-ish. And he's not getting paid for this.

Quick note: My stomach was growling at 3:00, so I grabbed an apple. I deviated from my normal cheap, from-wherever apples and splurged on organic Fuji apples. Let me tell you something: Yum. That thing was good. It was the antithesis to my bland eggs, dry toast, and avocado from breakfast. I'm feeling the love for apples. Let's see if it holds.

Reader, don't worry that I am going to bore you with the minutiae of every meal and snack for the next forty pages. I have other stuff to talk about. But it's Day 1, and the reduced menu is distracting me from (what will certainly be) terribly impressive spiritual observations. For today my head hurts, and ordering at a restaurant traumatized me. Give me grace to worry that starting tomorrow—Day Stinking 2—I'm speaking at an event for two days. My weird food limits are about to become someone else's minor problem. Can I pack a sweet potato in my carry-on? I don't even know.

Okay, back to today, dinner was somewhat of a nice surprise. Not nice like "a filet covered in peppercorn sauce" but nice like "this didn't stink as bad as I thought." I had a sweet potato and sautéed spinach. These food items are not unfamiliar, but the stripped-down cooking process was. Normally, I'd bake sweet potatoes in olive oil and sweet onions or slather them in butter and cinnamon. I love them whipped up with half-and-half and cream cheese. And spinach? Give me mushrooms, shallots, red pepper flakes, olive oil. Give me creamed spinach with nutmeg and butter.

A microwaved sweet potato with just salt and pepper? Spinach sautéed in water? Surprisingly, not bad. There is nice natural flavor in both, which I couldn't have possibly known since I condiment-up food (this *is* a verb) before taking my silverware out of the napkin. Again, it could be that I bought organic, local produce, notoriously more flavorful than its mass-produced, imported counterpart. But regardless, both tasted yummy, even though they were the not-as-cute wingman version of my usual hot chick dishes.

Admittedly, I felt unanchored in my own kitchen today. I had a cupcake—a strawberry daiquiri cupcake with cream filling and fresh strawberries I *made from scratch* yesterday—on my counter looking at me. It was strange not to pinch a bite off. I stared it down, trying to own it with my mind. I opened my pantry and uttered, "You're dead to me." It was all bizarre.

Which reminds me: I'm doing this for a reason. This is a fast, a major reduction of the endless possibilities that accompany my every meal. It is supposed to be uncomfortable and inconvenient. Not because I'm a narcissist but because the discomfort creates space for the Holy Spirit to move. This shake-up of my routine commands my attention. I can no longer default to normal, usual, mindless, thoughtless. It's like having an eyelash under my contact all day.

What will the Spirit do with this new space? I don't know. We'll see. It's His to engineer. I won't box Him in or assume I know what He'll say. I'm not going to project my goals onto His movement. I have simply said, "Jesus, may there be less of me and my junk and more of You and Your kingdom." I will reduce, so He can increase.

Admittedly, the spiritual waters were stagnant today. I was distracted by the mechanics, the launching. I struggled to find a spiritual rhythm. Ingredients and headaches sidetracked me. Perhaps this is the philosophy behind the biblical fasts of three days, seven days, and forty days in the Word. Maybe we need more than one day to push through the inauguration on to the business of communion. After the shine wears off, the real spiritual work begins.

And maybe these blasted headaches will wane.

Dear Coffee: I miss you already. We're just on a break. Don't worry. They say if you love something, set it free; and if it comes back to you, then it was truly addicted to you in the first place. Hold on to that. Mark it down: Jen/Java reunion in thirty days. Be strong.

LATE NIGHT E-MAIL FROM BRANDON HATMAKER

Dear Jen Hatmaker:

tor•ti•lla

—noun, plural -ti•llas [-tee-uhz; Sp. -tee-yahs] Mexican Cookery.

A thin, round, unleavened BREAD prepared from cornmeal or sometimes wheat flour, baked on a flat plate of iron, earthenware, or the like.

DAY 2

I'm sitting in the Dallas airport, happy to discover I've completed half a day on the road with no major incidents. I made my own breakfast, which was, well, exactly what I ate in the restaurant yesterday, but cheaper. I ate lunch during my layover, and this dawned on me:

I eat a lot of food in airports. Like, a lot. Layovers are the bane of my existence so I eat in airports or I don't eat sometimes. I walked past ten places before I found one that would work: That's right . . . Subway, Jared's yellow brick road to skinniness. *[Hey, 2010 Jen, Jared turns out to be supergross. He is in jail now. I'm not even ready to tell you about Bill Cosby. Just live your innocent life.]*

Wheat bread, chicken breast, raw spinach, and avocado. Dry. Not only were these fast-food-caliber ingredients; they were airport fast-food ingredients. Blech. The girl in front of me, possibly a lost sister, had not one, not two, but three sauces ladled on her sandwich: sweet chicken teriyaki sauce, honey mustard, and oil and vinegar. She even had the maker spread the sauces with a spatula for even coverage, which is exactly what I do (hello, OCD). I need my condiments and layers represented in exact ratios.

This is a good time to tell you that I take sandwiches very seriously. Ask my friends. I'm not going down with peanut butter and jelly or plain ham and cheese. Those are for amateurs. I pile up the ingredients: tomatoes, shredded Cheddar or Gruyère, thinly sliced honey ham, romaine, banana peppers, avocado slices, bread and butter pickles, honey mustard. The honey mustard is so essential that I would not make a sandwich should I find myself without it, which I would never allow to happen. Ever.

I like my bread lightly toasted, then I pile the meat and cheese on one slice and slide it under the broiler for a melt-down. The cold ingredients go on the other piece, and then they get married and live happily ever after in my belly. I am a sandwich diva. I eat one almost every day.

But I digress.

Once I arrived at the church where I was speaking, my adorable hostess had a plain grilled chicken sandwich for me from—wait for it—Chick-fil-A (be still my heart). [Oh man.] I'd sent an e-mail vaguely explaining my food limits and asking ever so nicely if I could stay within the boundaries of *Simple & Free*.

Insert the scenario I was dreading:

As we arrived at the church, my event planner said, "I want you to meet our pastor!" We trotted into his beautiful office, and he welcomed me by saying:

"We've been hearing all about your weird food requests!"

I knew it.

I won't be remembered as the funny author or the fascinating Bible teacher but as the high-maintenance girl who sent a list of culinary demands like I was Beyoncé. So I babbled uncontrollably, trying to explain *Simple & Free* (which I haven't done yet in under eight minutes), hoping to resurrect my reputation as low maintenance. I came across as a bizarre hippie who was a below average communicator.

Anyhow, I had a Spirit encounter later that redeemed the day. I spoke to a group of young women, and at the end I invited them to leave something at the altar: tangible sacrifices for a homeless mission—shoes, coats, gloves, scarves; or intangible offerings like a relationship, a habit, a heartache, a dream.

As I watched these dear girls leave their treasures for God's safekeeping, we sang:

I believe You're my healer.
I believe You are all I need.
I believe You're my portion.
I believe You're more than enough for me.
Jesus You're all I need.

So I stood there with tears, hands raised, trusting Jesus to be enough. As I reduce, He is enough. As I simplify, He is enough. He is my portion where food and clothes and comfort fall woefully short. He can heal me from greed and excess, materialism and pride, selfishness and envy. While my earthly treasures and creature comforts will fail me, Jesus is more than enough. In my privileged world, where "need" and "want" have become indistinguishable, my only true requirement is the sweet presence of Jesus.

So I wrote my offering on an index card and left it:

"All of me."

DAY 5

I ate a whole plate of nonsanctioned food today. I was still full five hours later. The only item remotely permissible was chicken, but it was covered with such rich sauce and exotic spices it isn't even related to my bland chicken-with-salt-only.

(Warning: impending justification.) The Council just transitioned to Ethiopian food, and they decided to experience genuine food prepared by a true national: enter Aster's Ethiopian Restaurant. Here's how the justification unfolded:

MOLLY: You definitely want to come. Just eat first.

ME: Of course I'm coming. Where is it?

MOLLY: Well, I-35 and something. I mean, come on! It's the little restaurant that faces the highway with the *giant picture of Africa and the Ethiopian flag.*

ME: Oh yeah.

I have an inexplicable, boundless love for Ethiopia, a country I have never set foot in. I've memorized pictures, I've pored over websites, read heaps of African books. I have bookmarked thirty Ethiopian blogs, which I devour with envy and pleasure. The beautiful people of Ethiopia frequent my dreams and nightmares. I know the country's history, nobility, its strength, its tragedies. I've mourned its losses and celebrated its triumphs. All this for a country I've never even been to.

But we are adopting two of its children.

Ironically, I mailed our adoption application today.

So I had a clear dog in this hunt. I couldn't miss an Ethiopian restaurant, a chance to breathe its smells, its character. I joined my girlfriends and enjoyed a fascinating tutorial by Judy Kassaye, Aster's daughter. She taught us about Ethiopian cuisine, how to eat it with injera bread. She explained each dish on the buffet, a veritable feast from the cradle of civilization.

When she left us to our dining, my girlfriends closed ranks.

"You have to eat this."

"It's a crime if you don't."

"You're going to have to cook this stuff soon!"

"We can't eat Ethiopian food before you do."

"We have Council Majority here. We say yes."

So we agreed on a *Simple & Free* moratorium, and I grabbed a plate, thrilled to share in the Ethiopian spirit and palate. On Judy's advice we took a spoonful of every dish, around twenty varieties of a few meat dishes and mostly vegetarian fare. Onions, garlic, ginger, turmeric, berbere, cinnamon, fresh lemon, tomatoes, green peppers; I died and went to flavor heaven. I'm an adventurous eater anyway, but this was a whole new frontier.

Admittedly, some got spit into my napkin. (I'm sorry, Ethiopia. You would spit out our processed American cheese food and McDonald's "chicken" nuggets, trust me.) We all had, um, intestinal issues by the day's end because I'd been eating bland whole foods, and The Council had eaten like homeless Haitians all week.

However, we marveled together and discussed favorites and surprises. In fact, everyone but me went back for seconds, because I was already in seriously gray territory and one round of prohibited food was all my Type A conscience could handle. The Council came back with desserts that looked like chocolate cake and lemon cake. When they pushed them over to me, I said: "That just looks like cake. Do you think it's uniquely Ethiopian?"

Silence.

Crickets.

"Whatever, Jen. It was made in an Ethiopian restaurant. Stop ruining our fun." All right. But I passed on what was clearly *chocolate cake and lemon cake* you could get at Applebee's.

Aster immigrated to the United States from Addis Ababa when Judy was two, but Judy didn't join her until she was nine. In so many ways she was like the children we're adopting: changing countries in elementary school, joining parents who were basically strangers, starting over with Ethiopia cemented in her blood, her language, her heart.

"Judy? I'm adopting children from Ethiopia who will be around the age you were when you moved to Austin. If you could give me one piece of advice, what would it be?"

"The kindest thing you can do is keep them connected to their country. Teach them the proud history of Ethiopia and instill love for their mother country. Cook our food. Pray our prayers. Take them back to walk on the soil where they were born. They might push back because sometimes adopted children just want to be American, no different from the other kids around them. But when they are grown, they will be so grateful you kept their heritage alive."

At this point Shonna and I were bawling (we're both adopting and that's what we do), and all of us were enraptured. I wanted to kidnap Judy and make her be my best friend. We came for Ethiopian food but left with Ethiopia in our hearts. Plus, I bought a pound of Ethiopian coffee beans and a hand-painted mug Aster made. It will be the first thing I enjoy twenty-five days from now, butwhoiscountingnotmeofcourse.

I came home floating.

Cut to dinner.

I made the kids breaded fish fillets, baked and crispy, which they have eaten a thousand times. I put a few goodies on the side (my seven-year-old, Caleb, loves "cold broccoli," which I consider a parenting victory and might mention on my adoption paperwork). Since we had finished our chicken and spinach, I ran upstairs to do something terrifically exciting like sorting laundry or washing it or drying it or folding it or putting it away. (Jealous?) I came down five minutes later to find all three kids in the living room.

"Did you finish eating already?"

"Yes."

"Did you eat everything?"

Long pause.

"Pretty much."

I went to the trash and saw five of the six fish fillets uneaten, even *unbitten*.

When the kids saw my face, they mumbled: "We didn't have any ketchup."

Maybe it was the headache I couldn't shake this week.

Maybe it was the pizza commercial I saw that caused me actual pain. But probably it was my afternoon in an Ethiopian restaurant, where I prayed for my African children and worried they were hungry and wished desperately they knew I was coming. It was probably the haunting knowledge that East Africa is suffering drought for the sixth year in a row. I wish I didn't know that Ethiopian Disaster Prevention Minister Mitiku Kassa denied reports that millions need urgent food aid and claimed the government was helping those hit by the drought. He argued, "In the Ethiopian context, there is no hunger, no famine."[3]

My children live in the ninth poorest country in the world, where 46 percent are undernourished with a Global Hunger Index listed as "extremely alarming." Tragically, the World Food Programme, which assists eleven million people in Ethiopia, reduced the emergency food ration by one-third, just when food assistance is critically required.[4] Meanwhile, embarrassed government officials are insisting the sky is not falling and international intervention is not needed. The chances my African children are going to bed hungry are so high I almost don't need to waste a line space speculating.

And tonight my kids here with me in the land of plenty threw away a pound of food because they didn't have ketchup.

How can we extract our children from this filthy engine where indulgence and ignorance and ungratefulness and waste are standard protocol? Where they know they can throw perfectly good food away because there is always more in the pantry?

I wept for all my children tonight, my Ethiopian children orphaned by disease or hunger or poverty, who will go to bed with no mother tonight, and my biological children, who will battle American complacency and overindulgence for the rest of their lives.

I don't know who I feel worse for.

"Tell me about the world before. What was it like?"

"We didn't even know what was precious. We threw away things that people would kill for today."

—*The Book of Eli*

[This whole entry makes me impossibly tender. It is hard to read. We didn't even know Ben and Remy yet. We didn't know why they were in an orphanage or how they got there. We didn't love their living parents yet or understand their suffering. I understood so little of the orphan crisis, the underbelly of adoption culture, and the best practices that would keep families together in the first place.

And reading about my very first Ethiopian experience here is so disorienting—we did indeed follow Judy's advice, and Ethiopia is like an eighth family member now. I later took a cooking class with Aster, for Pete's sake. We've been to Ethiopia so many times, we took Ben back to see his mother; it is all so much more complicated than I understood here. I feel deeply sad that the kids were suffering this year so much, in ways I know now but didn't then. I feel deeply sad that their living parents were suffering this year so much; what could help have looked like to them? My earnest 2010 self had an idealized, western, incomplete view of it all. I would have balked at this suggestion, but I saw myself as the hero of this story, no matter how sincere my intentions. International adoption was two-dimensional and laid flat on the page. Now I know it is flesh and blood, bones and heart, loss and pain, privilege and poverty.]

DAY 7

I could arguably be the Christian poster child. My dad is a pastor, and I went to church three times a week as a fetus. I am fluent in Christianspeak and can navigate the (wacky) world of Christian subculture blindfolded. I can still sing a few Petra songs by heart, and I used to pretend to be Sandi Patti belting out "Via Dolorosa." I burned my secular tapes and rebought them all twice. There isn't an Acquire the Fire, One Day, Passion, or Women of Faith conference I haven't sat through. I once wore a T-shirt to high school that read, "This is your brain. This is your brain in hell. Any questions?" I wish I were kidding. (If these references make no sense to you, then you obviously didn't grow up in the Bible Belt, or you've repressed the memories. Carry on.)

Consequently, I have heard more sermons, talks, messages, and lectures on Christianity than can possibly be impactful. I have spent half my life listening to someone else talk about God.

Because of this history, I've developed something of an immunity to sermons. Typing that is embarrassing; it makes me sound so unteachable. Teaching by example, radical obedience, justice, mercy, activism, and sacrifice wholly inspire me. I'm at that place where "well done" trumps "well said." When I see kingdom work in the middle of brokenness, when mission transitions from the academic soil of the mind into the sacrificial work of someone's hands, I am utterly affected. Obedience inspires me. Servant leaders inspire me. Humility inspires me. Talking heads dissecting apologetics stopped inspiring me a few years ago.

Like this rhetoric I stumbled on:

I have been thinking lately about how to classify different types of theology. What I am interested in here is only secondarily connected to the sorts of theological positions taken by those doing theology in any of the modes that I will explicate. The modes themselves are what interest me. It seems to me that one can fall anywhere on the continuum between orthodoxy and heterodoxy while working within any of these modes. Of course, some modes may make it easier than others to lean toward one or the other pole on this continuum, but that is beside the point.[5]

What the what? I would suggest this entire line of thinking is beside the point. I'm over this. Before I lose my doctoral students, trust me, I know theology has its place. And I appreciate the irony of a Bible student, paid speaker, and pastor's wife penning these thoughts. But when the exhaustive exegesis of God's Word doesn't create people transformed into the image of Jesus, we have missed the forest for the trees. Or perhaps Jesus explained it better: "You diligently study the Scriptures because you think that by them you possess eternal life. These are the Scriptures that testify about me, yet you refuse to come to me to have life" (John 5:39–40).

The careful study of the Word has a goal, which is not the careful study of the Word. The objective is to discover Jesus and allow Him to *change our trajectory*. Meaning, a genuine study of the Word results in believers who feed poor people and open up their guest rooms; they're adopting and sharing, mentoring and intervening. Show me a Bible teacher off mission, and I'll show you someone with no concept of the gospel he is studying.

The ivory-tower approach to sermonizing just wore me out after twenty-five years. I developed resistance to sermons because so many have been heard but rarely seen. This detachment is clearly not good. If I cannot be moved by God's delivered Word, I've set myself up as untrainable. That is some seriously dangerous territory.

So today in church, Matthew, our missions pastor, was at the helm. (A quick insert: My husband and our other two pastors are so on mission, they run out of time for church stuff. Two of them are bivocational, with their second jobs in non-profit work. These dudes are not just talking about it, yet my sermon resistance has flared up even at my own beloved church.) Matthew is our resident theologian-activist. He's the guy who reads Tozer, then drives off to work with refugees.

Note that *Simple & Free* is a one-week-old baby today. Spiritually, I've noticed a thaw. I can't pin it down yet except to describe a general softening. God has His eye on a couple of these hardened areas. He is showing me that my emotional barrier is throwing the baby out with the bathwater; I've missed some really good babies because they were once immersed in the bathwater of stale organized religion. The Spirit is whispering, "You are fighting a straw man here."

Matthew's sermon today confirms this. Or rather, my response to his sermon confirms this. After some smack-you-around Bible teaching on Acts, he asked three questions:

1. What in my life, if taken away, would alter my value or identity?

2. What causes an unhealthy change of attitude, personality, or focus when "it" becomes threatened?

3. What is the thing outside of God that I put everything else on hold for?

I sat there in a tsunami of convictions.

Rather than the arrogant, hard-edged, I've-heard-this-stuff-before reaction, I asked God the three questions. And lo and behold, He had some answers. Not surprisingly, I am unhealthily attached to the very things I'll be giving up during *Simple & Free*: approval, stuff, appearances, money, recognition, control.

That critical perspective has to go, too. Cynicism wreaked some havoc on my gentleness, my humility. When God interrupted our lives a couple of years ago, He deconstructed some toxic paradigms and rebuilt them on a sturdier foundation. However, unwilling to address them, I left a few in the rubble, never reconstructed or reimagined. The debris proved fertile soil for cynicism, as it always does for the obstinate.

So I repent today, acknowledging my reflection in the Scripture we studied: "You stiff-necked people . . . you always resist the Holy Spirit!" (Acts 7:51). That is not the legacy I want to leave. I want to live gratefully, humbly, hopefully. Clinging to criticism has not made me happier; it just made me cynical. It played a bit part when Jesus used discontentment to move me, but now it is simply baggage I must shed if I hope to carry on with integrity.

DAY 8

Hey, guess who I hate? That's right, you, Chicken Breast. I can't believe I ever had feelings for you. You're so dry, and you taste good only when someone covers up your blahness. Salt and pepper are just lipstick on a pig or, in this case, a fowl. I spent forever making a sweet potato and apple hash and stuffing it into your innards, only to be sorely disappointed by the Sahara Desert dryness of your boob meat. You need to be breaded, coated, injected, and smothered to be decent. We're going to have to part ways. I'm shacking up with your little friends Thighs, Legs, and Weird Parts Underneath That Taste Good. You've ruined my last dish.

However, I had a glorious culinary moment today, quite by accident. The way an addict returns to her crack house, I watched the Food Network during lunch. Listen, I can't quit the FN. Those people are my friends, my muses. I sent an e-mail to the Neelys once asking if they would adopt me. I mute Rachael Ray to avoid her wordy words but copy her oh-so-marvelous dishes. Giada gets lots of play as long as the hubs is gone, since I'm not all about her low-cut shirts near my man. There aren't words to express my devotion to Paula Deen. *[Oh, man. Dammit, Paula. Do better.]* I enjoy watching thirty minutes of food preparation as much as watching the kids do the dishes.

So while I dined on spinach (again) and half a sweet potato (again), what to my hungry eyes should appear, but Ina Garten, Mrs. Barefoot Contessa, pulling out ingredients for a dish that looked *Simple & Free*–approved. It was like watching lottery balls pop up while I held my precious ticket with its seven small numbers:

"Butternut squash . . ."

I can sub sweet potatoes!

"Nice tart apples . . ."

(gasp) Check.

"Sweet onions . . ."

(sigh) I can omit.

"Olive oil . . ."

Oh my stars.

"Salt and pepper . . ."

Come on, come on . . .

"And a little chicken stock."

Oh my gosh! Oh my word! I can't believe it! I won! These are all my ingredients! I called my friends and sent out a mass e-mail. It was thrilling. I emerged from food poverty with one magnificent windfall.

Following directions to a T, I roasted the cubed sweet potatoes and apples in olive oil and salt and pepper, making good use of their natural sugars as they caramelized in the oven. A quick buzz in the food processor to smooth it out. Back into a saucepan to thin out with chicken stock (which I made the day before) and cracked pepper.

GAVIN: What's chicken stock?

ME: It's basically chicken-flavored water.

GAVIN: Awesome! Will you put some in my lunch tomorrow instead of juice?

ME: You're telling me you want to drink chicken water?

GAVIN: Who wouldn't?

So anyway, the soup started bubbling, the caramelized bits rose to the top, and I did a happy hand clap. I sliced up half an avocado for the perfect topping, took a picture of my precious new dish, and let me tell you something: I blacked out a couple of times. It was soup divinity, and I became its disciple. I can't fathom how good it will taste when I add roasted onions and a dash of cream and fresh thyme. Oh, mama. Thank you, Ina Garten. Goes to show you: Never trust a skinny cook, but always trust one with a nice big squishy middle because *that* girl understands her some good food.

DAY 10

Brandon is insisting I tell you that I ate a tortilla in the airport with my eggs. They didn't have toast, okay? Plus, everyone knows a tortilla is a thin, round, unleavened bread prepared from cornmeal or sometimes wheat flour, baked on a flat plate of iron, earthenware, or the like.

DAY 11

I just got off the phone with Trina, and it's official: *Simple & Free* draws a strong response. Intentional reduction is so uncommon people just don't know what to do with it. Folks are adding, not subtracting.

We're encountering two responses. Those hungry for simplicity too beg, "Take me with you!" *Simple & Free* resonates with people already carrying tension about what *enough* really means. They immediately pledge devotion to *Simple & Free,* complete with a dissertation on how tired, broke, unhealthy, and disappointed they are with the American rat race.

"I'm doing this with you. Send me everything you have so far."

"My whole family is in."

"This is the best idea I've ever heard next to the Bible."

"I feel violated, like you've been reading my thoughts!"

"My wife came home ranting about gardening and adoption after eating lunch with you." (Sorry, Luke.)

Ironically, studies show that increased consumerism comes at a steep price. A rise in prosperity is not making people happier or healthier. Findings from a survey of life satisfaction in more than sixty-five countries indicate that income and happiness track well until about $13,000 of annual income per person. After that, additional income produces only modest increments in self-reported happiness. It's no wonder. We are incurring debt and working longer hours to pay for the high-consumption lifestyle, consequently spending less time with family, friends, and community.

"Excess consumption can be counterproductive," said Gary Gardner, director of research for Worldwatch. "The irony is that lower levels of consumption can actually cure some of these problems."[6] That makes sense: If we buy only what we need and can afford, debt becomes a moot point. When accumulation is not our bottom line, we are liberated to disperse our time and resources differently. I know working to pay off the Man and keep the house of cards intact has not made me a happy camper. A bunch of us are wondering if there is a better way.

But not everyone. I'm developing a thick skin for the other reaction *Simple & Free* draws. The Council concurs. It goes more like this:

"Why would you do that?"

"Weird."

"Don't you think this is a little extreme?" (Um, yes.)

"You're turning eccentric."

"What is the point?"

"Hmmm."

"You always have to have something, don't you?" (I don't even know what this means.)

I can tell who is going to dig it and who so isn't. I'm getting used to the "I thought you were normal but now I see I was plainly wrong" face. Maybe I *am* turning into a girl who always has to have something, I don't know. What I do know is that my "something" is a desire to look more like Jesus. I am pierced by Gandhi's astute observation: "I like your Christ. I do not like your Christians. Your Christians are so unlike your Christ."

Would Jesus overindulge on garbage food while climbing out of a debt hole from buying things He couldn't afford to keep up with neighbors He couldn't impress? In so many ways I am the opposite of Jesus' lifestyle. This keeps me up at night. I can't have authentic communion with Him while mired in the trappings He begged me to avoid.

I wouldn't dare call this reaction to *Simple & Free* persecution since that would be laughable. I'm not sure "I think you're stupid" is in the same category as "I'm going to kill you" as far as spiritual backlash goes. But it does forge a small sense of solidarity with Jesus, as He was always misunderstood for His countercultural ideas.

The least shall be the greatest.

Blessed are the meek.

Humble yourself like a child.

Sell all your things and give to the poor.

Don't gain the world only to forfeit your soul.

I can't imagine these were popular ideas either. I'm sure Jesus got the "I thought you were normal but now I see I was plainly wrong" face plenty of times. He seriously knew how to thin out a crowd. He always gunned for less, reduced, simplified. He was the most fully and completely unselfish, ungreedy, unpretentious man to ever live, and I just want to be more like Him. It's as simple and hard as that.

So if eggs and apples, bread and spinach, sweet potatoes and chicken, avocados and water can help Jesus overcome me, then so be it. I'm okay with my oddball label.

DAY 12

I had a glorious, marvelous *Simple & Free* evening.

It started with a dinner invite, although this would typically be disastrous. (When I consulted The Council on what to do when people cook for me or take me to dinner, they advised: "Don't be an imbecile.") I tell people the basics of *Simple & Free* and hope for the best when I'm not in control of the kitchen.

Sidebar: This position resulted in two extraordinary food oases this month. First, an event planner in Texarkana catered a dinner, anchored by chicken salad sandwiches. Striving not to be an imbecile, I ate it. Oh, did I eat it. Chicken and mayonnaise should spawn sandwiches like this one forever and ever, amen. Second, my event team in Columbia hosted a dinner involving creamed spinach. I couldn't speak because *there were no words*. I ate every bite before my fork acknowledged the chicken. I don't care what it is—drown it in cream and Parmesan, and, as we say in Texas: It'll eat.

Anyhow, this dinner invite was safe because it was Council Member Susana's parents, Dale and Laurel, who'd already navigated Pick Five with her. Laurel asked about my seven foods in advance, so I didn't waste any emotional space worrying about an impending evasion.

Dale and Laurel are Messianic Jews who go to our church along with most of their giant family/commune. We arrived at 6:00, just as the sun was setting. The table boasted a beautiful presentation of all seven foods. It was so dear and thoughtful, I almost burst into tears.

Traditionally, on Friday afternoon, observant Jews begin Shabbat, or Sabbath, preparations. The mood is like preparing for the arrival of a special, beloved guest: the house is cleaned, the family dresses up, the best dishes are set, and a festive meal is prepared—in our case, a *Simple & Free*–inspired meal. Shabbat candles are lit and a blessing recited just before sunset. This ritual officially marks the beginning of Shabbat.

The two candles represent two commandments: *zakhor* ("remember" creation and God's deliverance from captivity) and *shamor* ("observe" the day of rest God initiated at creation). Dale led us through a traditional Kiddush, a prayer over wine sanctifying Shabbat while passing a loaf of challah, a sweet bread shaped into a braid.

We shared some beautiful readings of Scripture together (until the Hebrew parts, when Brandon and I stayed silent to not butcher this lovely moment with atrocious pronunciation). Dale and Laurel sang a few sections, and the whole thing was beautiful. Between the communion, the food prepared with loving hands, the Scripture, and the ancient rhythm of it all, I was overjoyed.

There are many Shabbat readings available, but this one I love:

> *There are days when we seek things for ourselves*
> *and measure failure by what we do not gain.*
> *On the Sabbath we seek not to acquire but to share.*
>
> *There are days when we exploit nature*
> *as if it were a horn of plenty that can never be exhausted.*
> *On the Sabbath we stand in wonder before the mystery of*
> *   creation.*
>
> *There are days when we act as if we cared nothing*
> *for the rights of others.*
> *On the Sabbath we are reminded that justice is our duty and*
> *   a better world our goal.*
>
> *Therefore we welcome Shabbat.*
> *Day of rest, day of wonder, day of peace.*

DAY 16

Facebook status/thread by Brandon:

I'm tired of avocado and eggs. And I hate spinach without a bunch of ranch. There. I said it.

JEN HATMAKER: Don't forget dry chicken breast. I hate you, Chicken Breast.

BRIAN J: Try stewed spinach. Had some in grade school. Scarred me for life!

BECKY F: I love avocados and eggs, but I include sausage, sour cream, and cheese. Is that helpful?

MATT F: Are you on a reality show?

BRANDON H: Feels like it, Matt. Feels like it.

BECKY M: Dear Sweet Jesus, Please make the chicken juicy. Amen.

DAY 17

So I had my first *Simple & Free*–induced cry. I felt it coming on. I alerted Brandon that at some point today I would probably cry, and it wouldn't be his fault, but I might blame it on him. He was warned.

It was the perfect storm of factors. I was ousted from my house for the last three days, making *Simple & Free* adherence profoundly difficult. I've had five coffees/breakfasts/lunches in three days, meaning other people drank coffee, and I pretended to listen while fixating on their java.

Or they ate tomato-basil soup at la Madeleine's while I picked at plain chicken and dry spinach. Cashier: "So you don't want the bacon on your salad?" No. "What about the candied walnuts?" No. "Red onions or feta cheese?" No. Just spinach on a plate, dude! Gah! It still came out tossed in vinaigrette and I had to send it back. *[This sentence made a bunch of readers mad, and I still can't quit laughing. They found it wasteful. I was just following my own rules.]*

Plus, I burned my third batch of baked sweet potato chips. *I just want a snack food, for the love of Pete.* I need a handful of little somethings I can pop in my mouth. Listen, this is how sweet potato chips bake: too soft, too soft, too soft, burnt. I can't get it right. They need to be fried in oil, or just forget about it.

Then, last night, some pastor friends from Chicago were in

town for a conference and wanted to have dinner. "We've heard all about Hula Hut!" they chirped. "Can we meet there?"

%@*#!!

Hula Hut is the greatest Mexican-Hawaiian fusion restaurant ever, a total Austin icon. They make homemade tortillas and salsa I would commit actual murder just to have. My craving for tomato products is so severe, I think I've developed a disorder. I dream about salsa, marinara, spaghetti sauce, and pico de gallo. And ketchup. I feel light-headed just typing about it. Sitting at Hula Hut with its glorious salsa six inches away was torture. So was my condiment-free entrée while our friends were all experiencing food spasms.

Plus, it's been raining for five days.

Plus, Texas lost to Baylor in overtime. *Baylor*.

Plus, the Super Bowl is Sunday, and *Simple & Free* is going to ruin it.

So that's why I looked at an avocado next to yesterday's chicken and burst into tears. I just want to eat. Other stuff. All my foods except apples are soft and bland. (If it weren't for apples, I'd be bereft.) I had a nice, dramatic lament while Brandon commented helpfully, "This whole thing was your idea, you know."

I tried to redirect my emotions toward Jesus, but I struggled to maintain composure. Everything felt dark; I couldn't find center. I retreated to my bedroom and sat on the edge of the bed and prayed:

"Jesus, please help me find gratitude. This whole thing feels stupid."

It took a minute, but here is what came to mind:

I remembered how my friend Krista made a test version of her sweet potato soufflé with only *Simple & Free*–sanctioned ingredients, declared it still delicious, offered to bring it over, and sent me the recipe with happy thoughts and encouragement.

I recalled the twenty phone calls and e-mails this week from friends who love me, checking on *Simple & Free* and cheering me on.

I thought about these seven healthy foods jam-packed with nutrition, fueling my body. My energy has doubled and I feel really good. I have the luxury of eating healthy, organic food, an extravagance in most of the world.

I remembered The Council, sticking by this project with absurd enthusiasm. I recalled *their* diet as they ate like the poor: rice, cornmeal, some beans, simple breads. These girls are deeply living *Simple & Free* alongside me, and I'm so grateful.

I realized my slightly reduced life is still extraordinary in every way. There is no end to my advantages. For whatever reason I was born into privilege; I've never known hunger, poverty, or despair. I have been blessed, blessed, blessed—relationally, emotionally, spiritually, and physically. My life is so happy it's almost embarrassing.

So I thawed into a gratitude puddle, exchanging my physical aching for spiritual communion. It was a good trade. I exhaled and breathed, "Thank You."

Oh! I also remembered the dried apple slices I found at Sprouts, my favorite new natural grocery store, which I do believe count as a snack. Lots of little somethings I can pop into my mouth that don't taste like tree bark and make a decent substitute for the chips and salsa I would sacrifice a child to have.

Thank You, Lord.

DAY 19

At the DFW airport today, I almost bought a coffee. I stood four feet from Starbucks and nearly ordered. These were the sinister thoughts I entertained, nay, *coddled* for two minutes:

No one would ever know.

It would just be one cup.

I need the caffeine. For energy.

The letter of the law is not the point.

It would make me happy and, thus, a better speaker to-night.

I want a soy vanilla latte so bad I could spit.

In one teeny moment of resolve, I sent an SOS text to The Council: "I'm about to buy a coffee. I-am-this-close. Somebody help me." The texts started buzzing in.

SUSANA: It probably tastes like dirty underwear anyway.

SHONNA: Ask for hot water in a coffee cup.

BECKY: I should say something spiritual about Jesus being your caffeine, but really that just sux.

JENNY: I say coffee is acceptable. Love, Your Favorite Council Woman. (This permissiveness is why Jenny was selected for The Council.)

I escaped narrowly by chewing gum like a quitting smoker. I should tell you that every time I've been in Sprouts, I've put my nose directly on the glass cases of bulk coffee beans and inhaled like a deranged weirdo. I mean, deeply inhaled. For at least ten seconds. Nose to the glass. The only possible way I could act more disturbing is if I ground up some beans, made a line with a razor blade, and snorted it in the middle of aisle 9.

My gosh. I think I have a problem. A friend asked if I was quitting coffee after this month was up. I told her I'd considered renouncing coffee exactly zero times, and if she ever brought up such foolishness again, I was going to quit *her*.

Yeah. I definitely have a problem.

DAY 21

So, between my pantry, refrigerator, and freezer, I have around 240 food items. This is the kitchen my kids holler in about having nothing to eat. Nearly everything in my pantry is processed. We may not eat enough raw broccoli, but we are getting plenty of soy lecithin and sodium acid pyrophosphate. Most have at least fourteen ingredients, and there is an excellent chance our blood has turned to straight high-fructose corn syrup.

This bothers me.

Occasionally I come across a book that is so insightful it is a real struggle not to plagiarize the entire thing. If I could insert the entire content of *In Defense of Food* right here, I would do it. It has revolutionized my ideas about food and nutrition. This is the main premise: Eat food. Not too much. Mostly plants.

What author Michael Pollan means by "food" is "real food" that came from the ground, a tree, a plant, or an animal without messing with it, food that hasn't been loaded with corn syrup or injected with hormones. He writes not as a nutritionist overcomplicating something simple, but on the authority of tradition and common sense.

By the 1960s or so it had become all but impossible to sustain traditional ways of eating in the face of the industrialization of our food. If you wanted to eat produce grown without synthetic chemicals or meat raised on pasture without pharmaceuticals, you were out of luck. The supermarket had become the only place to buy food, and real food was rapidly disappearing from its shelves, to be replaced by the modern cornucopia of highly processed food-like products.[7]

Our grandmas ate local meat and vegetables from their gardens; we eat Pop-Tarts and Velveeta. Today in America the culture of food is changing more than once a generation, which is historically unprecedented. This machine is driven by a $32 billion food-marketing engine that thrives on change for its own sake, not to mention constantly shifting nutritional science that keeps folding in on itself every few years.

Pollan explains:

> Like a large gray cloud, a great Conspiracy of Scientific Complexity has gathered around the simplest questions of nutrition—much to the advantage of everyone involved. Except perhaps the supposed beneficiary of all this nutritional advice: us, and our health and happiness as eaters. For the most important thing to know about the campaign to professionalize dietary advice is that it has not made us any healthier. To the contrary: it has actually made us less healthy and considerably fatter.[8]

Clearly. Four of the top ten causes of death in America today are chronic diseases with well-established links to our industrialized diet: coronary heart disease, diabetes, stroke, and cancer. These health plagues remain rare in countries where people don't eat like we do, even if their local diet is high in fat or carbs, the two straw men America decided to fight. The basics of the western diet include:

- The rise of highly processed foods and refined grains
- The use of chemicals to raise plants and animals in huge monocultures
- The abundance of cheap calories of sugar and fat
- The massive consumption of fast food
- The shrinking diversity of the human diet to a tiny handful of staple crops, notably wheat, corn, and soy

(thanks to vigorous lobbying and strategic subsidization by our government)

- The conspicuous absence of fruit, vegetables, and whole grains[9]

This bodes terribly for us, and it is downright disastrous for our children. In fact, U.S. life expectancy was projected to rise indefinitely, but a new data analysis from *The New England Journal of Medicine* suggests this trend is about to reverse itself due to the rapid rise in obesity, especially among children. Our kids are the first generation in the history of America that has a shorter life span than their parents.[10]

There is a way out of this madness.

We get to vote three times a day against this toxic food supply with our forks.

Do you know what happened this month? After eating only whole foods and virtually no fast food, I feel my pants falling off. I feel energetic during my typical afternoon slump. My cheeks are rosy. My allergies have disappeared. I haven't had a single digestive issue. My canker sores went dormant. I swear, my eyes are whiter.

There's more. What used to take two hours shopping at the big store now takes thirty-five minutes at the farmers' market. I've spent only half my grocery budget by not buying extra garbage. Plus, you can't imagine how much we've saved by eating mostly at home. We're wasting less; you better believe leftovers get eaten—this was rare before *Simple & Free* because we had so many other choices. (Why eat yesterday's food when you could have new food?) More than ever, the family has gathered around the kitchen, chopping and stirring and rehashing our day.

Maybe food simplification is a good idea for all of us, and for more than one reason. Spiritual clarity and health come to mind. Waste reduction and time management and financial responsibility and gratefulness deserve some line space, too. There are other things, but that's a decent start list.

Barbara Kingsolver is a better foodie (and writer) than me, so let's wrap up with her oh-so-good thoughts:

> When my generation of women walked away from the kitchen we were escorted down that path by a profiteering industry that knew a tired, vulnerable marketing target when they saw it. "Hey, ladies," it said to us, "go ahead, get liberated. *We'll* take care of dinner." They threw open the door and we walked into a nutritional crisis and genuinely toxic food supply. . . . But a devil of a bargain it has turned out to be in terms of daily life. We gave up the aroma of warm bread rising, the measured pace of nurturing routines, the creative task of molding our families' tastes and zest for life; we received in exchange the minivan and the Lunchable.[11]

I'm hoping for a way back home.

[Since 2010, civic discussion has prioritized climate change, which is no longer an outlier concern. We now know that the earth is indeed in dire trouble, and either our care of the planet or our continued neglect will be our generation's greatest legacy. Scientists around the world agree, as reported in Time:

> If more of the world's population shifts toward plant-based diets and reduces their meat consumption, it could significantly boost the planet's ability to fight climate change. Meat, such as beef and lamb, is particularly inefficient to produce, because livestock need lots of space to graze, and that land is often space that used to be covered with forests. Lowering the amount of meat people eat

would also decrease emissions from livestock and the amount of fertilizer raising them requires.[12]

In a twist of injustice, the countries likely to be most severely impacted by climate change are often in low-income regions that have not been the leading contributors to global warming. Only around 25 percent of the world eats a great deal of meat, mostly wealthy countries like the United States. As Timothy Searchinger, a senior fellow at the World Resources Institute, says plainly: "The big beef eaters need to eat less."[13]

In We Are the Weather, *author Jonathan Safran Foer wrote: "We cannot keep the kind of meals we have known and also keep the planet we have known. We must either let some eating habits go or let the planet go. It is as straightforward and as fraught as that." A well-evidenced 2009 report by the Worldwatch Institute claimed that livestock-related emissions accounted for 51 percent of all greenhouse gases, "more than all cars, planes, buildings, industry and power plants combined."[14] Safran Foer's thesis is clear and compelling: By making "a collective act to eat differently" (he suggests "no animal products before dinner"), we can turn the tide of the climate crisis.[15]*

Michael Pollan's premise was right, and for more than one reason: Eat food, not too much, mostly plants. We have to resist the "not my problem" or "what difference will it make" narratives. We have to. American eating habits are a monstrous part of the global problem. It is incredibly possible to include meat in only one meal a day. It is incredibly possible to choose meatless days altogether. I have committed to this. I will do my part. I hope you'll join me.]

DAY 26

I've read *In Defense of Food, Animal Vegetable Miracle, The Maker's Diet, Fast Food Nation,* and watched *Food, Inc.* with my horrified children, who I am not ashamed to brainwash. Here's my conclusion:

I feel had.

I've been drinking the Kool-Aid the marketing industry, food lobbyists, nutritional "experts," and the FDA have been selling. You say oat bran is the new messiah? Check. Include in every recipe from 1988 to 1991. Fat is our enemy? Got it. Enter margarine, only one molecule away from plastic. Now carbohydrates are evil? Delete from menu. Insert angry feelings toward orange juice and other sneaky foods conspiring to make me fat. High-fructose corn syrup is healthy because it's made from corn? Bring on the, well, 10 million products it is pumped into.

After all, according to this campaign[16], high-fructose corn syrup *can* be part of a balanced diet, and these people would never lie to us. Evidently, our obesity epidemic has nothing to do with a highly processed sugar diet, but "a decrease in PE classes and other plausible explanations." (I know I haven't had a decent PE class since 1991.) Also? Good news! The FDA's expert panel concluded that frequently consuming soft drinks will not increase our obesity risk at all. Sweet surprise indeed! Dr Pepper for everyone, and pass the Oreos.

But beware of the carrots. They have an *agenda*.

Honestly, I have swallowed this whole. I haven't had a glass of orange juice in four years, but I've had no problem drinking Diet Coke, with substantiated links to cancer and kidney failure. But it's sugar-free. My nutritional perspective is so tainted by marketing I've lost touch with common sense.

I thought I was safely bubble-wrapped within *Simple &*

Free since my menu contains all whole foods except bread, but that's as wholesome as a toddler with dimples, right? Then I read this little gem under Pollan's food rule of thumb:

> Avoid food products containing ingredients that are a) unfamiliar, b) unpronounceable, c) more than five in number, or that include d) high-fructose corn syrup.

Consider a loaf of bread, one of the "traditional foods that everyone knows." As your grandmother could tell you, bread is traditionally made using a remarkably small number of familiar ingredients: flour, yeast, water, and a pinch of salt will do it. But industrial bread—even industrial whole-grain bread—has become a far more complicated product of modern food science (not to mention commerce and hope). Here's the complete ingredients list for Sara Lee's Soft & Smooth Whole Grain White Bread:

> Enriched bleached flour [wheat flour, malted barley flour, niacin, iron, thiamin mononitrate (vitamin B1), riboflavin (vitamin B2), folic acid], water, whole grains [whole wheat flour, brown rice flour (rice flour, rice bran)], high fructose corn syrup, whey, wheat gluten, yeast, cellulose. Contains 2 percent or less of each of the following: honey, calcium sulfate, vegetable oil (soybean and/or cottonseed oils), salt, butter (cream, salt), dough conditioners (may contain one or more of the following: mono- and diglycerides, ethoxylated mono- and diglycerides, ascorbic acid, enzymes, azodicarbonamide), guar gum, calcium propionate (preservative), distilled vinegar, yeast nutrients (monocalcium phosphate, calcium sulfate, ammonium sulfate), corn starch, natural flavor, beta-carotene (color), vitamin D3, soy lecithin, soy flour.

There are many things you could say about this intricate loaf of "bread," but note first that even if it managed to slip by your grandmother (because it is a loaf of bread, or at least is called one and strongly resembles one), the product fails every test proposed under rule number two.... Sorry, Sara Lee, but your Soft & Smooth Whole Grain White Bread is not food and if not for the indulgence of the FDA could not even be labeled "bread."[17]

For the love of Michael Pollan.

Sure enough, my 100 percent whole-wheat bread had thirty-nine ingredients. I counted. I felt smug about this choice just weeks ago, but it has more ingredients than the most heinous box of sugared cereal I've ever bought.

So I decided to make my own bread. This sounds like nothing to you who roll out piecrusts and can your own tomatoes or whatever, but this was seriously new territory for me, so give me this Laura Ingalls Wilder moment. When I mentioned this brainchild to my girlfriends, I had a tsunami of offers of bread machines:

- "I have one in storage."
- "I have one in the attic."
- "I have one I couldn't sell in my garage sale."
- "I have one to set out when my mother-in-law visits."

So I borrowed a bread machine, and with four days left I've made six loaves. I want to report that homemade bread has changed our lives, making us more grateful and connected to the earth. I'd planned to wax nostalgic about the smell of baking bread and the delectable, warm goodness of eating the first piece. I mean, if homemade bread isn't the bull's-eye of domestic excellence, I don't know what is. Reading Barbara Kingsolver's accounts of rising dough and general delight in hearth and home made me want to build a brick oven and milk some cows. Here is my actual report:

My loaves have been gross.

I've used different mixes and different settings; I've sliced it superthin and as thick as bricks. I've eaten it warmed, toasted, baked, and room temp. I've tried wheat, half wheat, nine-grain, and rye. My bread was slathered with baked apples, used for a sandwich, toasted as croutons, and employed as a sponge for over-easy eggs. I've tried, people. *I've really tried.*

But it's just icky. My first loaf was as hard as cement and about as flavorful. The next four didn't fare much better. Maybe the wheat mixes are the problem. There is a reason people love white, fluffy bleached flour—nutritionally void but oozing with white-bread deliciousness. Perhaps I'm so used to bread sweetened with high-fructose corn syrup and lightened up with chemicals that I can't appreciate four-ingredient bread anymore. Maybe the omission of butter on fresh bread is just too criminal. Maybe this just needs to be done the old-fashioned way, um, whatever that is.

I don't know.

My sixth loaf came out an hour ago, I spent twenty minutes chopping apples and cooking them down into a spread, only to take one bite and nearly gag.

I guess I need to call my mom for cooking instruction like I did during the first few years of marriage, when I was a domestic tragedy. I still believe in you, Homemade Bread! I know you can be delicious and soft. I won't be thwarted by my false starts, because clearly I have no idea what I'm doing in the baking department. I need to be trained before handling another innocent mound of dough. Bread will not defeat me, I say! I have a college degree, I'm raising three decent humans (and none have perished), and I haven't run out of gas in six years.

I can make bread.

DAY 29

I recant. The homemade bread is cement. I'm buying my bread. So what.

DAY 30

God bless The Council. What began as an innocuous e-mail ("Hey girls! Anyone want to come over for appetizers and brainstorm an idea with me?") turned into a group project that involved me getting avocados and sweet potatoes while they ate cornmeal. After letting this first month settle a bit, Shonna wrote her thoughts on the food fast, and I dropped it back in here for your reading pleasure:

> Fasting has always seemed like a radical thing to me. People like Gandhi fast. Not people like me. I have never really even considered a fast as a way to gain clarity or to better hear God's voice. My biggest problem with fasting is: I like to eat! I have seriously considered keeping breakfast bars in my nightstand. When my belly is empty, I feel less clearheaded, not more focused. I get grouchy and quick-tempered when I have not eaten in a few hours (or so I'm told).
>
> When I volunteered to be a part of *Simple & Free*, I thought, *Sure, this is really not about me, it will be easy!* I figured my participation would be in the support role. During the month Jen ate only seven foods, a small group of us chose an alternative. We selected seven countries and ate what the poorest residents of each country would eat for three days.
>
> There was rice and plantain. There was rice. There was rice and plantain. People in underdeveloped countries don't eat much, and when they do, it's most commonly rice.

I ate rice at home, I ate rice with my friends, I even ate rice at a restaurant. That last one got a funny look from the waiter; he must have thought that I was trying a new diet fad to lose weight. To be honest, I got a lot of comments. One friend even told me that I had become a bit "eccentric." I mean, look at me: eating rice and talking about Haiti and Ethiopia!

I found out so much about these seven countries. I was spouting facts left and right at people. When someone asked why, I talked about the countries and how little the people eat every day. I have never visited a single one of them, yet I love them all. And I yearn for the day when I can travel to each one and experience them firsthand.

So how did a girl like me, one that eats and eats, manage during these four weeks? Prayer. When I felt hunger, I prayed. I prayed for the country, for the people, for their leaders, for the children. I prayed more during those days than I ever have. I had a physical reminder to pray. I felt no hunger after praying for a child in Haiti that would be going the entire day on a cup of rice or less. I was amazed by what God showed me during those weeks.

Simple & Free was my introduction to fasting. After those weeks of rice and prayer, I knew I could do it again. And I have. (I recently finished a twenty-day fast from one of my favorite things.) Yes, I am embracing my eccentricity. When I take away what I enjoy, what I feel like I need, and replace it with prayer, I have felt that clarity.

Fasting: it's not just for Gandhi!

DAY 31

It's the last day of Month One, and I have some conclusions. The ordering of the seven months was fairly random;

food received Slot 1 because I copied this concept from Susana, and that's what she did. Rest got the seventh slot because God rested on the seventh day, and that seemed poetic. Other than that, the months were listed in brainstorm order.

That said, I'm grateful food launched me out of the starting blocks. There was no shirking possible, no viable semi-attention. Seven foods required my concentration from morning until night every day. Each meal was intentional, each bite calculated. There was no escape from *Simple & Free;* I never had longer than five hours between meals to mentally slip away. The concept of reduction was never further than my next meal.

This held me fast to the heart of Jesus.

Just as a forty-day fast inaugurated His public ministry, this month has paved the way. It's gently erased parts of the palette. I don't know nearly as much as I think I do. My riches aren't genuine. My story includes some fraud. Certain elements don't belong on the canvas. I don't know what this means yet, but the counterfeit parts must be exposed before they can be redrawn.

In *Simplicity,* Richard Rohr wrote,

On the way to contemplation we do the same thing that Jesus Christ did in the wilderness. Jesus teaches us not to say, "Lord, Lord," but to do the will of his Father. What must primarily concern us is that we do what Jesus has bidden us do. Jesus went into the wilderness, ate nothing for forty days, and made himself empty. . . . Of course, emptiness in and of itself isn't enough. The point of emptiness is to get ourselves out of the way so that Christ can fill us up. As soon as we're empty, there's a place for Christ, because only then are we in any sense ready to recognize and accept Christ as the totally other, who is not me.[18]

Honestly, I've said a lot of "Lord, Lord" without simply doing the will of my Father. My mission is clouded by a thousand elements with no eternal value. The canvas is muddy. I know the correct Christian rhetoric—emptiness, surrender, humility—but those words are meaningless until they are more than words. While my life is marked by ambition, accumulation, and perceived success, then no matter how much I squawk about Jesus, I'm a resounding gong, a clanging symbol; I am nothing.

After Jesus' fast, He began healing, rescuing, redeeming. The Spirit filled up the emptiness Jesus created, launching Him into ministry. In some supernatural way the abstinence from food was the catalyst for Jesus' unveiling; the real fireworks were next. Never again would Jesus fly under the radar. His powerful ministry was activated, inviting worship and opposition, salvation and death. After thirty years on earth, His story truly began.

> He ate nothing during those days, and at the end of them he was hungry. (Luke 4:2)

> I am hungry.

CLOTHES

This morning my seven-year-old, Caleb, went to school in "matching clothes": a green camouflage T-shirt, brown camouflage cargo shorts, and a gray camouflage hoodie. Back in the day I would've marched him upstairs to change into some Gymboree collection. But now? I'm over it. This is not the hill I'm going to die on when I have bigger fish to fry, like raising them to leave my house one day and not move back. *[All three of these children have now graduated and left the house. Ten years is the difference between a second grader and a college student. Jesus, be a Kleenex box.]*

Frankly, I've always taken my son to Target in his Batman costume and let my daughter wear a leotard and boots to church. It was never worth the drama; plus, there would always be another mom pushing a little Teenage Mutant Ninja Turtle around.

On any given day I wear jeans and a T-shirt. My style is utterly unsophisticated; I look like a college girl who rolled out of bed five minutes before class—but who has prematurely aged. Anyhow, I'm a simple or possibly lazy dresser who doesn't spend much time thinking about my wardrobe.

Clothes are just not a huge deal to me.

So, why clothes then? Why reduce radically in a neutral category I say I don't care about? Because although that sounds true in my head, my closet tells me a different story. I walked through all five of our closets, and I realized we spent real cash on every single item. I did some fuzzy averaging, and if we spent around ten dollars on each item, our closets represent an expenditure of, well, a *lot* of money. (I'm a writer not an accountant.) It is such a high total I had to sit down. Especially considering we don't wear half of the items.

I counted, and I have 327 items from which to choose. You read that right. No other category even comes close to this one in quantity. And let's be honest, most of these didn't average $10. If I spent $20 on each item, that's $6,540 spent on just my clothes in about the last five years. If the average is closer to $30, that means I've spent $9,810. This doesn't include anyone else in the family.

Sadly, I only wear a tiny percentage of these clothes. So while my mouth is yammering about my laissez-faire attitude toward my wardrobe, my hand keeps reaching into my wallet to buy more. If I am serious about addressing overindulgence and irresponsible spending, I need not look any further than our closets. I spend more just on clothes in one year than the average Ethiopian family earns in almost five.

So we are starting Month Two: seven articles of clothes. Besides the obvious crazy factor, the main wrench in the machine is speaking engagements. I have three this month. I live two separate fashion lives: my daily, one-notch-above-a-vagrant wardrobe, and my weekend, speaker-on-a-stage collection. These two styles are so opposite I've lost sleep trying to choose seven items that will work for both.

Advising me this month, The Council is divided between the permissive girls and the "Catholic nun slap your hand with a ruler" girls. Half think this month should be duplicable should any brave reader want to try it. The other half just want me to suffer (this is my assessment). So we've compromised on a couple of items.

Shoes will count as one item. However, I will rotate through only two pairs of shoes: my cowboy boots and my tennis shoes. Every working woman has two fashion lives, so two pairs of shoes is not an indulgence on par with 327 items of clothes. This still leaves twenty-one pairs untouched, lined up on shelves in my closet like I am Imelda Marcos.

Underwear doesn't count. It just doesn't, okay? Between bra, panties, and socks, I'd use up half my allotment before I got my pants on. I considered omitting understuff from my wardrobe, but unleashing my free-swinging lady self onto this innocent world is probably a felony. No one deserves that kind of visual assault. So undergarments get a free pass, and if that makes me a *Simple & Free* slacker, well, at least I'm a slacker wearing a bra.

Here are my clothes for the month:

- One pair of jeans, dark wash, kind of plain
- One long-sleeved solid black T-shirt, fitted
- One short-sleeved black "Haiti relief" T-shirt with white print
- One short-sleeved gray "Mellow Johnny's Bike Shop" T-shirt with yellow print
- One pair of gray drawstring knit capri pants
- One long silk dark brown dress shirt
- Shoes: cowboy boots and tennis shoes

At one point I was going to designate a scarf as one item, but Council Member Molly told me she was losing sleep over the scarf; that it wasn't *substantial enough*. So I replaced it with a second T-shirt, which was probably a good move so I don't wear my Haiti shirt for thirty straight days. In case you don't fully understand some of the core items I'm leaving out of life for the next month, here are a few pieces that will remain in the closet:

- No coat (it's February)
- No jewelry, except my forty-five-dollar wedding band from Walmart
- No accessories
- No belts

The Council is doing a few variations of this month along with me. Jenny and Shonna are also sticking to seven clothing items, but they are adding seven accessories, each from a different country. Every day, they'll pray for the country that produced the hat, scarf, earrings, necklace, or bracelet they are wearing. Molly and Trina are putting each item they don in a separate part of their closets to determine what percentage they actually wear, suspecting their closets are full of clothes that cost real cash but never even get worn. Susana is wearing only handmade clothes for seven straight days. Incidentally, the fact that I have a friend with enough handmade clothes to last her a week is hysterical since my children have to bring pants to my mother-in-law to sew on missing buttons.

Month Two begins with this wee pile of clothes. I'll turn a blind eye to the four bars, six shelves, and one dresser full of other garments and make my peace with these seven items, which I just realized are all black, gray, and brown. I'll look like a member of the Addams family or a mime. Maybe I'll just tell people I'm having a mid-thirties crisis and going emo. If I start wearing black nail polish and wallowing in an imaginary quagmire of torment, someone intervene.

[Reading that list of selected items to wear puts me in a time machine and zips me right back to 2010. I am there wearing that black T-shirt basically every single day. Also, why on earth do my friends support me so much? I have been such a menace to their daily lives. I can't believe they ever answer my texts.]

DAY 1

I already broke the rules. I didn't mean to. It was less than sixty seconds. We were getting an assessment on our back-yard for a garden (much more on this later in the month of our foray into green living), and it was 8:30 in the morning. It was cold and I hadn't had any coffee. I'd obediently dressed in my Haiti tee and jeans, so all started well.

But when gardener-activist Steven showed up to measure our yard and take soil samples, all I could see were the piles of dog poop my kids did *not* scoop. We appeared to be savages who couldn't be bothered to clean giant piles of feces from their living space. He acted like he didn't notice, but he drove himself here so he clearly wasn't blind. And I'm pretty sure his nose worked. As if on cue, my dog Lady walked right where he was digging and took a giant dump. I whisked the poop away, professing disdain, which sounded rather empty with the fourteen other mounds of excrement existing hap-pily in our yard.

It was the poop's fault. It distracted me.

When I went inside to wash my hands, all I could think about was redeeming myself. I conjured up a story about how I'd been in Zimbabwe digging wells and just returned and found my family let everything run amok. I would reclaim our normally immaculate house, of course, but *I just hadn't had a chance yet.* All I'd had time for since returning from Zimbabwe was preparing my typical vegetable frittata with freshly squeezed orange juice for my family's nourishment because I care about their health and stuff. That's how I am, Steven.

While inventing a detail about eco-friendly cleaning supplies, I snagged a jacket before rejoining him in the backyard. I slipped it on, tra la la. As Steven was talking about afternoon sun exposure, I realized I was wearing a non–*Simple & Free*–sanctioned item. And it was 8:30 A.M. on Day 1. I'd managed a whole two hours of obedience. Strike up the band.

I ripped it off and threw it on the trampoline, and Steven looked up with what I recognized as alarm. Like maybe the skittish dog-poop lady lured him here to bury him in the backyard. I stammered through a quick explanation of *Simple & Free,* which did nothing to increase my normal quotient. I came across as an eccentric narcissist who lives in doo-doo and lies about global relief work. And by "came across as," I mean that I am.

So Month Two is off to a smashing start.

DAY 2

"Make a coat one of your seven things."

"Aren't you going to have a coat?"

"Why didn't you include a coat on your list?"

"What about a coat or at least a jacket?"

"No coat?"

Yeah, I've been hearing this comment for the last two weeks. Maybe because this is February and my friends care about my discomfort. Or maybe these people are just extraordinarily bossy. Here's the deal: I'm not a coat wearer anyway (despite my jacket failure yesterday). I don't like to keep up with it. I'd rather be semi-cold from my car to the door of wherever I'm going.

Plus, I live in Austin. "Winter" is a loose term here. I habitually brag to my northern friends about our mild weather, and I'm certain to post pictures of us in T-shirts on Christmas morning. Winter in central Texas kisses and makes up with us for the brutal summer punishment it inflicts. Yesterday, yes, in February, my son wore shorts to school.

Today, however, it snowed all day.

In the last ten years, it has snowed a total of six days in Austin. The last recorded "snow accumulation" was one-tenth of an inch in 2007. This means that when there is a snow dusting, our schools close down, panicked Texans clear the stores, and some poor soul will wreck his car. The overreaction is apocalyptic.

My kids think a zip-up sweatshirt is a coat. They don't know about frozen snow toes. No one has gloves. They've never wiped out on an icy driveway. Snowmen are just something lucky children in books get to build. Their greatest seasonal hardship is packing away flip-flops for a couple of months, though that's a risky action since we often hit 70 degrees in the dead of winter.

So yesterday when our weathermen predicted snow, we rolled our eyes. We know better. We've been their snow pawns many times before. We know they are hogging airtime with their "extreme weather warnings" only to crush our little hearts with *rain*.

But lo and behold, the thermometer hovered at 32 degrees, and it snowed for five straight hours in Austin, Texas, today. It barely stuck since it was 54 degrees yesterday and the ground is basically an oven, but still. My second grader's teacher took the kids out to catch snowflakes on their tongues. My daughter put seven snowballs in our freezer. My middle schooler put on shorts and jumped on the trampoline bare-foot with his buddies to see who could last the longest. (Sixth-grade boys. I'll say no more.)

And I was seriously cold. I put my long-sleeved T-shirt under my short-sleeved T-shirt and shivered. Jenny, the most lenient member of The Council, sent this text: "I think Jen gets a green light on a jacket and gloves so she can play in the snow with her kids. Council?"

I declined and instead put my arms through my capri pants for reinforcement. I slipped my other T-shirt over my head with my face peeking through the neck hole. I looked like a nun with pants on my arms. With that, I headed outside, where my kids politely asked me to go back in before anyone saw me.

As always, when the weather is frigid, I think of our friends in the homeless community: Shoeshine, Red, Bridgette, Mike, David, so many others. I was outside in inadequate clothes for less than ten minutes, and I was chilled to the bone. It took me an hour to warm up and I had a roaring fire and a 72-degree home. Our church has supplied the homeless with coats and gloves and scarves for two months, but that's putting a Band-Aid on a hemorrhage. No outerwear can protect against sleet and punishing wind for long. Austin has between 3,800 and 4,500 homeless people, but only 803 shelter beds are regularly available. Additional beds are offered when the temperature drops below freezing and a few downtown churches open for emergency shelter, but thousands are still out in the cold.

More than one hundred people perished on the Austin streets last year; they died alone huddled in doorways and alleys. With one bed available for every five who need it, death by exposure is a certainty. For the homeless, extreme weather goes far beyond inconvenience or thrill; it is perilous.

I'll never truly identify with those who lack sufficient

clothing and shelter. *Simple & Free* is temporary; I have 320 clothing items awaiting my return. When I got too cold today, I retreated inside the home I own. Problem solved.

I'm going to bed tonight grateful for warmth, an advantage so expected it barely registers. May my privileges continue to drive me downward to my brothers and sisters without. Greater yet, I'm tired of calling the suffering "brothers and sisters" when I'd *never* allow my biological siblings to suffer likewise. That's just hypocrisy veiled in altruism. I won't defile my blessings by imagining that I deserve them. Until every human receives the dignity I casually enjoy, I pray my heart aches with tension and my belly rumbles for injustice.

> The first question which the priest and the Levite asked was: "If I stop to help this man, what will happen to me?"
> But the good Samaritan reversed the question: "If I do not stop to help this man, what will happen to him?"
> —Martin Luther King Jr.

DAY 5

I think it's worth mentioning that I'm developing a rather uncouth habit. Additionally, this habit confirms that I'm a lazy dresser who doesn't place nearly enough priority on decorum fitting for a thirty-five-year-old.

As you know, I have two pairs of shoes at my disposal—cowboy boots and tennis shoes. Both require two feats of Herculean effort: putting on socks and pulling on or tying shoes. Evidently I can't be bothered with this sort of exertion.

Anytime I'm not required to get out of the car, I'll choose to drive barefoot rather than put forth the effort to dress my feet. If I can't slip on flip-flops like usual, then I guess I'll slip on nothing. This habit is not thwarted by rain or freezing temperatures apparently. Zipping through the bank? Picking a kid up from school? Dropping someone at practice? Naked feet.

My friend told me, "You know driving shoeless is illegal." Okay, really? Listen, I can't follow every law. I'm not a Pharisee.

No shoes? No problem. At least not for me.

DAY 6

So today was my first speaking engagement during clothes month. I was set up for success. It was a one-day, semi-local event, eliminating the need for two days' worth of clothes. Not only that, but it was at a retreat center in the piney woods with zip-lining and horseback riding and such, so I assumed the dress code was casual.

I wore my jeans, boots, and long-sleeved black shirt under my black Haiti tee. I couldn't accessorize with a scarf or jewelry or any of my usual tricks to make Target clothes passable as event wear. As I walked up to the lodge where the women were eating breakfast, I checked the wardrobe vibe, worried I was grossly underdressed and needed to start explaining myself. (I have *never* worn a T-shirt to an event, even at a camp facility like this.)

I saw a sea of black T-shirts with white scrolly writing on the front. Just like mine. The graphics were nearly identical. It was the retreat shirt every registered woman received. On a quick glance, my event planner thought I'd snagged my retreat shirt early somehow. Ninety percent of us were wearing the exact same outfit. I was slightly fancier because of my cowboy boots; everyone else was in tennis shoes.

It was awesome.

We were a crowd of women in ponytails and old jeans, not trying to impress one another or paste on a Christian face. It was the feminine group dynamic at its simplest, and it appealed to the truest part of me, which loves authenticity. I wish women could regularly enjoy this freedom together, liberated from competition and comparison. There is something so marvelous about women comfortable in their own skin.

As we worshipped and studied the Word and enjoyed good weather and even better company, God reminded me that gathering the saints is powerful not because we look our finest or make a big production of the details but because we unite to seek Jesus. *That's* the magic. I suspect God is more glorified in a humble room of earnest worshippers than a massive production designed to sound "relevant" to the listeners but no longer relevant to God. When the worship of God turns into a "worship experience," we have derailed as the body of Christ.

Scripture describes the people who drew Jesus' eye: the poor widow, lepers, the lost and hungry, adulterers, the outcast, the sick and dying. The already dead. Finery and opulence never impressed Jesus; quite the opposite. He lambasted religious leaders for their fancy robes, strutting around as if their ceremonial dress had any bearing on the condition of their hearts.

There is something noble about an assembly of believers in simple clothes, where the lobby isn't filled with people saying "You look pretty" to one another. Maybe looking pretty isn't the catalyst for the Spirit's movement. Perhaps an obsessive occupation with dresses and hair and shoes distracts us from the point of the gathering: a fixation on Jesus. When the jars of clay remember they are jars of clay, the treasure within gets all the glory, which seems somehow more fitting.

[Because it keeps rising up in me, I wanted to add a brief word about all the ministry travel I wrote about in Simple & Free. *Ten years ago, these types of events for women composed the bulk of my work. They were primarily weekend church conferences or retreats, and I would teach three one-hour sessions plus always some other stuff. I'd fly out Friday morning and back late Saturday, depleted beyond words but home in time to get three kids to church on Sunday.*

Reading about them now has me in my feelings, because I travel so differently now. Two main reasons: (1) This combination of weekends, two-day events, and no one else to share the teaching load wore me and my family down to the bone, and (2) even if I wanted to continue this pace, I am no longer invited to these because I affirm the LGBTQ community in identity, full inclusion, and belovedness. So these Simple & Free *entries exist solidly in "my last life."*

Trying to locate the source of my feelings as I recall this season, it is primarily relief . . . with a tiny touch of wistfulness. That time in my life was the beginning of where I am now, and I couldn't have gotten here any other way. So although I would not go back to this season for literally anything on earth, and I am entirely free, thanks be to God, I am also grateful for everything this time taught me, what it offered me, and how it stretched me. It gave me what it had to give, and I received it.]

DAY 9

Council Member Becky patronized the Austin Women's Clothing Swap, benefitting Women for Women International, Safe-

Place (domestic violence intervention), the Center for Women's and Gender Studies at the University of Texas, and of course, participating women, who get free stuff. The concept: Contribute gently used clothes and accessories, then rummage through everyone else's junk and take what you want. It's a brilliant way to unload clothes you hate or that don't fit, get new-to-you things that don't require a rubber band around the button (if you don't know this trick, then you're too skinny to be my friend), and not feel like a wasteful glutton. All unclaimed items plus a five-dollar donation from each person go to the nonprofits. This was Becky's assessment:

The idea really is genius . . . in theory. Clean out your junk, shop through other people's junk. It would have been great if I had no time constraints or went when it opened. As it was, it left me wondering if maybe I really have OCD.

The website listed two drop-off sites, but as is often the case with well-meaning philanthropists, there was misinformation at both sites. So there I was, hauling my three bags of carefully selected castoffs, the ones that made the cut from the scrap pile and the Goodwill pile. This was the good stuff. Not everyone was so selective I found out.

I hauled my bags to the "sorting zone," which is code for a beehive of women trying to find treasures before they hit the racks. I asked if there was any order to this, which almost brought the bedraggled volunteer to tears: "There was," she kept saying. "There *was*." God love her.

Here are some things you can always expect to find in a gaggle of women:

- An eighteen-month-old kid, strapped via sling to his mama, enjoying a little snack from her exposed boob.

- A totally chic outfit that appears to have started from a bath rug.

- Total cooperation: I can't even begin to count how many times I heard, "Wanna trade?" as we did the dance in the ten inches of space between racks.

- Stranger commentary: "That pink looks great on you!" or "You should rethink the high-waisted jeans." I love that we feel morally obligated to keep a perfect stranger from lookin' a fool.

Not only can you see why I love Becky, but her experience got me thinking: Why don't we do this among friends and neighbors? You know that scarf you hate because the color makes it appear your liver is failing? It looks awesome on me. These pants that fit until I discovered how to mix the buffalo sauce and blue cheese sauce at Chick-fil-A? They're the bomb on you. What is tired for you might be the piece I adore. My trash could be your treasure.

Unlike my sons, who retire jeans with both knees blown out and bottom hems shredded, most women cast off clothes we're just tired of or outgrew. They're usually in great condition or could be reclaimed with one good dry cleaning. I have brand-new-looking clothes in my closet I haven't worn for three years. I say they're "old," but since they endured maybe a dozen wearings, let's call a spade a spade—they're practically still new.

Without spending a dime, we could freshen up our wardrobes and not feed the consumer machine more than it has already been fed. Clothes and accessories could be reincarnated into their second lives. Whatever isn't claimed can go to women's shelters and nonprofits.

I mean, seriously, do we really *need* more new clothes? When do we put the brakes on this runaway train? When I consider our resources, buying more clothes to add to the 327 I already own is positively stupid. That's just gross. My closet could easily clothe ten women with plenty of margin. Frankly, having thirty items sounds downright gluttonous to me, as I sit here in the same outfit I've worn three days straight.

You could host your own clothing swap with friends and neighbors and coworkers. Bring snacks, chill the drinks, put on the music, make a girls' night out of it. The more the merrier. Set up different stations: pants, purses, shoes, jewelry, shirts, accessories. Laugh and pretend you're kidding when you tell another woman if she touches that shirt, you'll cut her.

It's the smallest idea, but it suspends fashion spending that should bother us far more than it does. It's a start. Maybe once we slow the cash hemorrhaging, some buried issues could surface, interrupting our default settings and raising questions we've never asked.

And hey, at least someone would haul off the twenty items you've been waiting seven years to fit back into. Time to give up the dream, pretties.

[My daughter Sydney is, ridiculously, in college now. She is the greatest at this. She buys almost exclusively thrift, and in the rare moments she buys new, she is utterly careful about how it is sourced. She spends a little more on fair trade, handcrafted pieces and follows the supply chain all the way to the ground level. Her friends are all like this too. This next generation takes a lot of crap for being entitled or lazy, but let me tell you: They are a thousand times more sophisticated than we were when it comes to conservation, consumerism, and wastefulness. They care. They are paying attention to the planet and supply chains and their own carbon footprint. I have a ton of faith in them; I believe

they'll do what our generation has been unwilling to do in order to rescue this groaning earth.]

DAYS 12–13

Pick the worst place imaginable to show up underdressed as a "professional Christian speaker," anchoring a two-day event for a bunch of women. Let me help you: Atlanta, Georgia— a city where little girls in fifty-dollar smocked dresses romp around on filthy playgrounds. Where every freshly birthed Southern baby gets two names and women wear pastel pantsuits to lunch. These ladies instinctively understand closed-toed shoes and slips and no-white-after-Labor-Day-unless-it-is-winter-white. It's places like Atlanta where Brandon's observation becomes starkly apparent: "It's so weird that God called you to women's ministry because you don't even speak the language of your own tribe." *[Big love to my Native readers, who gently asked me to stop using the word "tribe" as an appropriation of their culture. In her 2005 book,* Who Owns Culture?: Appropriation and Authenticity in American Law, *Susan Scafidi defines cultural appropriation as "taking intellectual property, traditional knowledge, cultural expressions or artifacts from someone else's culture without permission."[1] When a member of a community with a history of oppression or racism asks you to consider their perspective, you do it. There are no exceptions. You center their experience, recognize your own privilege, and you do better. So now I say "squad" or "crew" or "people"... see how easy that was, 2010 Jen?]*

Indeed.

In the South you dress right. Their customs run deeeeeeeep, and you don't mess with them. The house where I stayed for this event sported paintings of Confederate battles in every room. *Yikes*. I didn't reference that pesky Yankee victory, old news to the tune of 145 years. Anyhow, if I were in laid-back California or no-nonsense Wisconsin, it would be a different story. But I was headed to a region where I once overheard this dialogue:

"So, are you a Christian?"

"No, I'm Southern Baptist."

Okay then.

I still hadn't decided if I should wear my nice shirt on Friday to make a good initial impression or wear it on Saturday to make a lasting impression. (The fact that I was worried about my impression at all should tell you this month hasn't sunk in yet.)

In the end I wore my Haiti T-shirt on Friday night, and although I told The Council I wasn't going to explain myself, my first sentence was a description of *Simple & Free* with a "What was I supposed to do?" reference to my outfit. I couldn't help it. Okay, I could help it, but I had a social compulsion to defend myself, utterly vain and reminiscent of middle school.

Blame it on the Deep South.

Blame it on my need for approval.

I blamed it on "respect for my audience," but that may or may not be genuine.

I couldn't gauge their response. There was some polite nodding but definitely nothing to really put me at ease. Then I remembered that wearing seven items of clothes for a month on purpose sounds superweird.

But just as quickly as the insecurity wave crested, it receded, because we opened up God's Word and let it speak. The clothes and the project and making an impression just went away because we immersed in Isaiah 58. What I'm wearing and what you think of it pales next to loosening the chains of injustice and setting the prisoner free.

Interestingly, in Isaiah 58, God is describing the kind of fast He actually requires. Not unlike people who are practicing *Simple & Free,* they were abstaining. They were reducing. They were going without. The Israelites were certainly uncomfortable, unmoored a bit. And yet . . .

> *Why are we fasting*
> *and you have not seen it?*
> *Why have we humbled ourselves*
> *and you have not noticed? (Isa. 58:3)*

Don't you see our good behavior? Don't you notice all we're forfeiting? Their spiritual house seemed in order, stamped and certified by self-denial and physical sacrifice. I mean, if we can't even feel smug about our abstinence, what is the point? It was all there: the hunger, the heads bowed low, the sackcloth, the ashes. All the external signs of piety were in place (like pointing out my reduced wardrobe to a room full of women).

> *"Is that what you call a fast,*
> *a day acceptable to the Lord?" asked God. (Isa. 58:5)*

Ouch.

Oh, how we love our religious yokes, not for what they communicate about God but for what they say about us. This is the kind of people we are. We say "no" when everyone else says "yes." We don't do *that.* We don't watch *that.* We don't vote *that* way. We don't go *there.* We don't include *them.*

But God's idea of a fast is less about what we're against and more about what we are *for.*

Is not this the kind of fasting I have chosen:
to loose the chains of injustice
and untie the cords of the yoke,
to set the oppressed free
and break every yoke?
Is it not to share your food with the hungry
and to provide the poor wanderer with shelter—
when you see the naked, to clothe him,
and not to turn away from your own flesh and blood?
   (Isa. 58:6–7)

When we hear "fast," we put on a yoke of self-denial. When God said "fast," He meant to take off the yoke of oppression. The Isaiah 58 fast is not about the mechanics of abstinence; it is a fast from self-obsession, greed, apathy, and elitism. When it becomes more about me than about the marginalized I've been charged to serve, I become the confused voice in this passage: "Why have I fasted and you have not seen it?"

I don't want *Simple & Free* to become a modern yoke because that'll only result in useless self-obsession (and that from a girl who wrote an entire book about myself already). While fasting from futile things, I don't want to fixate on them, missing the forest for the trees. The compulsion to defend my clothes to a roomful of women reveals a heart that isn't there yet.

In the yoke-on/yoke-off equation, I'm still on the wrong side.

I hope one day clothes and appearance and everyone else's assessment don't even occur to me. I would like to be so focused on the valuable that what I am wearing doesn't even warrant mental space. Not the fussy, concerned, indulgent obsession with clothes; not the conspicuous, public, distracting reduction where I am now . . . but the zero balance of priority is where I hope to land.

DAY 15

Conversation with Tray, Council Member Jenny's husband:

TRAY: Hey, *Simple & Free*!

JEN: Hey.

TRAY: Nice shirt.

JEN: Shut up.

DAY 16

I wanted to say this earlier, but I gave it two weeks to see if it held. Sometimes you draw premature conclusions about something. You pledge your dying allegiance and make puffy-paint posters and get a tattoo declaring your loyalty, only to discover the meaning of the term "honeymoon phase" three weeks later. By then you've broadcast your opinion and made a fool of yourself, and you're either stuck in the bed you've made or eating a lot of crow.

But since my parents got engaged after two weeks of dating, I figure sixteen days is enough time to make a call with profoundly less serious consequences than sixty future years of monogamy. Here it is: I'm loving this month.

It's awesome. Month Two, how do I love thee? Let me count the ways: I love the zero wardrobe planning that graces every morning. I love the teeny tiny pile of laundry in our basket. I love wearing jeans and a T-shirt every day. I love the simplicity and ease of it all.

Much junk took shelter under the "too many choices" umbrella: wasted time and energy, more pointless work, self-obsession, the ironic "the more I have, the more I want" cycle. It's helped that The Council is participating, since I see these people daily and no explanation is ever required, but still. I'm pretty down with seven pieces of clothing.

I obviously don't value clothes like food since Month One was 10 billion times harder. To discover what matters to you, take it away and see where the chips actually fall. Before *Simple & Free* started, I predicted Month Two would be one of my hardest. I was way off. I'm usually fairly self-aware, but I really miscalculated. I guess that's good news. While my closet reveals that I am still clearly caught in the machine, its grip is looser than I imagined. I might untangle without severing a limb.

Then again, maybe it should bother me a tad to wear the same outfit four days in a row without washing it. I don't know. I don't know what balance is here. I'm not sure what appropriate attention looks like.

I will confess: I was working at a coffee shop yesterday and kept smelling mildew. I looked behind me for the offender and even leaned down and smelled my laptop (my kids spilled milk on it once, so a curdled computer is within the realm of possibility). Finally, I raised my leg up and smelled my knee; it was my jeans. I had worn them not only every day this month, but also the last few days without a dunk in the washing machine.

So that's disgusting. I don't want to become a stinky girl with mildew jeans. Maybe I should aim for "mildly concerned" instead of zero.

DAY 19

Part of this month's restrictions is the no-jewelry clause. I'm a jewelry minimalist, but I normally wear earrings every day. My face looks disproportionate without earrings framing it. My head is abnormally large, and big hoops counterbalance my enormous noggin. It's like wearing vertical stripes; earrings provide smoke and mirrors for my cranial mass.

Outside of that I have a tackle box full of cheap jewelry, mostly supplied by Target. I have a couple of long, funky necklaces I enjoy, some chunky rings, a few big bracelets to cover my wrist tattoos when I'm speaking at First (fill-in-the-denomination) Church, USA. I have a few black and silver pieces from my Brighton knockoff days and some seriously flamboyant earrings. Nothing spectacular, but a month without it has left me feeling quite unadorned. And very bigheaded—physiologically, not egotistically.

So today I was in adoption dossier purgatory, on hold with the police department trying to figure out how to get fingerprinted. This, and three thousand other measures, is to ensure the lovely children of Ethiopia don't get adoptive parents who flash elementary school kids or enjoy a larceny habit. Good practices, all, but believe me: International adoption is not for the faint of heart. It's like the first year of law school, where the main objective is to weed out the slackers.

What is a dossier, you ask? It sounds so pretty. *Doss-ee-ay,* a beautiful French word, like "bourgeois" or "café au lait." France entices you with its lovely language, but "sabotage" is also French, gentle reader. Dossier = doctors' clearances, employment verification (oh so fuzzy for an author who kind of works sometimes), police reports, reference letters, fire inspection, new birth certificates and marriage license, residential history from age eighteen (you can't understand how many houses we've lived in), a "rough sketch" of our floor plan, home study with a social worker, proof of pet vaccinations, health insurance documents, a picture album, passports, essays, fifty other forms . . . all notarized and less than six months old, or—you guessed it—redo.

This is where my head is.

Trying to determine if we needed a state background check

or state *and* federal, the lady at the police department asked, "Do you have a fast pass?" which I've never once heard of; then she put me on hold. This was the crazy-eyed state of mind I was in when Brandon got home. Just as I was cut off after all that, Brandon redeemed the day.

What you need to understand is that my husband is an exceptional gift giver. This is his thing. Everyone knows it. Giving is Brandon's love language; he waits for the actual day to give his present around 13 percent of the time. He tracks down the most meaningful, exactly right gifts for me all the time; it's almost embarrassing.

So he sat down with a big ol' grin, holding a cutesy bag, and said: "I've had the worst day, but this *finally* came in the mail, and my day turned around. I've been dying to give this to you."

I mean, seriously.

Out pops a gorgeous handcrafted silver necklace in the shape of Africa, "hope" engraved across the front, "Ethiopia" the back. People, he found it on *Etsy*, handmade vintage online marketplace. (After I posted its picture on Facebook, Susana commented: "You got a man who knows 'bout Etsy? What?")

After a day of adoption labor and "Please hold" and phone calls and paperwork, I was reminded why this is worth it with one beautiful necklace. I cried, of course, which is part of his reward. You better believe I slipped it on quick as greased lightning, rules shmules.

Completing "meaningful necklace day," two hours later Susana surprised me during Sewing Night (tomorrow's gem) with precious Etsy gift 2: a long necklace sporting an old-fashioned typewriter key. The chosen key?

7.

Slipped it on, quick as greased lightning. What dear people are in my life.

My Ethiopia necklace reminded me it's not about the maddening paperwork; it's about two babies waiting for a home. *[As you will soon learn, 2010 Jen, they had homes. They had parents. Their families did not have resources. You'll spend the next decade supporting a business empowerment program in Ethiopia so that families won't be separated in the first place. Ben's mother will be one of the first graduates.]* My 7 necklace reminded me it's not about adorning myself for attention; it's about simplifying for God's glory.

I plan on wearing them both every day, and if you don't like it, you can call me a Heinous Breaker of Rules. But they tell of the things that matter, that count, that are lasting and lovely. They represent people who love me and don't think I'm crazy for adopting children 4 and 5 from an impoverished country or wearing seven pieces of clothing for a month. Sometimes life feels lonely and radical; my necklaces remind me I am neither.

Rather, I belong to a husband and faith community who embrace the grave challenges of the gospel and shore up my defenses. They inspire me. They travel with me. Remarkable, courageous people surround me. I am honored to be on mission with such extraordinary saints. While my stuff is decreasing, what matters is increasing in equal measure.

Plus, my necklaces are suuuuuper cute, so I'll just have that cake and eat it too. I can't help it if my husband and friend have great taste.

DAY 20

Susana volunteered to host a sewing tutorial to demonstrate it is possible to buy fabric and run it through a serger and create something. We were below-average students, but oh did we laugh. Our evening kicked off with an honorary clip from

Pretty in Pink, drawing inspiration from Molly Ringwald and reviving our crushes on Blane. Then we laughed some more. In the end we were seamstresses, I tell you.

Susana, our muse, captured the evening:

Tables were set up, snacks laid out, fabric, scissors, pins, extra bobbins, and measuring tapes properly placed, and sewing machines ready. My kids were miraculously asleep by 7:45 P.M., fun music was streaming on the stereo, and my house gleamed from its first professional housecleaning *ever*. (Thanks, Mom!)

I had been wearing my handmade clothes all week but saved my favorite item for this day: an exactingly tailored khaki and cream A-line skirt with orange piping and beautifully detailed exterior pockets, like a retro diner uniform. Oh, you know. Something I just threw together one day.

I patiently awaited my six pupils for the evening and checked my hair in the mirror. I made sure my phone was set to "loud" and checked e-mail to ensure no one needed directions.

Stop right here. Let me assure you I'm not a Type A. I'm normally unpolished, unorganized, laid-back, and easy. I like messy crafts, chaotic afternoons with children and dirt, and big kitchen messes. But if my biological makeup were faintly Type A, that teeny tiny, anal-retentive chromosome would have teeny tiny letters that read "punctual."

And everyone was late.

Twenty minutes late.

"Susana, we're so sorry. We feel like total jerks."

"No. Come in! I'm just glad you're here!" (Jerks.)

But resentment lasted thirty seconds, because when you're with such amazing, hilarious women, well, it's hard to hold a grudge. So we sewed. And laughed.

"Come here. Show me again."

"Fix it!"

"Hers looks better than mine."

"Susana, the thingie keeps getting stuck in the thingie!"

Wait, what?

Shonna wanted to give up first: "The machine keeps breaking." Jenny kept fixing it while Shonna went on to break the next machine. Then she'd go back to the first, and Jenny would fix the second. This cycle continued for some time.

And then there was quiet, confident Trina. Everyone insisted her purse wouldn't work. She had the wrong fabric. She cut her pieces askew. The seams didn't match up. What's this extra thing you've got hanging here? But Trina, quiet, confident Trina, just kept pinning and stitching. And you know what? She didn't make a fold-over clutch. My dear friends, hers was an elegant evening bag. Just like she planned.

In fact, everyone finished the projects. Two "pillowcase" shirts and four fold-over clutches later (well, three clutches and an evening bag), they had enormous smiles and something to show off to husbands: "Honey, look what I made."

Remember that feeling from grade school? "Mom, look what I made!" It's that unadulterated sense of accomplishment. Visions of art galleries and coffee table books floating in your head. That is, until your older brother says, "What's that supposed to be? It looks like you pooped on it." And you run crying to your room swearing off future creativity.

Yeah. It's the same feeling when you're older. Exactly the same.

DAY 22

I've spent half this month in wet clothes, and it's getting old. When you have only seven pieces of clothing, and one is shoes, another is a dress shirt, the third is threadbare yoga pants, and the fourth is an irrelevant long-sleeved shirt as it's mid-March and summer has begun in central Texas, what you basically have are three items: a pair of jeans and two T-shirts.

Seven items of clothing is essentially three.

I don't have a dirty clothes pile to wash at leisure. I am literally wearing these daily. And to bed. This has created a washing dilemma. If I was a preplanner like Brandon, who organizes every day in fifteen-minute blocks, creating short-term, mid-term, and long-term goals with corresponding to-do lists and relevant details in his synced iCalendar with reminder alarms and color-coded details (you think I'm kidding), then I might have clean clothes that I'd had the foresight to launder during the night.

Instead, I'm a spontaneous zero planner who has the Mac and iPhone but uses a paper calendar circa 1987 because I can't understand the Apple calendar feature and it won't obey when I try to enter a "New Event," so I have eleven "untitled" entries that never landed on the actual calendar. You might think the "+" sign under "New Event" would add a new event, but you would be wrong. So while my wireless gadgets were purchased to streamline travel, instead I call Brandon from airports to rummage on my computer for information.

He L-O-V-E-S this about me, and it never frustrates him.

I start thinking about my day right when it's happening. Which is why I remember not more than—but possibly less than—one hour before I need to be somewhere that my jeans smell like mildew (hence the unfortunate Day 16 entry).

So with my clothes on the shortest cycle, I walk around in a towel. Wearing other clothes is cheating. And I can't waste a wash-dry session without laundering *everything* because heaven knows it's all dirty.

You might have deduced, forty minutes is not enough to

wash and dry a load of clothes. It is enough to get them some-where between sopping wet and uncomfortably damp. At least six times this month, I've pulled soggy clothes from the dryer, struggled into them (wet jeans don't cooperate), and dashed out the door.

Listen, lambs, wet jeans don't dry when they're on your body. Walking into Hill's Cafe with friends, I hollered, "My butt is wet!" while the husbands hid. Well, it was. I would feel sorry for them if their butts were wet. I sat in the front seat and pointed the air vents at my rear to dry out. This was met with not compassion so much as outright mockery.

Dear wet clothes, I won't miss you.

DAY 25

I've slogged and underlined my way through Benjamin Bar-ber's *Consumed,* a remarkable book on the shifting nature of capitalism. After I'd read most paragraphs twice, the facts settled nicely in the brain space between the "Common Sense" and "Don't Be an Idiot" sections.

Like this obvious commentary:

Once upon a time, in capitalism's more creative and success-ful period, a productivist capitalism prospered by meeting the real needs of real people. . . . Today, however, consumer-ist capitalism profits only when it can address those whose essential needs have already been satisfied but who have the means to assuage "new" and invented needs—Marx's "imag-inary needs." The global majority still has extensive and real natural needs mirroring what psychologists T. Berry Brazel-ton and Stanley L. Greenspan have called "the irreducible needs of children." But it is without the means to address them, being cut off by the global market's inequality from the investment in capital and jobs that would allow them to become consumers.[2]

In other words, marketing used to represent basic needs of humans, without much embellishment or hyperbole. Certainly, the Third World still has these needs in spades—to the detriment of life and health and family—but no consumer power. Thus, Big Marketing turned to the wallets of the privileged, invented a bunch of fake needs (prepackaged sugar water, collagen moisturizer, Tide to Go pens, the slanket), and disregarded the people who were actually dying every day for lack of basics, exposed to the seductions of the consumer marketplace but without the means to participate in it.

In this new epoch in which the needy are without income and the wealthy are without needs, radical inequality is simply assumed. . . . Inequality leaves capitalism with a dilemma: The overproducing capitalist market must either grow or expire. If the poor cannot be enriched enough to become consumers, then grownups in the First World who are currently responsible for 60 percent of the world's consumption, and with vast disposable income but few needs, will have to be enticed into shopping.[3]

This is why I have 327 items of clothes in my closet.

With my genuine needs met but so many dollars yet unspent, shopping has become a stronger marker of freedom than voting, and what we spend in the mall matters more than what we're accomplishing together as the church. I am a part of the problem, a contributing member of inequality. Every time I buy another shirt I don't need or a seventh pair of shoes for my daughter, I redirect my powerful dollar to the pockets of consumerism, fueling my own greed and widening the gap. Why? Because I like it. Because those are cute. Because I want that.

These thoughts burden me holistically, but the trouble is, I can rationalize them individually. This one pair of shoes? Big deal. This little outfit? It was on sale. This micro-justification easily translates to nearly every purchase I've made. Alone, each item is reduced to an easy explanation, a harmless transaction. But all together, we've spent enough to irrevocably change the lives of a hundred thousand people. What did I get for that budgeting displacement? Closets full of clothes I barely wear and enough luxuries to outfit twenty families.

This is hard to process, so it helps to imagine standing in front of the families of my Ethiopian children, who I imagine were too underresourced to raise their own beloved babies. I imagine them calculating what I've spent on clothing alone, realizing that same amount would've kept their family fed and healthy for thirty years. *[This is so devastating to read. I know now what I didn't know then, and their pain haunts me. Family disruption and economic disempowerment are such complex problems, without easy solutions. Keeping families together (or reuniting them) has to be our first priority. I've written extensively about adoption ethics on my blog, and this is a tension I will always carry.]*

What if all my silly little individual purchases *do* matter? What if I joined a different movement, one that was less enticed by luxuries and more interested in justice? What if I believed every dollar spent is vital, a potential soldier in the war on inequality?

When thirty-five years of choices overwhelm me, Jesus makes it simple again: "Love your neighbor as yourself." If you read the story, you'll see that Jesus takes a broad, global, interracial view of who our neighbor is. In other words, what standard is acceptable for my own life? My own family? This is the benchmark for everyone else, which necessitates a decrease in the definition of *necessary* (for us) and an increase in the definition of *acceptable* (for everyone else).

The average human gets around twenty-five thousand

days on this earth, and most of us in the United States of America will get a few more. That's it. This life is a breath. Heaven is coming fast, and we live in that thin space where faith and obedience have relevance. We have this one life to offer; there is no second chance, no Plan B for the good news. We get one shot at living to expand the kingdom, fighting for justice. We'll stand before Jesus once, and none of our luxuries will accompany us. We'll have one moment to say, "This is how I lived."

More than thirteen thousand of those days are over for me. I'm determined to make the rest count.

DAY 30

Here we are, the end of the road for Month Two. Here are my observations:

First, wearing seven pieces of clothing was way easier than I expected. In my self-important mind, everyone would notice my repetitions and whisper about my wardrobe. People would obsess about my attire. You know what I discovered? Others aren't thinking about me nearly as much as I thought they were. Blending seamlessly into my environment, I brought up "my clothing situation" 100 percent more often than it was observed by anyone.

No one really cares. Shockingly, even I don't care as much as I thought. With the boundaries locked in, I lived this month unattached to "looking cute." And no one died. Ministry continued untainted. Life carried on. I could live my real life on a fraction of my previous wardrobe, and nothing significant would be altered. In fact, the simplicity was a blessed relief.

In the grand scheme of things, "how I look to people" all of a sudden just seems ludicrous. Listen, if my influence is linked to my wardrobe, then my ministry is falsely inflated and built on sand. A well-known ministry leader pulled me aside after I received my first multibook contract and said: "Jen, stay especially connected to Jesus from here on out. With your age and persona, they will try to make a starlet out of you." *[Lady, you have no idea how completely I will burn the whole thing down one day.]* At the time that sounded ridiculous. I was a twenty-nine-year-old nobody with a vague notion of my mission. Yet that statement lodged deeply, and I was never able to shake it. In a culture that elevates beauty and style, the Christian community is at genuine risk for distraction, even deception. What do we truly admire in our leaders? Are we no different from the secular population, drawn to charisma and style above substance and integrity?

I hope not.

I want to belong to a Christian community known for a different kind of beauty, the kind that heals and inspires. I can't help but remember Jesus, and how God made sure to mention He was plain and simple by human standards:

> *He grew up before him like a tender shoot,*
> *and like a root out of dry ground.*
> *He had no beauty or majesty to attract us to him,*
> *nothing in his appearance that we should desire him.*
> *He was despised and rejected by men,*
> *a man of sorrows, and familiar with suffering.*
> *Like one from whom men hide their faces*
> *he was despised, and we esteemed him not.* (Isa. 53:2–3)

There was nothing physically attractive about Jesus. He wasn't rich or notorious, well dressed or handsome. At first glimpse Jesus was forgettable, standing out for neither beauty nor charisma. Maybe this is why the widowed and marginalized and sick and outcast flocked to Him. He was approachable in every way.

Jesus didn't garner esteem the conventional way, but make no mistake: He was noticed. He was loved by the outsiders, hated by the religious elite, revered by His followers, and killed by His enemies. For a plain carpenter from Nazareth, Jesus sure found His way to the center ring; not through power or ruthlessness but by subversion and truth. His humility appeals to the unloveliness in us all. We are drawn in by His simplicity, then transformed by His magnificence.

Oh sure, there will always be people who want Jesus in the Oval Office, on *Primetime,* across from Oprah, on the red carpet, spruced up by a stylist, and touched up for the cameras. They try to assign Him the power and public sway He always resisted; people want to make a starlet out of Jesus. But He insisted His power was activated in the margins. Jesus redeemed the world not on the throne but through the cross.

I don't want to consume the redemption Jesus made possible then spurn the methods by which He achieved it. Jesus' kingdom continues in the same manner it was launched; through humility, subversion, love, sacrifice; through calling empty religion to reform and behaving like we believe the meek will indeed inherit the earth. We cannot carry the gospel to the poor and lowly while emulating the practices of the rich and powerful. We've been invited into a story that begins with humility and ends with glory; never the other way around. Let's align ourselves correctly, sharing in the humble ministry of Jesus, knowing one day we'll feast at His table in splendor.

After the suffering of his soul,
he will see the light of life and be satisfied;
by his knowledge my righteous servant will justify many,
and he will bear their iniquities.
Therefore I will give him a portion among the great,

and he will divide the spoils with the strong,
because he poured out his life unto death,
and was numbered with the transgressors.
For he bore the sin of many,
and made intercession for the transgressors. (Isa. 53:11–12)

POSSESSIONS

2,465 square feet.

Four bedrooms.

Two living rooms.

Two and a half bathrooms.

Nine closets.

Twenty-six cabinets.

Three bookshelves.

Ten dressers and armoires.

Every last one of them packed full. I invented an engineering trick to get them closed that I should patent. Some cabinets are stacked so high I have to remove forty pounds of stuff before I can retrieve the bottom dwellers. I don't even know what's in some of them.

About three times a year, I rant around the house, screaming at our stuff: "What is all this? How did this get here? Why do we have so much junk? How am I supposed to keep up with all this? Where did this all come from?" And then I remember:

I bought it all.

I suppose acting like someone snuck into my house while I was feeding the homeless and filled my shelves with more black shirts and a fourth set of Legos against my will is probably ignoble. To hear me fuss, you'd think I was a victim of drive-by consumerism. Guess what, doves?

I'm a part of this little game.

I see it (on you, on them, in their house, at Target, on TV). I manufacture a need for it. Then I buy it. I use it a little or not. I store it/shelve it/stack it/stuff it/get tired of it, then wage war against it one day when all my little things are strewn about as escapees from their shelves and drawers.

I could blame Big Marketing for selling me imagined needs. I could point a finger at culture for peer-pressuring me into having nicer things. I might implicate modern parenting, which encourages endless purchases for the kids, ensuring they aren't the "have-nots" in a sea of "haves." I could just dismiss it all with a shrug and casual wave of the hand. Oh, you know me! Retail therapy!

But if I'm being truthful, this is a sickening cycle of consumerism that I perpetuate constantly. I used to pardon excess from the tension of the gospel by saying, "Oh, it doesn't matter how much you have; it's what you do with it." But that exemption is folding in on itself lately. Plus, let's be honest: what does "it's what you do with it" even mean? Are we really doing something honorable with our stuff other than consuming it? I'm not sure carting it all off after we're bored with those particular items is a helpful response since we just replace it with more.

Anyhow, I'm getting ahead of myself. So here's the word of the day: "giddy." That's how I feel about this month. I originally planned on doing this as the fourth month, but I moved it up after the realizations from the last month horrified me. I am starving for reform. Here is the deal:

- One month.
- Give seven things away that we own.
- *Every day.*

Yes, I've done the math: 210 items out the door. This is a whole-family project, and there won't be a drawer left untouched. I predict the first half of the month will be a cakewalk. I'm a purger by nature; ask anyone. Everything goes. When my friends keep sentimental baby clothes and old newspapers, I threaten to call *Hoarders* on them. Clutter stresses me out. I like clean counters and labels. I'll gladly purge the first round of stuff.

It's the second round I'm guessing will pinch. When the obvious things are gone and things move into the sacrificial zone, let's see what a peppy cheerleader I am. (My friends have gently skirted my treasures: "So, um, what about your books, Jen?" Back off or you're dead to me.)

This month will be executed with The Council and other participating friends. Some will be generic donations, and others will be specific; I'm looking for the perfect recipient. Donating everything through a third party removes the relational magic when one human connects with another. Donating to Goodwill is fine, but I read the following quote three years ago, and it changed my life:

> I had come to see that the great tragedy in the church is not that rich Christians do not care about the poor but that rich Christians do not know the poor. . . . I long for the Calcutta slums to meet the Chicago suburbs, for lepers to meet landowners and for each to see God's image in the other. . . . I truly believe that when the poor meet the rich, riches will have no meaning. And when the rich meet the poor, we will see poverty come to an end.[1] (Thank you, Shane Claiborne, for messing me up.)

So off we go. Seven things a day. Clearly missing the point, my friends asked to paw through my stuff in case they want something before I give it away. Nice. This reminds me of Caleb, who asks *every single time* we feed the homeless if he can have a burger. One night when I refused, he mumbled: "The homeless get everything."

Well, this month they certainly will.

DAY 1

I wanted for this first entry to be charming and hilarious like the others have been (and clearly humble). I thought I'd share a cute anecdote or let my freak flag fly, easing into Month Three, warming up for this monstrous giveaway. But here is what happened:

I cleaned out my closet and I am sick.

Sick to death.

I couldn't even count the items or get them organized. They are piled on my closet floor and spilling into my bedroom as we speak. I had to walk away and breathe and sort through my emotions, which are churning too fast to keep up with. So many issues surfaced, I don't know where to begin. They're all screaming, "Pick me! Pick me!"

Okay, here's one: I grossly underestimated how much I've spent on clothes. I pulled out clothes I haven't worn in three years: Limited, Express, BCBG Max Azria, Seven (hello irony), Banana Republic, Caché, Nordstrom, Lucky, Steve Madden. These did not average ten dollars each, dear reader. And because I buy at the eleventh hour, moments before I need them, I mostly paid full price. No time for frugality when you're panic shopping.

Here's another reality check: I counted around forty items I've worn fewer than five times; four with tags on, never even worn. I might as well have sautéed that money in olive oil and eaten it. I think this bothered me most. *Forty items barely worn.* How indulgent and irresponsible and wasteful. Careless, that's the word. If I bought something that didn't warrant more than three wearings, I did not need it. That is thoughtless, default consumerism: see it, like it, buy it.

Cleaning out clothes that represented "my last life" kept me on a low simmer the whole morning. This was the bulk of all I purged, and I felt sad. These were beautiful clothes from another time, what I wore before we started Austin New Church—gorgeous, expensive clothes from a gorgeous, expensive season.

I don't know why I felt so sad. Maybe because these are the last reminders of a formative time. I wore these the first time I taught women, the first time I spoke, the first time I had a book signing, the first time I taught in church on a Sunday morning. These pretty clothes gave me confidence when I was terrified and uncertain. I look at them and see Christmas brunches, women's conferences, memorable weddings, the church lobby. I lived my life in these clothes for seven years, and getting rid of them is a final farewell to our old life.

After this there is nothing left from "before."

Clothes used to define me when my genuine identity was fuzzy. When I didn't know who I was or what I was here for, I dressed like someone who did. I dolled up the container, but I'm learning that I'm really just a jar of clay. Because that was all I was ever supposed to be. It will be my pleasure to give these beautiful, well-crafted clothes to someone who needs them.

Because I don't need them anymore.

[I have had four large, sweeping acts in my adult play. Act I was early adulthood, first job in the classroom, Baptist

church world. Act II was big cool church world, babies and toddlers, and the beginning of my writing career. Act III was deconstruction, missional reposturing, Austin New Church. Act IV is Black Lives Matter, LGBTQ rights, systemic injustices, and utter freedom.

Don't resist the movements in your adult life. This is called growing. And learning. And listening. And learning to be an ally. I suspect, if we are doing this right, we will increasingly care about people, justice, love, and this earth we were given to steward. I hope our tables will get wider, not smaller. May we find the courage to bless and release seasons when they have run their course. Let's show up for our lives with conviction and kindness. What is my Act V going to be? It is so exciting.]

DAY 2

125 things.

That's how many items survived the closet cut. It was easier to count what was left than what I donated, a 62 percent reduction. I came off the ledge and got to business. Yesterday was a mess, meaning I was. I left everything everywhere, and we stepped over/on it until this morning. My paralysis receded today, and I engineered a massive Sort and Organize. I had so many clothes that subcategories were required:

- Trendy dressy
- Dressy dressy
- Out-of-style dressy
- Ten-pounds-ago clothes

- Cute sleeveless
- Ball diamond sleeveless

And on and on. Good grief. I could've opened a boutique with this inventory. There were two categories: business appropriate and everything else. "Everything else" was loaded into my car (seats laid down to accommodate the plunder), and off I went to SafePlace.

What is SafePlace? you may ask. Well here you go. SafePlace's vision, as they report it, is:

> Working toward a community free of rape, sexual abuse and domestic violence. SafePlace provides physical safety for women and families affected by sexual and domestic violence.[2]

The abused find immediate shelter at SafePlace; the staff intervenes in the hospital and counsels children through trauma. Working to break the cycle, SafePlace provides community outreach, Expect Respect program for teens and youth, disability services, deaf services, and community dialogue. Violent patterns won't be repeated on their watch.

I thought about how my lovely clothes propped up the outside while my inside was struggling to find its way. I smile to think of a broken, abused woman slipping these pretty things on and propping up the outside a bit during her healing process. I pray they remind her that she is beautiful, she is valuable, she is worth it.

In the giant pile was my second pair of cowboy boots. If you read *Interrupted,* you've been here with me once, but let's go again (the following is excerpted from *Interrupted*):

> Easter snuck up on us—the day that changed everything. Deeply moved by Shane Claiborne among others, evidently

Brandon sent him an e-mail through dubious channels basically telling him *The Irresistible Revolution* was messing his wife up, and now he was reading it and didn't know what to do with it in this context. But we were wrestling and asking new questions, so that was probably good. He just wanted Shane to know that his message mattered to a pastor in the suburbs, even if it was driving us crazy. Sent and forgotten.

Ring-ring-ring. "Hi, is this Brandon? This is Shane Claiborne . . . yes it is . . . oh, I got your number off your e-mail . . . no, your wife is not involved in this. . . . Anyway, I'm going to be speaking at a small Asian American church in Austin Easter night, and I thought maybe we could have coffee afterward. . . . no, you're not being punked . . . okay, I'll see you in a couple of days."

Seriously? Who does that? I get e-mails from strangers all the time, and I was feeling good about responding to them, much less pilfering their numbers off their signature lines and scheduling coffees with them when I come to their cities. (As a traveling Bible teacher, Shane also convinced me to imitate the hospitality model of the New Testament and stay in homes when I travel instead of hotels. Best decision I've ever made. Guess what? There are people who actually have the gift of hospitality and are really good at it! Who knew? Paul and Jesus. And Shane.)

Anyhow, there was a 100 percent chance that coffee was happening, so we cleared Easter evening to spend with the members of Vox Veniae and Shane. (Check out this cool church at voxveniae.com—if I could, I would eat their website.)

Easter weekend, we blew the six services out of the water at our church: big, incredible, fantastic production, guest musicians, "When the Saints Go Marching In," trumpets, lights, gospel singers, rappers, sweet videography, killer. We herded approximately 10 billion people in and out of there like cattle, clearing out as fast as possible for the next service. As far as wow factors go, no one left disappointed. You got it, Jack. And Jackie.

Fast-forward to a few hours later, and we changed into jeans and drove downtown for Vox Veniae's one little Easter service with their guest speaker, Shane Claiborne. The church rented this crappy space on the University of Texas campus, and we parked in a ramshackle-looking parking lot a block away. As we walked up to the church, we saw a homeless-looking guy with weird hair, wearing what appeared to be a burlap sack in the shape of pants and a tunic. This was, of course, Shane. (He's been "escorted out" of several churches before they realized he was their guest speaker. Claiborne: Making Deacons Feel Awkward Since 1998.)

Maybe 150 people were at this Easter service, and it was simple and stripped down. There were candles, an unscripted welcome. The worship was so unself-conscious and pure, maybe three or four guys in the band. It was completely unproduced and humble, all of it. It smacked of regular people and simple church; their only preoccupation was this obsession with Jesus. It was tangible. I loved every molecule of it. I wanted to sell my house and move into this room.

Toward the end of Shane's talk, he mentioned his time that morning with a large homeless community in San Antonio. He had asked their spokesman what their main needs were. Above all else, they needed good shoes. He explained how they were on their feet all day, and the shoes they got from shelters and Goodwill were everyone else's castoffs, worn down, worn out. (Members of the homeless community have chronic leg and back pain from long days standing in inadequate shoes.)

As we were about to take Communion, Shane said, "You are under no coercion, but if you want to, you can leave your shoes at the altar when you take Communion. Oh! And leave your socks too. We'll wash them and deliver them all to the homeless community in San Antonio tomorrow."

Two significant particulars: One, Easter 2007 in Austin was unseasonably, crazy cold. Like 31-degrees-that-morning cold. Understand that in April in Austin, we would all typically be wearing shorts and flip-flops. Guaranteed. From the youngest to the oldest. As it was, every person there had on real, substantial shoes because it was freezing outside.

Two, Brandon and I looked down at our shoes in unison and just started laughing. Why? We were both wearing our brand-new cowboy boots we'd given each other for Christmas. By a huge margin, they were the most prized and expensive shoes we'd ever owned. I loved them so much, I gave them their own special box in my closet where moth and rust could not destroy.

Having thrown myself into this arena for a few months, I thought I would be thrilled to rip those boots off my rich feet and happily give them over to the homeless (who would promptly sell them since they are entirely impractical and worth a pretty penny—I've learned a few things). But I was discouraged to feel the twinge of selfishness rear its head first. Seriously? I'm going to make a deal over boots? Have I come only this far, God? I suck.

Jesus, unwilling to entertain my melodrama, cut to the chase: "Give them up. I have something to teach you." Evidently, this moment was not about me and my urban cowgirl boots. So I took them off, raised them to my lips for a farewell kiss, oh okay, and an embrace, and Brandon and I left my boots and his at the altar along with our socks and the last remaining thread of reluctance.

I'll not do the moment justice, but at the close of the service, I watched all these smiling people gladly walk barefooted out into the cold, and I heard Jesus whisper: "This is how I want My church to look. I want her to rip the shoes off her feet for the least every single chance she gets. I want an altar full of socks and shoes right next to the Communion table. I want to see solidarity with the poor. I want true community rallied around My gospel. I want a barefooted church."

A barefooted church.

Brandon replaced those boots on Mother's Day, and today I gave them away again. As we inventoried my things, I told this story to the SafePlace volunteer. He promised to personally ensure my boots found the right feet, someone who needed reminding that though she feels like the least, she is loved by a Savior whose eye is on the sparrow.

I pray for the woman who will literally walk in my shoes. Jesus, embrace her with safety and healing. With every step she takes, wrapped in my clothes, may she know Your faithfulness and experience Your redemption. Take her to that sacred place with You where there is no more abuse, no more violence, only the sweet rescue of salvation.

DAY 3

Since I gave away 202 items from just my closet, and Month Three requires 210 giveaways, we're going to adjust. The Council decided one week can involve clothes. The end. So even if we purge one thousand shirts, they will count toward only seven days.

Now I have to tell you something, and it's bad.

Three months ago I was cleaning out the kids' drawers as the season was changing from warmer-cool to cooler-cool. Out came shorts that didn't fit, T-shirts inching up their bellies, jeans from last year, and other outgrown items. I pulled at least twenty-five items per kid.

Every mom engages in this purge twice a year. There is nothing noble about it. It's out with the old and outgrown, in with the new and shiny. It's not about reducing, simplifying, or sharing; it's really a function of our kids growing two sizes every three months while we research gland disorders and reswear off GMO products.

But I did something bad. I knew this month was coming, and I wasn't sure we'd have enough to purge so quickly after that cleanout. So I stored the piles to donate should our options become too slim. That's right, my trusting friends:

I prehoarded.

I'm sorry, okay? I won't count them. Sadly, I don't *need* to count them. We will exceed 210 items by a landslide. I told you I'm the type to cheat in advance, and now it's confirmed. Two hundred and ten sounded like a lot! I was scared we'd be leaning against the walls where our couches used to be by the end of the month.

But yet again, I underestimated how much we've bought.

Criminy.

DAY 6

I am a schizophrenic consumer.

I have an overabundance of certain items as unnecessary as diet pills for a supermodel. For instance, I have about a hundred books. On God. I have another sixty on women's issues. This doesn't include my fiction, memoirs, essays, global issues, cookbooks, biographies, and reference books. Oh okay, and commentaries, mysteries, poetry anthologies, parenting books, and autobiographies. And history books. And maps and atlases. And humor essays. Books on tape. You get the picture.

Also, I have lots of movies. Like four drawers full of VHS

tapes and no VHS player. Included is *The Next Karate Kid,* a straight-to-video tragedy starring young Hilary Swank, who was ridiculously annoying and also managed to seriously overact in said movie, which I spent actual money on. That is an hour and a half and ten dollars I'll never get back.

And don't get me started on blankets. I am *uptohere* with blankets. It's not like we live in the frozen tundra or don't enjoy a $250+ a month electric habit. We are not the Ingallses living in the Big Woods while our children, Laura, Mary, and Carrie, huddle together for warmth. I should invite Michael Jackson's son Blanket to live here among his own kind (and maybe Gwyneth's daughter, Apple, could live in our refrigerator and Frank Zappa's daughter Diva Thin Muffin can stay in my pantry).

However. I am downright destitute in other categories. Most black holes exist in my kitchen. For example, I have two pot holders. Two. One is a Christmas-themed gem complete with mildew polka dots. It is as thin as a Kleenex, so it withstands actual heat for about three seconds, then no longer protects my hands from burning metal. The other is a crocheted mini–pot holder I bought from Trina's daughter. It is 1 millimeter wide, so I've burned myself innumerable times because it doesn't cover the surface area of my hand (too bad for you, Bottom of Palm and Tips of Fingers).

My reaction to the pot holder conundrum is nonsensical:

Scene: Jen suffers ninety-fourth burn, extracting dish from oven:

"Aaaaaaghhhh! I burned the tips of my fingers again and now I won't have fingerprints! I can't be searing my hands all the time! I just ca-a-a-a-an't!" (Holding up hands dramatically, perhaps shaking them for effect.)

"This is how I make a living! This is my livelihood! I'm a word surgeon. . . . I need my hands to execute my craft!

These ten fingers are how the magic happens, and without them I might as well cut out my voice box too, because that's how useless I am on earth!"

Brandon, fantasizing about the missing voice box, "Here's ten dollars. Go buy some."

I can't explain why I haven't bought new pot holders. I guess it's laziness. What else could it be?

The pot holders aren't in that category by themselves. The same is true about bath towels (seven in the whole house), mixing bowls, cooking utensils (I have one half-melted spatula), and pots and pans. As a matter of fact, I still use a 1993 wedding shower pan that adds so much flaked Teflon into every dish, I'm certain I've seeded us all with cancer.

So evidently, I'm of the feast-or-famine variety.

DAY 11

It's Easter.

Between ages zero and thirty-two, I celebrated Easter the fun way: with bunnies, baskets, and expensive clothes. What better way to say "Jesus reigns" than dressing my preschooler in a forty-five-dollar dress to show her off in the church lobby? (You're welcome, Jesus. Be blessed.)

Now let's be clear: If you had asked me what my Easter priorities were as I stood all fancy in the lobby, I'd've become grave and mentioned the resurrection. For crying out loud, I'm a Christian. But to tell the truth, between the outfit shopping, the Easter baskets, the egg _____ (dyeing, stuffing, hiding, hunting), the pictures, the lunch menu, and the gift buying, Jesus was flat last. I started thinking about Him as the band began playing at church, and I thought about Him for a whole hour.

That's just true.

But for the last three years Jesus has messed with me. Frankly, He's hijacked all my holiday endeavors. I've always celebrated holidays with a cultural major and a spiritual minor. Take Christmas, for example. I endlessly spent on garbage no one needed and worked myself into a December frenzy and oh well. La-di-da. Now I'm overwhelmed by the poor and the disgusting consumerism cycle and the heinous neglect of Jesus and the appalling nature of it all.

Then we got to Easter, or as God called it, Passover. Easter is a little name picked up from the Anglo-Saxon fertility goddess of spring, Eostre, who saved a frozen bird from the harsh winter by turning it into a magical rabbit who could lay eggs. Hence: "Easter" bunnies and eggs. Why are elements of a pagan religion associated with the highest holy day of the Christian faith? Oh bother. Can't we just carry on and dye our Eostre eggs in peace?

Assessing the typical American Easter, on one side I see Jesus on the cross, humiliated and mutilated, bearing the failures of every person past and present, rescuing humanity through an astonishing miracle of divine redemption, splitting history in two and transforming the human experience for eternity. On the other side I see us celebrating this monumental heroism with chocolate bunnies and boiled eggs, with Jesus as an afterthought. It doesn't make sense. (Insert some of you tossing this book in the garbage. *Don't mess with my Easter fun, you hippie chick.*)

This year, Austin New Church decided to rethink "The Traditional Easter Service That Brings in More People Than Any Other Day of the Year." It is our church's two-year anniversary, and certainly we could stand more foot traffic, but I'm not sure Passover is best celebrated by a high-attendance Sunday of people who won't be back until Christmas Eve.

We literally asked ourselves . . . What would Jesus do?

Would He drop a bunch of cash on fancy clothes? Buy out the chocolate and plastic egg supply? Find the biggest church in town and spend twenty minutes posturing in the lobby?

Who in Austin might want to celebrate the astonishing hope of resurrected Jesus but might feel uncomfortable surrounded by beautiful people dressed to the nines? Who needs the gospel spoken into their brokenness but might not be welcomed by the saints in the sanctuaries? It came quickly to us:

The homeless.

If Jesus came to proclaim freedom for the captives and good news to the poor, then Passover uniquely belongs to the bottom dwellers. *[2010 Jen, please see my earlier note on "the least." . . . We don't call people bottom dwellers. I don't mean to talk down to you, but this is incredibly condescending.]* So we canceled our service and took church downtown to the corner of Seventh and Neches, where our homeless community is concentrated. We grilled thirteen hundred burgers and ate together. Our band led worship; then in a powerful moment of solidarity, we shared Communion. It was a beautiful mess of dancing, tears, singing, and sharing. It wasn't an *us* and *them* moment; it was just the church, remembering the Passover Lamb and celebrating our liberation together.

Now, if we get one repetitive request when serving our homeless friends, it's this: "Do you have a bag?" (Could also be: "Can I have that bag?" "Can I take that trash bag?" "Do you have a bag I can put this bag in?") So this was the perfect moment to give away seven of my nine purses, which were nice and roomy, just like the ladies want.

When the gals had a perfect view for maximum impact, I hollered:

"Hey, girls! Anyone want one of . . . these?"

Cranberry red leather.

Green with gold buckles.

Chocolate brown bohemian bag.

Turquoise with short handles.

Burnt orange across-the-shoulder.

Shiny black backpack bag.

And one little purse I debated bringing. It was a tiny thing, hot pink crocodile by Gianni Bini, functionally useless but fashionably magnificent. Our street girls want the biggest bags possible, since they carry everything they own. A wheelbarrow would be a huge hit. So my little vanity purse was a wild card, but at the last second with a conspiratorial nudge from the Spirit, I threw it in.

Not surprisingly, it was the last purse left. What self-respecting woman picks a hot pink purse that would barely carry her bus pass? Glamour handbags are only for women who have eight others and a house in which to stash them. So I was standing there with my one little purse, when its rightful owner, the one for whom I daresay that purse was stitched together, made a beeline for me.

She had on her Easter finest, tights included, though it was ninety degrees. Flouncy dress with—what else?—hot pink flowers. Hair done in sections with matching beads, pink floppy hat on standby. Leather dress shoes polished to a sheen. Dainty ribbon necklace and rings on four fingers.

She was six years old. Her name was NeNe.

Never has a purse better matched its owner. She slipped that hot pink number over her arm and never put it down, not even to eat. Her mom looked at me and no words were necessary; mothers speak a silent language. I took her picture and fussed over her beauty and breathed a thank-you to Jesus for the nudge.

I serve a Savior who finds a way to get pink purses to homeless six-year-old girls.

Jesus is a redeemer, a restorer in every way. His day on the cross looked like a colossal failure, but it was His finest moment. He launched a kingdom where the least will be the greatest and the last will be first, where the poor will be comforted and the meek will inherit the earth. Jesus brought together the homeless with the privileged and said, "You're all poor, and you're all beautiful." The cross leveled the playing field, and no earthly distinction is valid anymore. There is a new "us"—people rescued by the Passover Lamb, adopted into the family, and transformed into saints. It is the most epic miracle in history.

That is why we celebrate. May we never become so enamored by the substitutions of this world that we forget.

> It was just before the Passover Feast. Jesus knew that the time had come for him to leave this world and go to the Father. Having loved his own who were in the world, he now showed them the full extent of his love. (John 13:1)

DAY 13

I have a growing number of friends joining *Simple & Free*. I casually mentioned it on Facebook, which started a firestorm of questions. Which begat more e-mails. Which led to rogue groups joining the fray. Which led to one group in Nashville demanding the outline because they couldn't wait for *Simple & Free* to become a book.

Our ANC friend circle is joining, and I get e-mails from all over the country telling me their *Simple & Free* moments and following along. God is rewriting so many of our stories at once.

My girlfriend Amanda discovered the Prom Project, which collects formals and all the fixins for underprivileged girls to wear to prom. If you only understood how perfectly this nonprofit fits Amanda. She donated not one, not two, but *twelve* formals complete with gloves, heels, jewelry, and shiny hair ornamentation.

ME: Amanda! *Twelve?* Have you been attending the local proms on the prowl? Does Ryan know? Why on earth do you have twelve formals?

AMANDA: I used to do a lot of fancy things!

ME: I do a few fancy things, and I've worn the same dress for seven years, making me a social tragedy. No long silk gloves or bejeweled heels either. Explain.

AMANDA: I'm from the Valley, okay! We learned to be gaudy at a young age. I grew up with a "more is more" mentality. Between everyone's quinceañeras and Los Días de los Muertos and cotillion and all my real estate cocktail parties and Renaissance fairs, I have a bunch of costumes, I mean, formals.

ME: Wait, Renaissance fairs?

AMANDA: The Dark Ages are done. *Fiat lux.*

Thanks to Amanda, twelve skinny high school girls will attend their proms in the highest fashion without spending a penny. She made a prom memory possible, a rite of passage for the American teenager but impossible for girls in poverty.

This is why the body of Christ is so essential. I could no more meet the needs of teenagers attending prom than I could recount the basic years of the Renaissance. (1500s? 1700s? I vaguely recall the word "mutton" and a movie with Heath Ledger.)

But this is Amanda's offering. She's doing her part. We each meet unique needs in our cities and our world. If we all raised others up instead of raising ourselves a little higher, there would be few needs left on earth. I marvel at what God accomplishes with the generosity of His sons and daughters. I'm proud they are brothers and sisters. What a family.

And hey, if you need any elbow-length satin gloves or chandelier rhinestone earrings . . . I know a girl.

DAY 17

Were it not for the intervention of the Holy Spirit, my girlfriends and I would end up on *Jerry Springer*. We are loud and silly. When one friend volunteered to move in with me so that together she and I might make one whole wife, Brandon said, "Oh yeah, that's exactly what I need. One more woman in this house who thinks she's hilarious."

Admittedly, we skirt the edges of inappropriate and hold some pictures as leverage against one another, but let me tell you: If you're ever in a crisis, we're as effective as the Red Cross. We can mobilize in four minutes.

This month of *Simple & Free* created plenty of opportunities to team up. Susana sent an SOS e-mail about her single-mom friend, Staci, and her two daughters who'd lived with someone for a year, all three in the same room. Staci left a destructive marriage with whatever fit into the car. She was working, putting herself through college, and trying to rebuild a healthy life for her girls. She'd saved for a small apartment—a thrill—but she literally had nothing. No beds, no furniture, no silverware.

The working poor get lost in the shuffle. Susana and Staci were friends for six months before Susana realized Staci was struggling. Their girls were in a club together; there was plenty of laughing and banter. By all appearances Staci's station seemed "normal." The usual clues that point to poverty are ambiguous for those in the gap.

The working poor are one missed shift from homelessness,

one lost paycheck from hunger, one overdue bill from repos-
session. However, they learn to camouflage nicely into society. They laugh at the right jokes and deflect questions with
sarcasm or silence. The children are ashamed to admit they
haven't eaten all weekend or can't afford to play soccer, so
you'd never know. In many ways they are invisible.

Had Susana not asked for a plate at Staci's house, and had
Staci not pointed to the two plates holding snacks and said,
"You're looking at them," she wouldn't have known the family
was hanging on by a thread. Susana urged (read: bullied) Staci
into making a list, and she rocketed the needs out to our
friend tribe.

We had her apartment furnished, stocked, filled, and deco-
rated in four days. Because of *Simple & Free,* we'd liquidated
tons of items, awaiting the right recipient. Beds, linens, microwave, couches, TVs, tables and chairs, dishes, pictures, all of it.

Staci sent Susana this e-mail on Monday:

We were so overwhelmed yesterday that I am not sure I
even said thank you. Thank you for listening to that still
small voice from God. Thank you for inviting your prayer
group into your vision. Thank you for setting such a wonderful example of Christian service and womanhood. Dylan
notices EVERYTHING and she told me, "Those people are
Christians." Yes, honey, they are. And God said we will be
known by the love we show one another. How nice to lay in
that bed and sit at that table and stare at those groceries in
the cabinet. This is the best vacuum cleaner I have ever had.
The microwave and the trash can and bowl of apples (my
favorite red delicious apples) and the brown smooth sheets
all scream GOD LOVES YOU AND YOU ARE NOT ALONE.
Who knew apples could say so much? I have an overwhelming feeling that everything will be fine for the first time since
I moved back to Austin.

This was one of those moments when my mission became very clear, very concentrated, very unambiguous. Static has always surrounded the Christian life; so much threatens to distract us from the main point. People have always preferred details and complications and rules, but when Jesus was pressed, He said (Jen translation), "Love God and love people. That's pretty much it." Staci's story reminds me:

This is what we do, and this is why we do it.

Sometimes the best way to bring good news to the poor is to bring actual good news to the poor. It appears a good way to bring relief to the oppressed is to bring real relief to the oppressed. It's almost like Jesus meant what He said. When you're desperate, usually the best news you can receive is food, water, shelter. These provisions communicate God's presence infinitely more than a tract or Christian performance in the local park. They convey, "God loves you so dearly, He sent people to your rescue."

I guess that's why "Love people" is the second command next to "Love God." And since God's reputation is hopelessly linked to His followers' behavior, I suspect He wouldn't be stuck with His current rap if we spent our time loving others and stocking their cabinets.

But there I go, off on another tangent, imagining apples can be part of the gospel.

Next I'm going to tell you *the last will be first* or something crazy.

DAY 18

I'm two and a half months into *Simple & Free,* and I'm noticing some things. God historically moves epically in my life. I don't have subtle seasons of change. Our rhythm works like this: I experience a maddening tension I can or can't exactly put my finger on, and then *BAM*. God kicks me in the teeth and things change.

Simple & Free is becoming epically transformative. Tension led me here; now God is making a mess of things. I sense God preparing us for change. My sensitivity is peaking; noteworthy, because I have the sensitivity of a thirteen-year-old boy. I feel raw and less and less attached to my stuff. Scripture is pouncing on my brain like a panther. It's like when I first got glasses and couldn't get over how clear everything was. And I walked weird because my perception was altered. I kept shouting, "Look at all the leaves! I can see every leaf on the tree!" like it was a miracle after having been impaired so long.

I have no idea what this means, but my hands are opening. I know my next phase of life is not going to look the same.

I'm scared. Hmm. When I first typed that, I accidentally spelled "sacred."

Perhaps those have always been flip sides of a coin. Like my friend says, "Obedience isn't a lack of fear. It's just doing it scared."

DAY 20

"God? Connect us with people who need our stuff."

"Okay. Hey? How about these refugees?"

Refugees are an invisible population, marginalized by language barriers and ethnic stereotypes. They disappear into society, unseen as they clean our hotel rooms, flip our burgers, and sweep our airports. We look right past them, unaware of the trauma they've endured or the countries they've left behind. Their stories are lost to people who see only their function—Please leave us extra towels. Take us to Fifth and Broadway. One Coke and the paper.

Austin New Church is learning about refugees the way we

do: stalking experts and attaching like barnacles. The Refugee Services of Texas is teaching us how to support this forgotten group. Typically, RST is understaffed and overworked, the plight of the average nonprofit. So we jumped from "Hi! We'd like to learn about refugees, please" to "Good! A Burmese family is flying in Friday with the clothes on their backs. Can you furnish their apartment and pick them up at the airport?"

Oh lawd.

Insert: e-mail frenzy, harried administrating, and a massive clearing of calendars. Off the list I spotted some items I'd been waiting to give away, one in particular: bedding. This Burmese couple and their two teenage daughters needed everything, and this was something I had to share. In addition to one full-sized bed, out went:

Seven sheet sets and the fixins.

We supplied furniture, dishes, toiletries, groceries, clothes, and accessories. Obviously, that is only the beginning of this family's journey. The true challenges are yet to come: financial independence, language acquisition, education, empowerment, community—an overwhelming transition in an unfamiliar country. They'll need us more in the coming months, but for tonight they'll sleep on their own sheets in their own beds at their own apartment for the first time in years.

So once again, we pray God is evident in every pillowcase, each fork, all the simple comforts we take for granted. While this family has known violence and fear, we hope tonight they'll experience safety and love.

DAY 25

For the last three years, God used Easter to mess me up. I've mentioned the Easter I gave my boots away and life was forever altered. The next Easter we launched Austin New

Church, and my story divided in half: before ANC and after. The following Easter was our church's one-year anniversary as God delivered on His promise, and ANC was legit, a monumental lesson on His faithfulness.

So let me finish the story about this Easter; there was more than NeNe and her little pink purse. When you bring your entire church downtown to feed eight hundred homeless people including a band, worship, a message, Communion, and resource stations, it gets . . . messy. The sanitized version of church goes out the window. The rules to maintain an organized service simply don't apply to an outdoor service dominated by the homeless.

So during Brandon's brief message, one very sad, very lost woman screamed, *"Where were all of you when these men were violating me? Where were you?"* There was more, none printable. It was raw and desperate, littered with expletives and sorrow. If we came to proclaim freedom for the oppressed like Jesus said, then we didn't need to look further than this broken woman.

What did I do? How did her grief move me? Well, I motioned for Tray to "take care of her." My instinct was to protect the service, keep everything decent. I mean, a shattered woman screaming during church is just too messy to indulge.

My church family, however, responded with grace befitting the Bride. Brandon spoke gently to her, Christi tried to embrace her, Ryan held out his hand, others interceded for this daughter. If Jesus really meant the church was a hospital for the sick, not a showcase of the healthy, then we were seriously having church.

Cut to the next day.

I was preparing to be the keynote speaker at a monstrous event two weeks away, the Ladies' Retreat for the Baptist General Convention of Oklahoma, around three thousand women. I was locked into Mark 10, where Jesus engaged blind Bartimaeus a week before He went to the cross. I got down to business studying.

I had so much to teach. Other people.

Ahem.

Bartimaeus: poor, blind, beggar. Probably looked like every homeless person I know. Outcast, shunned from the temple, unclean, discarded in every way—a true societal reject. And here comes Jesus with His entourage, headed to Jerusalem to be "king" (oops, they had a little misunderstanding about what that meant—their bad). Everyone is excited, everyone is cheering. Yay, Jesus! We're getting our king and we'll be free!

> As Jesus and his disciples, together with a large crowd, were leaving the city, a blind man, Bartimaeus (that is, the Son of Timaeus), was sitting by the roadside begging. When he heard that it was Jesus of Nazareth, he began to shout, "Jesus, Son of David, have mercy on me!" (Mark 10:46–47)

Whoa up. Yikes. This is awkward. This is embarrassing actually. There is nothing dignified here. This reeks of desperation. I mean, Bartimaeus? Poor, blind Bartimaeus screaming at Jesus? Sheesh. What a mess, Jesus surrounded by normal, decent followers, forced to deal with this sad, sorry homeless guy screaming bloody murder.

> Many rebuked him and told him to be quiet, but he shouted all the more, "Son of David, have mercy on me!"
>
> Jesus stopped and said, "Call him."
>
> So they called to the blind man, "Cheer up! On your feet! He's calling you." Throwing his cloak aside, he jumped to his feet and came to Jesus.
>
> "What do you want me to do for you?" Jesus asked him.
>
> The blind man said, "Rabbi, I want to see."
>
> "Go," said Jesus, "your faith has healed you." Immedi-

ately he received his sight and followed Jesus along the
road. (Mark 10:48–52)

And bam, right in the middle of my important studying to
teach others how to follow Jesus, the Holy Spirit leveled me.
Who was I in this scenario? Not Jesus, mercifully pausing for
a blind beggar *on His way to the cross,* but the embarrassed
"Christ followers," who scorned this humiliating interrup-
tion during their Christ-following and sanitized this awkward confrontation to get on with their holiness.

I cried for an hour.

I have so far to go.

"Rabbi, I want to see." Bartimaeus asked for the most basic
human need. In biblical times blindness meant he was considered cursed by God, which made him unclean, which
made him an outcast, which made him a beggar. Unlike James
and John, who twelve verses earlier asked to sit at Jesus' right
and left hand in glory (preceded by the awesome demand
"Teacher, we want You to do for us whatever we ask"), Bartimaeus asked only for mercy.

This is like the starving asking for food, the orphan asking
for parents, the homeless asking for shelter, the sick asking
for medicine; basic human needs—food, shelter, care, love.
These aren't tangled up in power or position; they aren't born
out of entitlement or greed. They are a plea for mercy, the cry
of every human heart.

Decorum has no relevance for the mother who prostitutes
to feed her children or the nine-year-old who eats trash to
survive on the streets. The "rules on how to behave" are
meaningless for the sixty-six children infected with HIV in
the last hour or the twenty-five thousand people who died
today from starvation.

The poor world is begging for mercy like Bartimaeus, while
the rich world is asking for more favor like James and John.

I taught this mess at the BGCO Ladies' Retreat, including my dismal failure on Easter two weeks ago. I wondered if the American church was like well-mannered nice-talkers, sitting in a living room sipping coffee, talking about choir practice, while the world burns down outside our windows. While the richest people on earth pray to get richer, the rest of the world begs for intervention with their faces pressed to the window, watching us drink our coffee, unruffled by their suffering.

It's just not right.

So I blubbered in front of three thousand women, bawling for the anguish of others and my own heinous disinterest, worried we were missing the point. I told the story about giving away my boots and asked if a similar moment wasn't in order—not that shoes will change anyone's life, but there is something spiritual and submissive about offering the shoes on your feet, the sweater off your back. It tells Jesus: I'm in.

It's the engine behind this month of *Simple & Free*: giving away is somehow sacred, connecting to the sacrificial heartbeat of Jesus. It's as transformative for the giver as it is a blessing to the receiver. When God told us to give, I suspect He had spiritual formation in mind as much as meeting needs.

You might want to sit down.

Before I formalized this or offered any structure, women started pouring down the aisles, pulling their shoes off. They left jackets, Bibles, purses, diamond necklaces, wedding rings, cameras, iPhones, bags—I have never seen anything like it. Eventually, I just turned off my microphone as hundreds of women lay facedown, sobbing, barefoot. The stage was covered in their offerings, falling onto the ground and taking over the room.

It filled seventy large moving boxes.

It was the greatest possible giveaway of Month Three.

I learned something: There is much hope for the American

church. It's too soon to declare the Bride hopelessly selfish or irrelevant. The fear my message would be received poorly was so debilitating I hadn't slept for a week. When women are accustomed to beauty and happiness messages, discussing a crumbling world caused me no end of anxiety.

I'll repeat: seventy moving boxes full of offerings, thousands of women going home in the pouring rain barefooted. The church is not beyond the movement of Jesus. A stirring is happening within the Bride. God is awakening the church from her slumber, initiating a profound advancement of the kingdom.

Please, don't miss it because the American Dream seems a reasonable substitute, countering the apparent downside to living simply so that others can live at all. Do not be fooled by the luxuries of this world; they cripple our faith. As Jesus explained, the wrong things have to die so the right things can live—we die to selfishness, greed, power, accumulation, prestige, and self-preservation, giving life to community, generosity, compassion, mercy, brotherhood, kindness, and love.

The gospel will die in the toxic soil of self. Paul wrote, "We were therefore buried with Him through baptism into death in order that, just as Christ was raised from the dead through the glory of the Father, *we too may live a new life*. If we have been united with Him like this in His death, we will certainly also be united with Him in His resurrection" (Rom. 6:4). We want the life part without being united with Jesus in the death part, but that version of Christianity doesn't exist—that is a false gospel, void of sacrifice.

The fertile soil of death is where the gospel forms roots and actually bears fruit. We have to die to live; we have to die so others can live. It almost sounds like Jesus' mission. This is the church He was willing to die for, a Bride that inspires and changes the world. This vision is worthy of radical obedience. Don't give up on the church.

There is hope for her yet.

DAY 27

CONNIE: I know you're giving stuff away, and I have some really underresourced kids at the school where I teach.

JEN: What do you need?

CONNIE: One of my boys wears his sister's old jeans every day. They are so small he can't button them, so he pulls his shirt down.

JEN: Bring him to me. I'll be his mother.

CONNIE: That's one idea, but maybe just give him clothes.

JEN: Perhaps.

CONNIE: We also need girls' clothes. And boys' clothes. In basically every size.

I delivered three boxes of my kids' clothes and shoes. There is no reason for any boy to wear his sister's jeans when we dump kids' clothes at Goodwill twice a year. Calling the counselor of an underresourced school about felt needs takes three minutes. Meeting a need directly is a guaranteed solution, getting nothing lost in the shuffle.

DAY 30

After a month of liquidating, my friends and I still have stuff to give away. I am not even kidding. Our closets, drawers, cabinets, garages, attics, and shelves have been purged, and the volume created a pit in my stomach I can't shake.

When did this lose relevance for me?

Do not store up for yourselves treasures on earth, where moth and rust destroy, and where thieves break in and steal. But store up for yourselves treasures in heaven, where moth and rust do not destroy, and where thieves do not break in and steal. For where your treasure is, there your heart will be also. (Matt. 6:19–21)

I've creatively distanced myself from this, namely, a strategic focus on the "treasures in heaven" with a blind eye to the contrary "treasures on earth," addressing the spiritual list, ignoring the tangible list. But Jesus set these two in opposition, much like:

You can't serve God and money.

You're either a sheep or a goat.

There is only a wide road and a narrow road.

Either you love your brother in Christ or you're a liar.

We've invented a thousand shades of gray, devising a comfortable Christian existence we can all live with—superawesome, except the Bible doesn't support it. According to Scripture, no real disciple serves God while addicted to the dollar. There is no sheep-goat hybrid. There is no middle road. There is no true believer who hates his brother.

Grayed-down discipleship is an easier sell, but it creates pretend Christians, obsessing over Scriptures we like while conspicuously ignoring the rest. Until God asks for everything and we answer, "It's Yours," we don't yet have ears to hear or eyes to see. We're still deaf to the truth, blind to freedom, deceived by the treasures of the world, imagining them to be the key when they are actually the lock.

Nothing like handing over a big pile of your stuff to drive this point home! After we've given away one thousand items this month, there is still more. Ditto for my friends. (Insert pit in stomach.) So Molly, with her "bonus storage room" that would make pack rats weep with envy, devised a plan: Let's organize her space and use it as a supply room for streamlined giveaways from here on out.

The storage room was solitary confinement for Molly's junk, so everything had to come out first. Fortuitous, since we found a trunk packed with high school memorabilia. The six of us plopped down and roared with laughter for an hour. We summoned her husband, Chris, and demanded an explanation for his long, middle-parted hair from 1996. We returned his stored pager; I've told him to "page me" seventy times since. He pretends to keep laughing.

We purged and organized and rearranged and categorized, and now Molly's storage room houses home accessories, toiletries, jeans and shoes, kitchen appliances, linens, and toys. No more scrambling when someone needs our stuff; we can go from phone call to delivery in ten minutes.

But now here's the real issue: Will I just replace all this? Will I purge another one thousand items three years from now? Will I slowly refill the empty spaces? Or will my family disconnect from the machine, creating a more courageous legacy than simply consuming? I want to confront the big part that says "more" with the smaller part that says "enough."

Believers, let's oppose the powers that manipulate us, lying about our needs, our responsibilities, our neighbor. Let's challenge the laissez-faire response that dismisses our consumerism with a casual shrug. But be prepared for the upstream struggle. The keepers of the market want us to spend. In a typical year the United States spends about $16 billion in foreign aid and $276 billion on advertising. Like Benjamin Barber wrote in *Consumed*, "How much easier it is for the keepers when their task is to let Peter Pan fly free and keep Wendy cartwheeling under Peter's careless gaze rather than contain narcissism and help children grow up. For the keepers know the risk that comes with helping children grow up: they do not necessarily grow up into consumers. They sometimes become citizens."[3]

Paul put it this way: "When I was a child, I talked like a child, I thought like a child, I reasoned like a child. When I became a man, I put childish ways behind me. Now we see but a poor reflection as in a mirror; then we shall see face to face. Now I know in part; then I shall know fully, even as I am fully known" (1 Cor. 13:11–12).

A child says "me." An adult says "us." Maturity distinguishes need from want, wisdom from foolishness. Growing up means curbing appetites, shifting from "me" to "we," understanding private choices have social consequences and public outcomes. Let's be consumers who silence the screaming voice that yells, *"I WANT!"* and instead listen to the quiet "we need," the marginalized voice of the worldwide community we belong to.

We top the global food chain through no fault or credit of our own. I've asked God a billion times why I have so much while others have so little. Why do my kids get full bellies? Why does water flow freely from my faucets? Why do we get to go to the doctor when we're sick? There is no easy answer. The *why* definitely matters, but so does the *what*. What do we do with our riches? What do we do with our privileges? What should we keep? What should we share? I'd better address this inequality since Jesus clearly identified the poor as His brothers and sisters and my neighbor.

What if we tried together? What if a bunch of Christians wrote a new story, becoming consumers the earth is groaning for? I suspect we'd find that elusive contentment, storing up treasures in heaven like Jesus told us to. I'm betting our stuff would lose its grip and we'd discover riches contained in a simpler life, a communal responsibility. *Money* is the most frequent theme in Scripture; perhaps the secret to happiness is right under our noses. Maybe we don't recognize satisfaction because it is disguised as radical generosity, a strange oxymoron in a consumer culture.

Richard Rohr described American Christians in *Simplicity*: "We're just about to become adults, to honestly let the Gospel speak to us, to listen to what Jesus says, in no uncertain terms, about poverty and about leading a simple life in this world, a life that shows trust in God and not in our own power and weapons. God never promised us security in this world. God promised us only truth and freedom in our hearts. What does all this mean for us? It means that we're on the way."[4]

Let's prove that theory correct.

[An update if I may: Here is what strikes me as I reread this chapter. Ten years later, my career has grown enormously. When I wrote Simple & Free, *I had a regular Facebook account with three thousand or so followers. Today, I have a million and a half followers on social media. In every category of work, I make more money now. And yet the increase in fame and income did not shield us from loss, pain, trauma, or suffering. Nor did it make us categorically happier. It really didn't. The goodness of life is still located where it always was: in family, friends, memories, Jesus. In fact, revisiting parts of* Simple & Free *has been hard because things felt simpler, smaller, and slower then. I have more income now, but I also have more pressure, more critics, more responsibility, and more obligations.*

Here is my point: Everything I concluded above is true. None of it delivers what you think it is going to deliver. Money doesn't solve life's dilemmas. Its power is in generosity, in the mystical ability to hold it loosely and share it

freely. That's it. After that, it is just an exercise in diminish-
ing returns. I hope God finds us faithful with what we have.
But if it all went away tomorrow, I know for sure that I still
have everything that matters. I suspected it back in 2010,
but now I know.]

MEDIA

Excerpted car conversation:

> CALEB: I wonder what it feels like to die?
>
> GAVIN: I wouldn't want to die of constipation like Elvis did.
>
> ME: Wait, what?
>
> GAVIN: Dad told me Elvis died on the toilet.
>
> CALEB: Gavin, Elvis isn't even real!
>
> GAVIN: I thought he was the King of Rock?
>
> CALEB: Gavin, do you really think someone would name their baby Elvis?

These used to be funny stories to tell grandparents; now they are sound bites for Facebook. Spam and Jesus forwards hijacked regular e-mail: "Blah blah blah . . . forward this to all your friends. Remember, if you deny Jesus before man, He will deny you before the Father! PASS THIS ON OR ELSE! DON'T MAKE THE BABY JESUS CRY!" Three years ago we had four channels; now we have literally thousands with the dumbest shows ever conceived. (I'm talking about you, Lifetime, featuring *Mother, May I Sleep with Danger?* starring Tori Spelling.)

TV was innocent when our kids watched *Dora the Explorer* on Nick Jr. But now it's the Disney Channel, where you can bet the farm those little overactors will turn straight crazy the second they become eighteen and start their "music careers." It's awesome when the *High School Musical* stars post naked pictures on social media; thank you, young starlets! I was short on teaching moments for my daughter until you came to the rescue with your online boobies.

Don't get me started on gaming. This, I know, is ironic, since "someone" bought these systems and then waged Mortal Kombat against her kids' Xbox 360, Nintendo DS Lites, Wii, and computer games. Listen, the son who can't muster an initiative to wear clean socks can attend to complicated war games for two hours. It's a miracle.

We have:

- Four gaming systems
- Two MacBooks and one desktop computer
- Five TVs
- Three cell phones (two of the "i" variety)
- A DVR
- Two DVD players
- Three handheld Nintendo DSs
- Three stereos

Stunning, since I didn't have a computer, e-mail address, or cable until 2005. We went from zero to full-blown addiction in five years. Our family is now owned by the Man (Time

Warner Cable), and we're paying the piper, too (Hello, Apple, we're talking to you.) I don't know how we lived before Al Gore invented the Internet.

What the heck? I don't know how this happened; we hedged on boundaries one careless degree at a time, and now I hardly recognize our family rhythm. We have our own little screen worlds to immerse in; actual human contact seems optional.

Time to stop the madness.

So this month we're going radio silent. We're shutting down seven screens and muting the chatter. No:

- TV
- Gaming
- Social media
- iPhone apps
- Radio
- Texting*
- Internet*

The two asterisks involved much discussion with The Council and the hubs. Texting is a double-edged sword. Sometimes it is a time-saver; I can get an answer without talking for twenty-five minutes about hair products. So sometimes, it *adds* minutes instead of subtracting them.

On the other hand, sometimes texting is extraneous, even ridiculous. When I text this to a friend: "Friendship is like peeing in your pants. Everyone can see it, but only you can feel the warmth. Thanks for being the pee in my pants" then I have too much time on my hands. And also I need to grow up.

Asterisk 1: our texting rule: If it is a time-saver and/or necessary, then text away. If it's to be sarcastic, silly, or inappropriate, then pass. We're deferring to our own discernment, so someone should check my texts weekly because heaven knows, I need accountability.

Asterisk 2: The Internet is a necessary tool for our jobs and life. Event planners, the kids' teachers, our adoption agency, my Restore Group, agent and publisher, and my neighbors correspond through e-mail. Additionally, I research for my books and messages online. I can't ditch Internet for a month. Neither can Brandon for all the same reasons, except for "corresponding with the kids' teachers," who I'm 90 percent sure he couldn't name.

But we *can* go without Facebook, Twitter, SportCenter .com, adoption blogs, iPhoto, StuffChristiansLike.net (make sure you've emptied your bladder first), Hulu, scanwiches .com (recall my sandwich fixation), Amazon, twitter.com/ xianity (i.e., "Dispensational republican audience turns on Christian comedian after one joke too many about red heifers."), thepioneerwoman.com, and YouTube (I'll miss you most, Annoying Orange). Good-bye.

The Council is in various levels of participation. Becky and Susana are going Full Monty. Shonna and Jenny are limiting screens to seven hours a week. Trina is contemplating giving up her cell phone. Dear Molly is still traumatized—recall the three DVRs loaded with "her stories." She begged me to move media month out of May. Because of sweeps. Because of season finales. Oh, the humanity! I suggested reducing to seven shows, and she gave me the look that precedes an assault and battery charge.

So remote controls are stashed, Facebook notifications turned off and corresponding iPhone app dumped, gaming controllers locked up, and the kids' computer unplugged. I've certainly received an earful on this:

"This month is going to be terrible! What are we going to do? I don't even like to read! What else is there? I think *some*

TV would be fine! *No texting?* All my friends text me! You're going to have your nose in a book while I'm bored with nothing to do! How many weeks? *Four?*"

And that was just Brandon.

DAY 1

E-mail banter with The Council on our Facebook withdrawals:

BECKY: This Facebook-sized hole is causing me to send e-mails like this: "Chatted up AGAIN by the creepy pre-school dad! Eeewww!" (Only have a small case of the shakes today.)

SUSANA: Dude, I so get it. I have all this hilarious, self-aggrandizing drivel wasting away while I'm abstaining from the hive of Facebook. Like that statement I just gave. That's brilliant Facebook fodder. Wasted.

JEN: How will anyone manage without knowing Sydney and I made calzones tonight and that I have a fruit fly problem? What is the point of living if you don't get to hear that we took our first trip to the snow cone stand today? This is public FB material, and without posting it, it's like living our lives in privacy with no purpose.

SHONNA: What are we supposed to do with our witty one-liners? How is anyone going to know how funny we are?

JENNY: I had decided not to give FB up, but my Bible reading today was terrible: "Dear children, keep yourselves from idols." I decided FB is an idol of mine since it steals my attention and affections away from God. But then I thought: maybe He wasn't talking to me. It did say "DEAR children." I'm not dear.

MOLLY: I've been trying to figure out my contribution to media month, and I will definitely be signing off FB. I'm struggling with the rest, well not the rest, just one thing: . . . TV. You know how much I love TV. It's what my degree is in. I make a spreadsheet every fall with all my shows and new ones I want to try (check my kitchen cabinet where it's taped). I have three DVRs and have to watch two shows a day so my main DVR doesn't exceed 97 percent full. Clearly I need professional help. It's May, and that means all the season finales. (Thanks, Jen.) Who will be my next "American Idol"? Will the *Glee* kids win regionals? Will Meredith and Derek have a baby, thus ending one of their careers on *Grey's Anatomy*? And for the love of the land, I MUST know what that island on *Lost* is about! That's a five-year commitment I intend to see through. These are the questions that keep me up at night.

TRINA: Sent from your iPad. Clearly you love technology. I also am pondering our commitment. I'm considering ditching my cell phone for the month. The biggest worrier here is my husband—he calls Jen when he can't find me.

SUSANA: There's freedom from addiction. Trust me. I gave up my shows for no good reason other than to be obedient and see what happens. And so, after eight seasons of never missing an episode, I have not seen *American Idol* this year. And I'm still alive. Except *Glee*. I still watch *Glee*. Umm . . . (plastered smile, eyes shifting) I have no excuse for this.

JEN: I love you, *Glee*.

[Look at all the shows we were watching! I loved 2010, man.
Who knew Grey's Anatomy would still be on our televisions

ten years later? I think maybe it will never end because Shonda Rhimes is a freaking queen and her will shall be imposed. I still watch American Idol. *Bye.]*

DAY 4

Okay, it's Thursday. We started Monday. No one has died. With love and affection for this person, and devotion and respect, and tenderness and esteem, the only complaints are Brandon's. This morning:

BRANDON: (reading off open laptop) Jen! Avery Bradley is going into the NBA draft. Can you believe it? He only averaged eleven points this year! He needed another season with us, and he would've been clutch. But we recruited another stud point guard from Nevada of all places, and he's a shooter.

JEN: Um, what website are you on?

BRANDON: Rivals.com. Why? What? *What? This is off-limits? How am I supposed to get my news!*

Brandon gets his news from college sports sites and I get mine from Facebook, so I don't know how two news junkies like us will manage. What if something monumental happens, like preseason football polls drop or *The Voice* gets a new judge? How can we live in such ignorance? I suggested buying a newspaper, and Brandon said, "Do they still make those?"

Anyway, the kids are doing surprisingly well. In four days I've not heard one word. The boys organized airsoft gun wars, so eight sweaty, stinky boys are running through my house wielding semiautomatic pellet guns dressed in sweatshirts though it was ninety-seven degrees yesterday. My rule on this boy business: "Don't cry if you get pinged, and if one stray pellet hits me, I will run over your guns with my car." This is life with sons, people.

Sydney and I tackled ambitious recipes from my Pioneer Woman cookbook. We've rolled out crusts, made homemade calzones, chopped and diced, sautéed and baked. Report: homemade mac and cheese—FAIL. (I hate you, separated Cheddar cheese that ruined my creamy sauce. Why are you so temperamental about heat? Velveeta would never treat me like this.)

We've played Pictureka! with our (cheating) kids, and the boys trash-talked through HORSE on our "basketball court." The gang built a massive fort in the playroom (imagine over-turned couches and stacked chairs). I even mopped and dusted because I wasn't spending time on web surfing and the Food Network.

Maybe this month won't mean the end of the universe, after all.

DAY 5

I take back everything I said about my kids behaving.

From 3:00 to 4:00 today, my house was a war zone. Gavin and Caleb were "kickbox fighting" on the trampoline. I can't imagine why this ended in tears and yelling, but it did, the little one accusing the big one of "fighting me too hard." I made matters worse by laughing because Caleb's Six Stages of Anger are so funny (get hurt ➜ lie on the ground ➜ cry eyes out ➜ transition to "red rage" ➜ come up swinging ➜ shout something that includes the word "revenge"). The red rage—

also known as Going Mad Dog—certainly hints of anger issues but is hilarious nonetheless.

Sydney started a puppetry project, transforming a cardboard box into a stage with a pillowcase that sacrificed its life to become a curtain. It should've been sturdy held together with blue painting tape and wood glue (sarcasm intended), but it was rickety. This set her off and she became . . . difficult. All my suggestions were pure drivel. It was also my fault when she couldn't see the line I drew on the pillowcase and cut the opening too big. "Mom! You just don't get it!"

Between the fighting, crying, whining, and blaming, I hit a metaphorical wall. I wanted to turn on a movie and silence their little mouths. A nice screen trance would settle the tumultuous waters. Instead, I sent everyone to bedrooms until I gave the word.

We have to deal with tension rather than anesthetizing it with TV or videogames. It's easier to bypass relational snags with a convenient distraction, forfeiting the chance to improve problem-solving and listening skills. I don't want my kids to be more comfortable interacting with a computer screen than with a human being. We stay the course until we've resolved an issue, not allowing *Phineas and Ferb* to fill the space instead. This is harder and requires more time, but my kids will marry people and have bosses and children. Learning healthy relational skills is now or never.

Thirty minutes later we pressed the reset button. Perspectives were shared and apologies offered. All reengaged the puppetry project. The day was recovered: We collaborated on homemade pizza, and the puppet show was a smashing success. The kids reenacted "The Three Little Pigs" with some questionable alterations to the plot. Why did the boys' puppets have machetes? We don't ask these questions in the Hatmaker house. They just do. Thank you for understanding.

DAY 8

Take something away, and your habits become clear. Parts of my day I don't miss media because I'm working or running errands or meeting with people. But I can easily identify the sections when media is a habit, a faithful companion to that time slot or task:

- Morning coffee + the *Today* show
- Prewriting procrastination = Facebook and adoption blogs
- Folding laundry + *LA Ink*
- Mental writing break = cooking blogs and www.failblog .org
- Lunch at the table + Food Network
- Post–kid bedtime = TV shows

These are the wrenches in the media fast machine. Folding laundry today, I called Trina on speakerphone because I couldn't handle the silence. She commiserated, as our morning ritual includes a few segments of the *Today* show. Unanchored this morning without Matt and Savannah's company, she stood in the bathroom, watching her hubby, Andrew, shave.

ANDREW: I'm guessing you're bored.

TRINA: I don't know what to do.

ANDREW: Start tackling your tasks?

TRINA: I can't yet. I'm suffering *Today* show withdrawal.

ANDREW: Would it help if I gave a tech script overview of the likely programming?

TRINA: Yes, but don't make fun of my soft journalism.

ANDREW: Let's see, cheery good morning, one belly laugh and show summary, then cut to serious-faced anchor, most likely ethnic.

News: Somewhere in the U.S. a child is either missing or was horrifically harmed. Straight outta the trailer park, her grandmother will be interviewed with an attorney on one side, a T-shirt with the child's image on it, feather earrings, and bad dental work.

The oil spill is still a massive catastrophe, according to the individual in the live shot standing in front of distinctly coastal Louisiana scenery (shrimp boats are nice). We'll see images of oil-soaked birds struggling to escape caring hands and dead sea life on the beach.

The president will say something about something.

Then, in the weather, it will either rain or not rain locally, and we'll see footage of someone somewhere picking through the wreckage of a tornado-flattened house or being plucked from the rooftop of a flooded home by a helicopter or johnboat.

In celebrity news a much prettier person than we will ever meet in real life either did or did not have sex with someone, meaning there is either a scandal or a child on the way/newly born.

Cut to commercials, most likely Clorox, diaper, or menstrual related.

Back for a cooking segment, probably a summer-themed recipe, which means there will be fresh tomatoes in it. Pray the second-tier talent doesn't sever a tendon while clumsily chopping ingredients.

Cut to witty banter between the show's personalities either at the desk, in a faux living room setting, or outside, where regular people holding up signs are kept at arm's length by rope barriers and the veiled threat of ta-sering.

Repeat every half hour until *Ellen* comes on.

In a similar substitution Jenny's husband, Tray, sent me three pictures from awkwardfamilyphotos.com to view via e-mail, *technically* following the rules to abstain from time-wasting websites. (He sent me two, but I begged for a third to satisfy my sophomoric, inappropriate sense of humor.) There is nothing better than a family of eight, dressed in Star Wars regalia, posing at Olan Mills.

I am really, really immature.

DAY 12

This silence has been awesome. Our house feels peaceful—well, as peaceful as a house with three kids and all their friends can feel. I *like* the missing white noise of media. I *like* the silence during the day. I *like* the alternative rhythms we're discovering. Such as:

- Cooking together
- Walks after dinner
- Porch time with our friends
- Sydney's endless craft projects at the table
- Dinner with neighbors
- Actual phone calls
- Four books read, a fifth in queue
- Caleb's new obsession with fishing

These are emerging out of the black hole of media. It's not rocket science; there's just space for them now. With the TV off, we ask, "What else can we do?" With the Wii packed away, the kids invent their own games. With an hour to kill after dinner, we grab Lady and hit the sidewalk. Some of this is out of boredom, some out of desperation, but still.

Several times, as I realized I was caught up on correspondence, done with laundry, and finished with my to-do list, God whispered:

"Hi there."

My communion with God suffers not for lack of desire but for lack of time. And let's be honest: I say I don't have time, yet I found thirty-five minutes for Facebook and an hour for my shows. I found half an hour for YouTube videos on how to style black hair. I found fifteen minutes for the radio and twenty-four minutes for a missed *30 Rock* episode. So when I say I don't have time, I'm a gigantic liar.

I have time. I just spend it elsewhere.

God hasn't made a nuisance of Himself or given tasks for my newfound time. He's just been . . . extra there. Sort of like "Remember I'm here with you all the time? And I can help you choose kindness and patience during the day?" (Could also insert: gentleness, meekness, self-control, love, selflessness, forgiveness . . . you know, all the things that come so easily to us humans.)

God is using *Simple & Free* to transform the ease of my communion with Him. It's intimacy like a comfortable sweatshirt, beyond dressed up Sunday wear—past the formality, past the spiritual tasks. More like "Let's just live this life together." I'm not transferring this extra time to hard-core Bible study and theology formation. Honestly, that's already my bread and butter. I study God's Word for a living.

This is something different. Something more relational and daily. Something in the gaps of spiritual activities, in between the stuff on a calendar. It's just simple communion, the natural kind between people who spend a lot of time together. I'm pondering this:

> *He has showed you, O man, what is good.*
> *And what does the Lord require of you?*
> *To act justly and to love mercy*
> *and to walk humbly with your God.* (Mic. 6:8)

Without the noise and static, I'm learning about that "walk humbly" part. Frankly, justice and mercy are my first languages; I'm a doer. Acting justly satisfies the deep part of me that so wants a happier, safer, kinder earth. I feel productive with a task, a list, a project, a mission. I like the word "act" in this verse. (Gotta be honest, I've been trying to earn my salvation for some time.)

But God is teaching me *walk humbly*—daily, simply, quietly. It's in the walking humbly that God trains me for acting justly and loving mercy. Being aware of God's presence is a powerful catalyst for courage later. Acting on the latter without the former is just charity, not worship. Plenty of people enact justice without devotion to Jesus. There is no salvation in that, no devotion. That well of mercy will run dry without replenishment, without supernatural motivation.

If more of us took the "walk humbly with your God" part seriously, we might become agents of justice and mercy without even meaning to.

DAY 14

Straight up: I dreamed about TV shows last night.

I saw the *So You Think You Can Dance* premiere. Epic. There was an Animal Planet piece about an alligator I can't recall, but I remember thinking, *See? This is the kind of important science I'm missing.* I'm getting dumber during this media fast. I watched a sewing show (?). My REM mind was grasping at TV straws. It's very deprived. Last, I enjoyed *Law & Order* specifically starring Mariska Hargitay as Detective Olivia Benson and Sam Waterston as Executive Assistant District Attorney Jack McCoy; yes, I know they are on different *Law & Order* dramas, but the sleeping mind will have what it wants, and mine wants those two on the same show. (Can you imagine the snappy dialogue?)

The last thing I recall was the sharp realization I was doing something naughty. I was a TV-watching fraud. *Simple & Free* had been compromised. I swear to you, I was already making excuses in my dream ("I thought *Simple & Free* was over." "I didn't take my ginkgo biloba.").

I apologize to my readers for watching TV in my dreams.

DAY 15

Between *Simple & Free* tunnel vision and this media vacuum, my eighth book released today and I thought it was next month. My in-box started blowing up with preorder messages: "I got my copy!" "Guess what I got in the mail today?!" "Got my hot little hands on your book!" "I've already read half!" "The cover looks awesome, Jen!"

ME: Really? I can't believe you got it a month early!

FRIEND: It came out today, stupid. Don't you know your own release dates?

ME: Um, evidently not.

This is helping make sense of the blog tour I start next week. I *thought* it was dumb to promote a book that wasn't available yet.

Simple & Free will be my ninth book. As I type that, I am stunned. After my fifth book, I said I was done writing because I didn't know anything else. I'd mined everything in my brain, and there was nothing left. So God changed our lives. Then I had more to say apparently, although from book six on, my writing sounds like a girl who has clearly come undone and cannot communicate without an avalanche of emotion. I've bawled through the writing process on my last four books.

When I think about the girl who wrote *A Modern Girl's Guide to Bible Study,* my first book, I can hardly remember her. Recalling what I cared about, how I acted, how I spent money, what mattered to me, what I misunderstood about my mission, what I thought I knew, how I loved, how I lived . . . it's like describing another person.

If I could go back to the Jen of 2004, surrounded by babies and banging out that first book on a borrowed laptop, I would tell her a few things:

First, I would stroke her hair and tell her I know how hard she is trying. I know she genuinely loves Jesus and is trying to be obedient. I would be far more gentle with her than she was with herself during those years. I would remind her she is only twenty-nine, and managing three kids under five with a husband logging seventy-hour workweeks is ridiculously hard. It's okay to cry sometimes. This will pass. The kids will grow up and wipe their own butts soon. You're doing a good job. (Why is the current me so much kinder to me than the 2004 me was to me?)

Second, I would drive myself around the extravagant neighborhoods in west Austin, the houses I dined in and met with women in and brutally coveted while we baptized people in their multimillion-dollar backyards. I would note the meticulous landscaping and four-car garages and the beautifully groomed women with killer wardrobes and perfect bodies. Then I would gently tell myself: "This is all meaningless; substitute happiness. This vicious trap will capture you with no mercy if you get too close." I would describe the liberation of living below your means, something the 2004 me has never experienced. I would assure her that this affluent lifestyle is a horrible goal—go ahead and stop trying, stop dreaming, stop striving. You will be stunned where true happiness actually comes from soon.

Then I would link arms with myself and walk down the street we lived on. I would kindly explain that our neighbor to the left, the one who never mows and lets her house fall down around her, junking out the neighborhood, is actually a widow whose grown son and friends take advantage of her. I would go on to explain that she is all alone with a pastor's family next door who have never lifted a finger to serve her but only complain about her messy yard. I'd show 2004 Jen that the gospel is neutered until it grows hands and feet and actually becomes good news to someone, like someone whose only label was "irresponsible neighbor" when it should've been "widow in distress."

I would tell Jen:

It's okay to admit your worst struggles. To actual people.

You don't have to be awesome. You can be ordinary.

You can trust the Spirit when He challenges your interpretation of Scripture.

You can ask, "Why do we do this? Why do we think this? Why do we say this?"

Pastors aren't always right. God is your authority.

Jesus warned against wealth for a reason. Stop chasing it.

Next, with affection, I would ask 2004 Jen if she knows where Ethiopia is. She would lie and say yes because she hasn't discovered the freedom in admitting ignorance about anything yet. I would describe this beautiful, tragic country and the others like it. To her shock, I'd reveal that she would become so burdened by its poverty and enamored with its beauty that she would adopt two of its children. (2004 Jen tells me to get out at this point, as she has a one-year-old on her hip, a three-year-old on her leg, and a five-year-old whose exact location is unknown.) I'd kiss her overwhelmed cheek and assure her better days are coming, days that aren't so self-absorbed and lost and frustrating.

I'd tell 2004 Jen that one day she will garden. We'd laugh our heads off together.

Then I would call forth the best in her, and I would say: Guess what? Soon your whole life will be centered on justice. You're going to walk away from power and reputation, and you'll break bread with the homeless and give away the shoes on your feet. It will be awesome. You'll be free soon. This nagging tension that things aren't right, that life is more than blessing extremely blessed people . . . that's all true. A torrent of believers are demanding more from the indulged American life, daring to imagine that discipleship is adventurous and risky and sacrificial and powerful. You won't believe how many of them there are. You'll be drawn into a thrilling chapter God is writing in the church, with new and ancient themes.

Finally, I would hug 2004 Jen, understanding that discipleship is a journey, and each stage is a necessary precursor to the following one. God was right in Proverbs: our light is the dimmest at the beginning of salvation, but it grows brighter and brighter as we go. There is no wasted scene, no futile season. God gives us what we can handle, when we can handle it. We are drawn more and more deeply into the knowledge of Jesus. A baby can't handle a steak before she has teeth. The steak will come, but for today milk is on the menu. That's not an insult; it's biology. The baby will get there. Be patient. Do the best with what you know. When you know more, adjust the trajectory.

Self-hatred is not appropriate when God reveals a new angle. That is not the way of Christ, who abolished condemnation under the banner of grace. The wise responder humbly receives truth, allows it to supersede the version he or she is holding, and adjusts. This progression is cause for not shame but gratitude; thankful God never leaves us where we are but draws us into a richer faith. I giggle to imagine what 2017 Jen would come back to teach me; I don't even know what I don't know.

So for now I'll continue to reduce and simplify, fight and engage until I know what else to do. What I know now is this: less. I don't need to have the most, be the best, or reach the top. It is okay to pursue a life marked by obscurity and simplicity. It doesn't matter what I own or how I'm perceived. Whether I succeed in the market or land hopelessly in the middle is irrelevant, although this used to keep me up at night.

I'm just beginning to embrace the liberation that exists only at the bottom, where I have nothing to defend, nothing to protect. Where it doesn't matter if I'm right or esteemed or positioned well. I wonder if that's the freedom Jesus meant when He said, "Blessed are the poor in spirit, for theirs is the kingdom of heaven" (Matt. 5:3). In order for Jesus' kingdom to come, my kingdom will have to go, and for the first time I think I'm okay with that.

[Okay, I'll tell you what 2017 Jen would say: I feel supercompassionate toward 2010 Jen's understanding of God and inequality and faithfulness. I know this was as far as she had gone and as much as she had experienced. There is honor in doing the best you can wherever you are.

But inequality isn't easily reduced to just economic disparity, as she mainly thought. Her through line here was "rich and poor," which put her tidily on the side of rescuing. When she added an international distinction, it was downright White Saviorism. She hadn't yet learned to examine systems of oppression that actively marginalized people of color, LGBTQ people, immigrants, and refugees. White supremacy and unchecked capitalism and patriarchy and homophobia break more than economic equality; they break people's hearts.

So 2010 Jen, this may surprise you, but in 2016 you will stand on the side of the LGBTQ community as an ally, and it will split your story in half. They will teach you so much. You will love them dearly and serve alongside them. They will have a great deal of patience for you as you slowly reconsider a doctrine that produced no life, only death. This community will become your friends and teachers in ways you couldn't imagine. It will be hard and then beautiful beyond words. Don't be afraid.]

DAY 18

Last year our husbands left Jenny and Shonna and me unsupervised for too long, and we planned a Disney World Christmas surprise. My kids had never been, and after wasting colossal amounts on Christmas crap, I decided this was superior holiday spending. We got past the hotel-booking stage, even beyond the five-day FastPass investment, when Brandon and I said, "We're morons. We have a double adoption on deck. What kind of idiots spend their adoption money on Space Mountain?"

So with no small amount of disappointment, we pulled out.

Jenny and Shonna—best friends that they are—must have decided never to mention the trip again, as I was like the senior girl who didn't get to go to prom because she got mono. Being good friends, all her BFFs said prom was stupid anyway, the band was going to be lame, and they were going only because their moms were living out their unrealized dreams vicariously through them.

Jenny and Shonna were so tight-lipped that I forgot they were going. I'm certain this was intentional because we exchange 438 e-mails and initiate 762 conversations about every trip we take together. Our husbands beg us to stop talking about it two months before our plane leaves. The anticipation is half our fun, but I didn't hear one solitary predetail about their *five days at Disney*. I mean, come on.

This same emotional preservation is happening right now. I'm sure of it.

I know this because my favorite show—*So You Think You Can Dance*—is currently on its fourth week and I haven't heard boo about it from my friends. They are acting like they aren't watching. I mentioned it to my girlfriend Christi, and she shrugged it off: "Oh, it's just tryouts. Superboring. Who cares, right?" *As if* we haven't organized watch parties, dance contests (true story), show trivia quizzes, season soundtracks, and attended SYTYCD Live! in Austin for the last three years.

The same friends who call me to *watch a show together on the phone* are acting like they've lost interest in reality TV. I know they're reminding one another not to mention anything and to act like TV is for losers, pretending to wish *they* were on a media fast because there is nothing good on and they could spend more time in Bible study and meditation like I was getting to.

This is an elaborate conspiracy, and I'm onto them.

And I love them.

DAY 21

Is it really groundbreaking news that too much media is bad for us? Is anyone thinking, *You know what my kids need? More TV*. I see couples having dinner in silence, checking their phones, as if *anything* cannot wait one hour. Don't get me started on the Bluetooth guy; it makes me want to ask, "Have you always been a jerk?" Wear it in the car, dude; do not wear it into Jason's Deli and have a loud conversation while making the cashier wait for your order. If I am close enough, I will pinch you, and I don't even know you.

Lots of experts are weighing in. It turns out, all this input isn't just annoying; it's troubling. A recent *New York Times* article, citing dozens of sources, reported that *this is your brain on computers*:

> Scientists say juggling e-mail, phone calls and other incoming information can change how people think and behave. They say our ability to focus is being undermined by bursts of information.

These play to a primitive impulse to respond to immediate opportunities and threats. The stimulation provokes excitement—a dopamine squirt—that researchers say can be addictive. In its absence, people feel bored. The resulting distractions can have deadly consequences, as when cellphone-wielding drivers and train engineers cause wrecks. And for millions of people these urges can inflict nicks and cuts on creativity and deep thought, interrupting work and family life.[1]

Even after this multitasking ends, fractured thinking persists because evidently *this is also your brain off computers*.

In 2008, people consumed three times more information each day than they did in 1960. Computer users at work change windows, check e-mail, or switch programs nearly thirty-seven times an hour, new research shows. I am completely guilty of this, and it gives me ping-pong brain. It is increasingly hard to focus on one task for longer than twenty minutes without succumbing to an alternate source: Hey look, my in-box says "6," my favorite blogger posted something new, let me just send this quick text, what's the daily recipe on cooks.com?

Researchers at Stanford found that media multitaskers seem more sensitive to incoming information than nonmultitaskers, and that is not necessarily good.

A portion of the brain acts as a control tower, helping a person focus and set priorities. More primitive parts of the brain, like those that process sight and sound, demand that it pay attention to new information, bombarding the control tower when they are stimulated.

Researchers say there is an evolutionary rationale for the pressure this barrage puts on the brain. The lower-brain functions alert humans to danger, like a nearby lion, overriding goals like building a hut. In the modern world, the chime of incoming e-mail can override the goal of writing a business plan or playing catch with the children.

"Throughout evolutionary history, a big surprise would get everyone's brain thinking," said Clifford Nass, a communications professor at Stanford. "But we've got a large and growing group of people who think the slightest hint that something interesting might be going on is like catnip. They can't ignore it."[2]

I think these people have been spying on me. I've developed an addiction to input, and I'm not sure how to turn it off. It is worsened because I work on the computer. If my career involved art or labor or customer service or raising babies again, I'd naturally find myself unplugged more. But writing books and developing messages and corresponding with readers and event planners is all right here on my handy laptop, and oh, there's an iPhone alert, and oh, there's my in-box, and oh, here's Facebook, and oh, let me click on this article real fast, and oh, here's a sidebar link, and oh, I meant to check that website, and oh . . .

Do you remember when we used to mail letters and read the paper and leave messages on answering machines? We were not available every second, and my gosh, I miss that. I cannot be unplugged for three hours without someone asking, "Where are you? I've e-mailed you and sent you three texts." My time no longer belongs to me, and if I disconnect for a few hours, people take it as a personal affront.

This month has been heaven on a biscuit. *Simple & Free* gave me permission to say, "Don't text me, don't Facebook me, and don't e-mail me unless it's an emergency because I won't answer." And then everything went silent. As it turns out, I can set media boundaries and everyone will live. The instinct to check all my accounts and programs went dormant, because I knew nothing would be there, and I was like an addict taking my first deep breath of unpoisoned air in a while.

I don't want to be addicted anymore, and I certainly don't want my kids to be slaves to these compulsions. "Researchers worry that constant digital stimulation like this creates attention problems for children with brains that are still developing, who already struggle to set priorities and resist impulses," the *New York Times* article reported.

Do all these screens sabotage the neurological maturity our kids are already struggling to achieve? Well, I for one have given my son instructions while he was on the Xbox, found zero progress on said instruction fifteen minutes later, while he swears I never said anything. Really? What about when I stood twelve inches away and said in plain English,

"Go pooper-scoop the yard." He's making a good case for that lower-brain-function theory.

Now the question is: How do we remain unplugged after next week?

[Wow, do we know more now than we even knew then. Ten years have delivered a great deal of data on our plugged-in culture and its effect on all of us. In some ways, it is worse than we suspected. In addition to negative physical effects, like poor posture, strained eyesight, and chronic insomnia, Business Insider *reported that technology is seriously affecting our mental health, particularly that of our kids:*

> According to a national survey by the University of Pittsburgh Center for Research on Media, Technology and Health, young adults who use seven to eleven social media platforms had more than three times the risk of depression and anxiety than those who use two or fewer platforms.[3]

It is all just happening so quickly, research and data cannot keep up. We don't even know what we don't know yet. But as we consider our usage, I like this perspective from Michael Bess, historian of science at Vanderbilt University and the author of Our Grandchildren Redesigned: Life in a Bioengineered Society:

> I think each of us needs to ask, "What does it mean for a human being to flourish?" These technologies are forcing us to be more deliberate about asking that question. We need to sit down with ourselves and say, "As I look at my daily life, as I look at the past year, as I look at the past five years, what are the aspects of my life that have been the

most rewarding and enriching? When have I been happiest? What are the things that have made me flourish?" If we ask these questions in a thoughtful, explicit way, then we can say more definitely what these technologies are adding to the human experience and, more importantly, what they're subtracting from the human experience.[4]]

DAY 26

I pulled up Hulu.com, clicked on *Modern Family,* then turned it off.

There. I said it.

Brandon had been out of town for three days, I'd been wrangling these out-of-school kids who have no media to occupy their little minds (read: mouths), and it was 10:00 P.M. and everyone finally went to bed. I didn't want to read. I didn't want to write. I didn't want to tackle my e-mails. I didn't want to be productive.

I wanted to laugh at Phil and Cam and Gloria.

I stopped short of actually watching it. I know the universe wouldn't have imploded if I had. One thirty-minute episode of TV couldn't ruin the whole experiment. But my DNA won out (firstborn, Type A, selective rule follower). The principle of the thing fought its way to the top, shoving down the lesser players, like boredom and entitlement.

So let's review the months thus far:

I ate Ethiopian food on the fifth day of *Simple & Free.*

I wore a nonsanctioned jacket during Day 1 of the clothes fast.

I prehoarded piles of clothes for giveaway month, just in case.

I came this close to watching TV during media fast.

I warned you about these tendencies. I never pretended I had a will of iron, people. That I'm still doing this is a miracle. The threat of public humiliation keeps the wheels on *Simple & Free,* since waaaay too many people know about this thing. While drive and determination might fail me, people pleasing will never let me down as an excellent motivator. *[Guess what I know about myself now that I didn't know then? I am a textbook Enneagram 3, which means I am driven not just by success but by what everyone thinks of my success. Surprise! Public approval (and disapproval) is a mega-motivator for me. In case you are new to the Enneagram, it is the most comprehensive personality inventory I've ever used, and it read me my own mail so precisely, I was convinced they had hidden cameras in my house.]*

Is there something similar in biblical community? Does the collective will and watch of like-minded people keep us from derailing sometimes? Innumerable times I've grown weary, but the powerful backing of my faith community lit the fire, and I carried on.

Maybe "letting down my fellow journeymen" isn't such a bad reason for pushing through either. In my circle of Christ followers, we take turns being strong. While one of us is down, the rest rally. Later, we'll trade. The equation always balances in the end. Sometimes a second surge of effort affects another believer in profound ways. I can't count how many times I've thought:

If she can do it, then I can too.

If he can hold steady, then I should try.

If God is keeping them afloat, then He'll do the same for me.

Our stories affect one another whether we know it or not. Sometimes obedience isn't for us at all, but for another. We don't know how God holds the kingdom in balance or why He moves a chess piece at a crucial time; we might never see the results of His sovereignty. But we can trust Him when He says press on, cling to hope, stay the course. He is always at work, even if the entire thread is hidden. I might be just one shade of one color of one strand, but I'm a part of an elaborate tapestry that goes beyond my perception.

The power of the church has always been in its many, many parts. In a culture of hero worship and conspicuous rainmakers, this concept struggles to emerge, but the story of God's people comprises a billion little moments when an average believer pressed on, carried through, stepped up. In the quantity of ordinary obedience, the kingdom truly advances.

So in that one area where you are fatigued and considering surrender, remember this:

> Therefore, since we are surrounded by such a great cloud of witnesses, let us throw off everything that hinders and the sin that so easily entangles. And let us run with perseverance the race marked out for us, fixing our eyes on Jesus, the pioneer and perfecter of faith. For the joy set before him he endured the cross, scorning its shame, and sat down at the right hand of the throne of God. Consider him who endured such opposition from sinners, so that you will not grow weary and lose heart. (Heb. 12:1–3)

DAY 30

Whew! What a month. I know in the big scheme of things, a media fast is not headlining news, but I gotta tell you, we had to dig deep this last week. For me, it wasn't so much the media I was missing but the knowledge that I was the only one missing it. The party was going on outside my window, and I uninvited myself.

But the wiser (read: smaller) part of my brain interrupted this pity party with a question: What are you really missing? Asinine television programming? Websites that suck you in then waste your time? The Facebook knowledge that someone is "going to the store" or her "son went big boy poopy in the big boy potty today"? These bits of information don't enrich my life in the slightest. They do, however, steal energy from my home and family, substituting face-to-face time with screens. We're all losing on this exchange, and we won't revert to the plugged-in family we were before.

Enjoy this end-of-month summary by Brandon, of rivals .com fame:

> One of Peter's early leadership lessons from Jesus was about letting go. He said the things we hold loosely are more likely to have eternal impact than the things we bind. When we hold too tightly to things, we lose perspective as well. While Jesus was talking about the kingdom in this passage [Matt. 16:19, 18:18], His words certainly give us insight to our created nature.

We like our stuff. We need our things. Usually the things we think we need become the very things we need a break from. This was the case for me with media.

I remember when you wouldn't expect a return phone call for a day or two; now if it's not within minutes, people fear you're "screening" them. A letter response that might have taken weeks has morphed into an e-mail with an expected turnaround of hours. Media have changed the way we interact with one another and what we spend our time doing. Our social norms have changed. The pressure is on. We are being held at gunpoint by our technological expectations.

What began as advances in the ease of communication have become things that clutter and consume. Media "noise" is everywhere, and some perspective would do us all some good.

This month came with a surprisingly high level of prep work: updates on social media warning my peeps I was taking a break, scouting the month for any critical sporting events, and getting any necessary projects or anticipated recreational media out of the way before we started. In hindsight, this was feasible because I knew it was only a month. Truth is, most of us could do anything for a month, but very few of us could do without media for much longer. Like expecting my dad to learn e-mail or own a cell phone, it's unrealistic to expect society to reorient their norms around any of us.

That said, while beginning this month of *Simple & Free* was harder for me than for the others (and I gave Jen a harder time about it), it became a refreshing break from the norm. Everyone was respectful—if not envious—of my Twitter and Facebook "fast," few cared whether or not I watched TV, and surfing the Internet had already lost its flair for me. Honestly, my biggest fear going into media month was that the world might stop turning until I was done, but I discovered others didn't need me to be as wired as I thought. Most of my media involvement is simply about me (blah).

This is rarely a good thing.

All told, media month offered some pretty good perspective. Someone once said, "Think about the things you'd most hate to lose (outside of your family), and you'll identify your idols." These are not only the things we treasure too much but what we've likely lost perspective on. We place this stuff on a pedestal that wasn't built for it. If we're not careful, TV can become this. Facebook and Twitter can become this. Even the unreasonable pressure to respond to every e-mail immediately can become this.

The dangerous part of our social media and technologically saturated world is not its existence but what it distracts us from. We found quality time with family, focused attention to conversation and creativity in planning our weeknights and weekends—all refreshing additions to our month. And while the Hatmaker clan resumed a very abridged schedule of TV and Internet and gaming, we certainly gained a new perspective on them all.

[I dreaded giving an update on this month of Simple & Free. *I wish I had better news to report. I'd hoped to disclose a more permanent family revolution in terms of our technology usage. But ten years later, there is even more to manage. At the original writing, there were no Instagram, Snapchat, TikTok, Musical.ly, Alexa, iPhone whatever version is current, GIFs, Tinder/Match/Bumble/Hinge, Google Nest, iPad, AirPods, Twitter, Voxer, Candy Crush, Uber, PayPal, and tons more. Guys, we were all on 3G and didn't even know what we were missing.*

While some of these developments have improved our lives (I'm looking at you, Instacart!), my point is that our bandwidth and opportunity to be staring at our phones anywhere, anytime, and for any reason have only increased. We will never experience a reversal in technology, so our only hope is to manage our consumption in a world shrunk and sped up by automation. I wish I was a better guide here. I'm addicted to the convenience, the speed, the ease of it all. My career is largely located on the Internet; I owe a great deal of my success to it. My toilet paper is delivered straight to my front porch, man.

While I find a "good old days" approach overly sentimental and impractical, as technology is here to stay and an asset to global progress by any account, old-fashioned human contact cannot be replaced. Unplugged mental rest cannot be replaced. Experiencing the world through our senses cannot be replaced. We must be the grownups in the room; our technology cannot parent and rule us, or our kids. It is possible to put limits on our usage. The world will keep spinning. It is possible to delete apps from our phones. We can declare entire days or time slots screen free. We can charge phones overnight in another room in the house. We can limit our children's usage no matter what their peers say or do. This will all be increasingly countercultural, I'm afraid, but it is our responsibility to keep ourselves and families connected to one another, to other people, and to this gorgeous earth.]

WASTE

The motto of my city is "Keep Austin Weird." Austin is superbly bizarre because of our musicians, granolas, foodies, intellectuals, exercise enthusiasts, liberals, crazies, and environmentalists. Our nicest five-star restaurant would feature a couple dressed to the hilt next to five college frat boys in backward hats. No one thinks this is strange. Ask any local about Leslie—our cross-dressing homeless transvestite who once ran for mayor. *[RIP, Leslie!]* I love it here. I plan to live here forever and get buried in the backyard. When we moved to Austin ten years ago, I asked two questions:

Do I have to start running?

Do we need to start recycling?

Part of Austin's charm is its green obsession, I mean, consciousness. Our impervious cover law forbids residents or corporations from building on more than 20 percent of their land—you know, to save the trees. (A visiting friend as we drove down the highway: Where is the city? Me: Under all these trees. Look hard.) Austin is inhabited by recyclers, refurbishers, and repurposers.

And then there is me.

I'm less Mother Earth and more Mother Load, as in *Gah,* I can't be fussing with recycling bins and rainwater collection and remembering my reusable grocery bags and tree hugging. I mean, it's just the earth. If we use it up and trash it into oblivion, it will regenerate, right? Plus, I'm a Christian author, so my deal is to write Bible stuff, and the hippies can worry with creation.

Wait a minute.

Does "creation" have anything to do with God, whom I call "Creator"? Oh, pish posh. Surely God isn't worried about how we handle His creation that He created. His main concern is making His followers happy and prosperous, yes? And if we need to consume the rest of His creation to make us happy, then I'm sure God doesn't mind. I bet "creation" mainly refers to us humans, and the soil and rivers and animals and forests and oceans and wildflowers and air and vegetation and resources and lakes and mountains and streams are purely secondary, if not inconsequential.

If I'm taking cues from many mainstream evangelicals, then only Democrats and loosey-goosey liberals care about the earth. It's a giant conspiracy to distract us from the abortion and gay issues, which evidently are the only subjects worth worrying about. Ecology is for alarmists who want to ruin our lives and obsess about acid rain.

I'm beginning to wonder if the unprecedented consumption of the earth's resources and the cavalier destruction of its natural assets is a spiritual issue as much as an environmental one. Like Wendell Berry wrote: "The ecological teaching of the Bible is simply inescapable: God made the world because He wanted it made. He thinks the world is good, and He loves it. It is His world; He has never relinquished title to it. And He has never revoked the conditions, bearing on His gift to us of the use of it, that obliges us to take excellent care of it. If God loves the world, then how might any person of faith be excused for not loving it or justified in destroying it?"[1]

He might have a point.

This month the Hatmakers are doing their part, setting aside apathy and respecting the earth God made and loves, trying to care for it in a way that makes sense for our kids and their kids and everyone's kids. Because let me tell you something: We are wasters. We are consumers. We are definitely a part of the problem. I no more think about how my consumption affects the earth or anyone else living on it than I think about becoming a personal trainer; there is just no category for it in my mind. (Please revisit my introduction to *Simple & Free,* where I declared *repentance* the first motivation. Thank you.)

So, Month Five = seven habits for a greener life, a fast from assuming I am not a part of an integrated earth but somehow above it all, expecting that sacrifices necessary to accommodate humanity should be made by species other than me.

- Gardening
- Composting
- Conserving energy and water
- Recycling (everything, all of it)
- Driving only one car (for the love of the land)
- Shopping thrift and secondhand
- Buying only local

If you've implemented these habits for years, forgive me if I ever called you "earthy crunchy." We currently do none of these, so this is a giant departure from careless consumption that requires nothing of me. God's earth is like my kids' artwork:

Rather than briefly admiring it then throwing it away when they turn their backs because *my gosh* where am I going to put these handmade treasures that seem to have no end, instead I'll treat their creations respectfully. I'll carefully display their work and declare it all a masterpiece while realizing that though it seems production will last forever, it will run out as my kids grow older, and my days of enjoying the work of their hands will be over, and if I don't preserve their creations right now, one day I'll have bare walls because I squandered these beautiful offerings when they seemed plentiful.

I've got to separate myself from this astute observation by the writers of twitter.com/xianity: "Today is Earth Day, or as conservative evangelicals call it, Thursday."

Ouch.

DAY 1

My fingers are raw.

My back is aching.

My feet are throbbing.

My shoulders are burning.

As I sit in filthy clothes past the "wring the sweat out" phase but damp enough to chill me to the bone and also gross me out, I'm ruminating on the first day of Green Month/ Waste Fast.

It started with a trip to the Sunset Valley Farmers' Market with my produce sherpas, Gavin and Sydney. We brought the necessary tools: reusable cloth grocery bags and cold hard cash. (You want to draw scorn from the Austin local foodie community? Exit the farmers' market with fifteen plastic bags. Might as well dump oil into Lake Austin and drive a Hummer through the Earth Day parade.)

Austin is a very green city, so plenty of patrons at the farmers' market looked like average nine-to-fivers. However, there was an exciting contingency of granola people, which made for excellent people watching ("Mom! That lady's nursing her baby *while she's walking around!*").

It's July, so the farmers' market is in lovely form: tomatoes, English cucumbers, blackberries, melons, peaches, beautiful squash, green beans galore. Other local vendors bring artisan breads, gourmet olive oil, freshly ground flour, handmade hummus/salsa/pesto/pico, fresh eggs, organic meats and cheeses, fresh tamales (bliss). We devoured homemade tacos and hand-squeezed lemonade while a sweet little Birkenstock band played us some bluegrass.

I was in foodie heaven.

My perfect children improved this nirvana by freaking out over every eggplant and heirloom tomato. Whether this was sincere or satirical, I'm not certain, but still. We carried bags packed with produce picked in the last day or two, smudged with dirt, all delightfully messy and unpackaged.

With vendors like this, how could we go wrong? Acadian Family Farm, Fruitful Hill Farm, Full Quiver Farm, Engle Orchards, It's About Thyme Garden Center, Johnson's Backyard Garden, Kitchen Pride Mushrooms, Rocking B Ranch, Sandy Creek Farms—the farthest farm is an hour away, most within city limits or just outside.

We brought our bounty home and ate half immediately. It's peach season in central Texas, reader. Our Fredericksburg peaches lasted three hours. I sliced up cucumbers, onions, and tomatoes and immersed them in vinegar, sugar, fresh dill, salt, and pepper, and they'll be gone tomorrow. Everything else got chopped, peeled, diced, or rinsed, ready for quick consumption.

So I'll discuss this in detail tomorrow, but we planted a garden two months ago for this phase of *Simple & Free*.

I have so much to say about this.

Again, tomorrow.

Anyhow, today we edged our garden with two-by-fours. This involved a lot of digging, scooping, grunting, and lifting. The fingers on my right hand are so sore, I keep choosing words that are left-keyboard dominant. (My nemeses? The letters *i, k,* and *m. -y—ddle f-nger -s ach-ng*!) I'm such a garden virgin that I don't have proper tools; hence, ungloved hands that act as shovel, hoe, wheelbarrow, and vise.

The garden properly contained, I went inside to construct my first composting bin. Piece A to Piece B, snap in, snap down, slide on top . . . voilà! An overpriced plastic box. Considering my mom's compost is a huge pile of rot on the ground (this has a good connotation here), no one need overspend on a plastic box with "ventilation outlets" (holes) to contain it all.

BRANDON: Are you putting that together inside?

JEN: No, I just spread the parts all over the floor because I wanted more things to pick up around this house.

BRANDON: I'm picking up on your sarcasm. Are you sure it will fit through the back door?

JEN: Uh, I think I can accurately eyeball the basic width of a box and determine if it can fit through the door.

So I'm in the living room typing next to my compost bin, which won't fit through the door. Whatever. I've spent hours researching composting, and even though every website says, "This is the easiest thing in the world!" the next line includes formulas for the necessary carbon-nitrogen balance lest your compost turn into a slimy, stinky, rotten mess and attract every rodent and fruit fly in a ten-mile radius.

"Leaves = 60:1, Legume Hay = 15:1, Non–Legume Hay = 30:1, Sawdust = 400:1. A moisture content between 50 to

60 percent is desirable in an active compost pile." *What the what?* How do I know if hay has lost its leguminess? What does 60 percent moisture content look like? Somewhere between putrefied decay and damp rot? There is clear room for this project to turn nasty.

So for now, I'll just kick my feet up on my compost bin and watch a little Food Network (thank heavens media month is over).

DAY 2

I'm smart about a few things. I've managed my kids' math homework all the way to seventh grade with only a couple of meltdowns. I can talk pretty confidently about *Gilmore Girls*. I am now an expert on international adoption (I-600A? USCIS? DTE and RR? I know what all that means). Thanks to my girlfriend Laura, I can now "turtle down" with my head and make my face look skinnier in pictures. So clearly I've got some skills.

Gardening is not one of them.

Rarely have I encountered a subject I am more ignorant about. For three-quarters of all produce, I have no idea how it grows. I don't understand life cycles or know where anything is found in nature.

SYDNEY: Mom? Can we plant watermelon?

ME: Honey, I don't know if we have room for a watermelon . . . bush?

I've never plucked an eggplant off its vine/stem/root (please circle whichever system gives eggplants their life). Until now, my produce originated from the same place where it is all in season, all the time: the grocery store. Whether it is a hot-weather vegetable or a fruit that requires sandy soil, I haven't a clue. It doesn't matter because it can be prematurely picked, artificially ripened, and shipped from anywhere on earth if I need it for my cobbler that day. I've never picked something from my backyard and fed it to my family.

Thinking ahead to this month, I couldn't shake the idea of gardening, cultivating respect for the earth and the miraculous way it sustains humanity. I don't want to raise ignorant little consumers who think food is from the fridge, where produce angels magically deposit it. Appreciating creation means learning what it is capable of producing. I want to initiate the seed ➜ plant ➜ harvest cycle, like every generation in history has done until mine.

Here is the appropriate place to mention I kill all plants.

My mother-in-law gave me a cactus, which needs water once every two months, and it perished under my sustained neglect. Every plant in my home is plastic. Somehow I gave life to actual human children, but I cannot remember to splash water on a bougainvillea. I have a dismal history growing anything other than *Homo sapiens*. To be honest, while I was considering a garden, the voices in my head said, "You won't actually do this" and I was 95 percent sure they were right.

Enter the best thing that ever happened to Month Five. E-mail from my friend Amy:

> Hey Jen! Your mom said you were researching garden stuff but you were probably too garden stupid to pull it off. I am similarly inept but interested and just found a nonprofit that is the answer for remedial bleeding-heart gardeners.

It's called the Karpophoreō Project (pronounced car-puh-fuh-RAY-oh), a Greek word that means "to bear fruit in every good work." The KP Project bears genuine fruit, from the soil and in the lives of real people. This is their mission:

> KP and the HOW program work with a community of men, women, and families that once suffered from chronic homelessness, most having experienced at least one year on the street. The marks of such homelessness go much deeper than can be addressed solely by the acquisition of a home. KP is a community environment, fostering an environment for healthy interactions with each other and a positive contributor to the city. [2]

Willing partners offer KP their land for a backyard garden and/or backyard farm (the farm involves chickens, and I'm sorry, but I can only handle so much, y'all), and the KP folks *build and plan the whole garden*. Their team includes regular volunteers as well as formerly homeless men and women.

Then, they come out weekly and prune, treat, and harvest. Half the produce stays with the homeowner, and the other half is sold at the farmers' market or in subscription boxes. The formerly homeless who work the gardens keep 70 percent of the profit. Bam. Sustainable income from locally grown organic produce with nearly zero overhead.

Genius.

What a creative use of privately owned land in lieu of dedicated public property! What vision to connect privileged landowners with the chronically homeless, building relationships and making something beautiful together. KP just planted a huge garden at the Travis County Correctional Center, continuing their inventive mission of bearing good fruit in unlikely places with unlikely farmers.

Speaking of unlikely farmers, I have a garden, thanks to the KP team. I'll write about the garden inauguration tomorrow, but if you've paid attention, you realize I managed to mix local organic food (Months One and Five) with intervention for the poor (months all) where other people do the heavy lifting and I get to feel good about that instead of guilty.

And you should see my tomatoes.

DAY 3

You might recall from Month Two that in the midst of dog excrement, a legitimate gardener, Steven, founder of the KP Project, assessed our backyard. There was some digging, some looking at the sun, some staring at dirt. Outside of the obvious poo-poo situation, our space passed, and a date was set to install our garden as spring approached.

Our backyard is pretty small, so we planned a fifteen-foot-square garden. We bought two hundred dollars' worth of rich composted soil, which was unceremoniously dumped by our back gate. Twenty wheelbarrows full and a minor hernia later, we moved it *twenty feet* to the actual garden site. (Really, dirt guy?) We staked out the garden, which felt very farmerish and awesome.

Mississippi was one of the formerly homeless assigned to the Hatmaker garden, and he could've easily passed for James Earl Jones's brother. In the marathon dirt relocation process, he had a mantra for the females:

"Use your legs, girls. Use your legs. Easy. Eeeeeasy . . ."

I wanted to use my legs, Mississippi, but my arms were required in shoveling seven hundred thousand scoops of compost into wheelbarrows. (These arms could not be lifted the next day. Thanks for nothing, legs.)

About this time Steven busts out the tiller, and it had its way with him for twenty minutes. It was like watching the rider of an out-of-control bull hanging on for dear life. Thus, the sod we'd lovingly installed was churned into oblivion, reincarnated into its next life, where it will produce more than beautiful blades of Bermuda.

Hearing a low hum, I looked for a swarm of locusts or approaching tractor. The hum grew louder, picking up volume and definition. Our heads popped up as we attempted to identify the crescendo and conceal our alarm. The sound became chattery and high-pitched, causing a fight-or-flight response in me, left over from ten years in student ministry. Then they descended:

Twenty-five teenagers on a mission trip from Arlington.

Steven had failed to mention they were coming to "help."

Jen, the KP liaison (not me, Jen, as in the author, a second Jen, KP Jen), escorted them with what can only be described as wild eyes. With a frozen smile and post-traumatic stress, she said, "Yeah, I'm not as good with teenagers as I thought." Evidently, ours was the third garden install of the day, and this church group was assigned the heavy labor to provide a spring break option superior to starring roles in Girls Gone Wild South Padre.

Let me sum up their involvement: Twenty-three of them flirted with one another while the other two sporadically tossed aside grass clods (which I retrieved and put in trash bags). The event also included water poured on heads, cheerleading moves practiced on trampoline, and one girl who sat in my living room with sweet tea because she was *overcome*.

I fully remember why we quit youth ministry.

They left after thirty minutes, and the rest of us burst out laughing. (Is this at all like Americans who take international mission trips and make a giant mess of things and leave feeling good about themselves while the locals shake their heads and clean up the wake? Oh, surely not. We know what's best for everyone in the world, right?)

Anyhow, with Steven's careful instruction, he, Jen, Mississippi, my mom, and a handful of volunteers planted the goodies; in went squash, tomatoes, bell peppers, corn, basil, zucchini, green beans, arugula, and watermelon. Seeds the size of atoms stuck two inches under dirt. Yeah, I was 100 percent convinced this was so not going to work. I predicted crop failure immediately. I instantly became a farmer—tipped my hat back, looked to the skies, scratched my head. Like washing my car is the impetus for a downpour, planting a garden guaranteed a drought. I expected it to commence at once.

When the team left, it was exactly like the moment I was alone the first time with my baby. When the experienced mothers vacated, I was left with an infant no one was sure I could raise. (Ironically, we practically have to be sainted to get through the adoption process, but any fool can spawn and have a baby, tra la la.)

So I had a little come to Jesus meeting with my new garden:

"Garden? I'm really going to try here. I promise to care about you and feed you water and fight off your enemies. I can't make too many promises, Garden, because I once (allegedly) killed a cactus, but I'm turning over a new vine. I'll be there for you. These five words I swear to you. When you breathe, I want to be the air for you."

Garden just sat there looking rather embryonic, but I picked up on the signal it sent out. It said:

"I feel very scared."

[This section is making me laugh so hard. I want you to know something as you read about my amateur gardening journey: I continued to garden for five years after this until we moved. Please be impressed, reader.]

DAY 5

Garden update: My melons won't grow.

The last time I said this was seventh grade, with an eerily similar angst.

If I understand this problem like I think I do, Watermelon Vine is sick with envy, wondering why Tomato is ripe with plump, round fruits while she is still flat as a Kansas highway, developing gawky, awkward shoots everywhere, but no freaking melons. I bet she does a self-examination every morning hoping, *hoping* for development, a promising bud at least, only to discover a lengthening of her skinny vine in another clumsy direction, impossible to maneuver with any grace.

I keep telling my melon vine that her day will come; we develop differently, that's all. It's basic biology, nothing to fret about. Some vines sprout early, requiring wires and string to hold up their bulging fruits sooner than others. Not to worry, Watermelon Vine, soon you'll need your own wire and string, and your melons are going to be waaaay bigger than Tomato's. Trust me.

I know she looks smug, what with her perfectly rounded bounty that everyone admires while you're just a skinny vine without so much as a bud, but believe me, Tomato will be yesterday's news once your sweet fruits develop. I've seen the gene pool you came from; the future looks bright for you, WV. Your kind grows them big. (If you want, we can get you a wire and string like your more developed garden friends so Basil will quit mocking you; like he's so awesome—he's just a bunch of leaves.)

Parenting my garden requires way more emotional energy than I expected. It was easier when they were just little seeds and all they needed was water. Sure, I worried about them in their infancy, but at least it was *simple*. Now there's all this drama and competition: Who's sprouted, who hasn't, who is independent, who is more—how shall I say it nicely?—*needy*? Wow. It's a good thing we don't know all that is involved in raising a garden when we first conceive it, or none of us would bear any fruit.

DAY 8

So, one car.

I realize 86 percent of the world does not even own one car to squabble over, but we have been a two-car union since our dating years, when my hair took over the entire cab of my bad-to-the-bone RX-7.

When my friends and I were in Manhattan last year on a girlcation, we took public transportation everywhere, and it was both invigorating and slightly stinky. I like the idea of public transportation, the efficiency of it, the urban lure. Next to our mortgage, cars and their upkeep comprise the biggest slice of the budget pie. I'd gladly kiss gas stations, Jiffy Lube, and the DMV good-bye forever. If I never drove on I-35 in bumper-to-bumper traffic again, you could color me happy and maybe declare a moratorium on my little road rage problem.

But those urban transit alternatives do not transfer well to suburbia. We've made our master-planned community bed, and now we have to drive to it. Our suburb is not concentrated with little bodegas and boutiques within walking distance. We have big-box grocery chains. We have landscaping. We have a Cracker Barrel. We drive eight hundred yards to our neighborhood pool, for the love of the land. The American urban exodus came at a cost, and commuting was certainly on that bill.

We technically work from home, so you would think a one-car system would work, but you would be wrong. Especially since it's summer and I am in full mom mode. I'm neck deep in water parks, movies, swimming pools, camps, and "kids eat free" destinations. Perhaps this is obvious, but none of these are next door. The car has seen a lot of action.

Additionally, and again, perhaps this is obvious, but the working-from-home thing suffers with the offspring up in our grille every day. Every summer, I bid farewell to productivity. But because Sunday sermons and book deadlines are fairly inflexible, we vacate the house so we can keep our little jobs by actually doing them. We do this by driving away from home. In our cars.

Our first upset came courtesy of my travel schedule. I spend a decent amount of time flying somewhere to speak. I'm no stranger to the airport or its little cousin, Parking Garage, who babysits my car for ten dollars a day. So when packing for a convention in Orlando, I said, "Oh my gosh. You have to take me to the airport. This is so awesome for me! Uh, sorry for you." No parking garage, no smoldering walk to the terminal, no twenty-dollar exit fee, no where-did-I-park? dilemma, one husband and three little faces waiting for me at the curb when I deplane.

Yes, please.

Less driving is theoretically marvelous for me, albeit practically challenging. To reduce our dependence on two cars, we would need to reconsider how and where we live. We'd have to think like my friend Carson, who lives downtown with her little family, riding their bikes everywhere. (I ran into Carson at Target around Christmas with my basket burgeoning with presents. I asked her what she was giving her daughter, and she replied: "An apron." I just blinked at her dumbly, like a pigeon.)

Or we'd need to reconsider our availability, driving all over Austin for lunches, meetings, coffees, and sessions. Come to you? Yes. Drive to your part of town? Sure. Meet for coffee instead of talk on the phone? No problem. You need me? On my way. This has rendered us slaves to two cars. Leery of letting someone down or substituting a twenty-minute phone call for a two-hour lunch, we pass out our time like Halloween candy, traversing the city and feeding the odometer.

What if we said, "Wednesdays are for meetings, and the other days are off-limits"? If we stopped letting the tail wag the dog, could a one-car scenario work for us? It seems like simple planning, and a proactive stance could revolutionize the way we drive, maybe even the way we live.

Which reminds me, I need to text Brandon; I fly home tomorrow at 2:35, and he's picking me up. I'll be the girl on the passenger pickup curb casually checking e-mails and waiting leisurely for my driver.

[2010 Jen had three kids ages seven to eleven. Current Jen has five kids ages fourteen to twenty-two. Four of them drive. This brings the grand total of our cars to six. Dammit! We are going in reverse on this initiative. We don't have public transportation out here, two of these kids are at college, and the rest of them go in forty directions a week. I sound so defensive, don't I? Someone send help.]

DAY 10

The Council is split on green habits; five really try, and one doesn't at all (I shan't name names, but said person not only employs zero green efforts but also lies about it). The rest of us waffle between zeal and guilt, diligence and hypocrisy. Here are Becky's ruminations on going green:

Before I moved to Austin, I was in no way green. I wasn't even teal. Since then I have tried to live more responsibly. I keep shopping bags in the car, I recycle, I take old batteries to Radio Shack (meaning I keep a pile of batteries so long that my husband gets sick of it and takes it for me), and I send away my empty ink cartridges. Recently I joined the KP Project that tends my garden for half the produce. Therefore, I garden.

Since I garden (chuckling), I decided to compost. I feel very Ma Ingalls sending my daughters out to dump the countertop compost bin—an ice bucket I got at Goodwill—into the backyard "compost bin" (i.e., a trash can with holes punched in the side). I laugh every time the girls do the heebie-jeebie dance at the sight of God's little creatures doing their work.

Although I recycle so much more, there are four thousand ways I can live more green. One thing is sure: my carbon footprint will always lead back to Sonic until some tree-hugging hippie discovers a non-Styrofoam vehicle to deliver the icy perfection that is the Sonic soda.

Sorry, planet.

DAY 11

You know what's a layup for buying local in Austin? Dining out. *No hay problema.* Austin is a jackpot of locally owned, independent restaurants. This is a foodie town, so choosing Olive Garden instead of Carmelo's is like skipping a Jonny Lang concert for the Jonas Brothers—cause for great scorn. [*I love the Jonas Brothers reboot and I am not sorry.*] When discussing a good steak, a friend of ours asserted with absolute seriousness: "Well, you can't beat Chili's," and we have repeated that line behind his back one million times since.

Like music, we take food seriously here in the capital city. Plenty of remarkable chefs call Austin home. You're more likely to drive past Salt Lick, Magnolia Cafe, Iron Cactus, or Matt's El Rancho than an Applebee's around here. This gives us plenty of opportunities to eat creative, innovative food and act superior. (Notable exceptions to the chain aversion: Chick-fil-A, P.F. Chang's, and Whole Foods. I'm comfortable with some hypocrisy.)

So although Sonic and Starbucks are off the menu, I can still drive my (one) little car to Leaf, Moonshine, and Eastside Cafe. (Please come to Austin immediately and eat at these restaurants.) Circulating my money back into Austin's economy is thinly veiled as noble, barely disguised as purely preferential.

DAY 12

Why buy local?

FOOD

- Most produce is shipped an average of fifteen hundred miles to your grocery store, and that's just domestic produce. International mileage is substantially higher.

- We can afford this only because of the artificially low energy prices we currently enjoy and by externalizing the environmental costs of such a wasteful system.

- Cheap oil will not last forever though. World oil production has already peaked, and while demand for energy continues to grow, supply will soon start dwindling, sending the price of energy through the roof. We'll be forced then to reevaluate our food systems.

- By subsidizing large-scale agriculture with government handouts, we:

- Expedite the extinction of small farmers and diversified crops.

- Facilitate agriculture that is destroying and polluting our soils and water, weakening our communities, and concentrating wealth and power into a few hands.

- Industrial food production is entirely dependent on fossil fuels, which create greenhouse gases that are significant contributors to climate change. The biggest fossil fuel use in industrial farming is not transporting food or fueling machinery; it's chemicals. As much as 40 percent of the energy used in the food system goes toward the production of chemical fertilizers and pesticides.

- Food producers use large amounts of paper and plastic packaging to keep food from spoiling as it is transported and stored for long periods of time. This packaging is difficult or impossible to reuse or recycle.

- These large-scale, agribusiness-oriented food systems are bound to fail over the long term, sunk by their own unsustainability.

- Only eighteen cents of every dollar, when buying at a supermarket, goes to the grower. Eighty-two cents goes to various unnecessary middlemen.[3]

- Farmers' markets enable farmers to keep eighty to ninety cents of each dollar spent by the consumer.

GOODS AND SERVICES

- When you buy from an independent, locally owned business, twice the amount of your money spent recirculates through the community, doubling the positive impact on the local economy.[4]

- Nonprofit organizations receive on average 250 percent more support from smaller business owners than they do from large businesses.

- Our one-of-a-kind businesses are integral to the distinctive character of our cities.

- Environmental impact is reduced, as locally owned businesses generally make more local purchases, requiring less transportation.

- Small local businesses are the largest category of employer nationally and provide the most jobs to residents in our communities.

- A marketplace of tens of thousands of small businesses ensures innovation and low prices over the long term. A multitude of small businesses, each selecting products based not on a national sales plan but on their own interests and the needs of their local customers, guarantees a much broader range of product choices.

- Local businesses owned by people who live in the community are less likely to leave and are more invested in the community's future.[5]

DAY 13

We had our first cognizant *Simple & Free* fail. Okay, we actually had two. In the same day.

The first came courtesy of back-to-school shopping. Like all children, mine are mutants growing at unnatural rates. Overnight, their jeans become capris, and their big toes emerge from their shoes. It's ridiculous. Although we test the feasibility of last year's shoes at the end of every summer, it's like Cinderella's stepsisters jamming their hammertoes into the tiny crystal slippers that look like they were made for Cabbage Patch dolls. No dice.

This created quite a conundrum for "buying local."

I researched, I hunted, I made phone calls, I googled, but I couldn't find a local tennis shoe that wasn't made out of hemp or straw. The only option was RunTex, a local high-end runners' store, but the day I spend $110 on a pair of shoes for my eight-year-old is the day someone needs to slap the tarnation out of me. Sorry. Not even for *Simple & Free* will I turn into an imbecile.

I waited until the last second, hoping to solve the dilemma, but with school starting in four days, I went to Academy and bought them Nikes. *Just do it?* I did.

Failure 2 was a result of poor planning. I signed up to bring not one but two people dinner this evening. Somehow I imagined that back-to-school shopping, sour cream chicken enchilada creation, and food delivery could fit into a four-hour window. They might have were it not for that stinkin' recipe; www.cooks.com is a liar. Those enchiladas take "30 minutes to prep" only if Rachael Ray and Bobby Flay are my sous chefs chopping, pureeing, sautéing, and shredding while I'm executing the other forty-nine steps.

An hour behind, I realized I wouldn't make it home in time to hand the car off so Brandon could bring Caleb to his first football practice. Preparing them for this conundrum, I threw out an asinine question: "Can you go twenty minutes late?"

Three seconds of stunned silence followed while one thirty-eight-year-old and one third grader tried to comprehend the blasphemy I'd just uttered. Then their brains recovered and the crap hit the fan:

"It's my first practice!"

"He's getting his uniform!"

"I wouldn't even miss five minutes!"

"I want to stake his place on defense!"

"The coach will think I'm a slacker!"

"We're not going to be that family who traipses in late!"

"This is football, Mom! It's not like school!"

"This is football, Jen! It's not like church!"

Reader, allow me to explain the seriousness that is football in Texas. There are things we take lightly here, like education and soccer. Texas ranked forty-eighth among the states on SAT scores, but who cares when UT has the number one college football recruiting class in the nation? So what if he can't read; our incoming offensive lineman ran a 5.10 40 at the combine. In Texas, football is first. Decrease the enthusiasm by 86 percent, and you'll find every other sport.

Of course I know this, even subscribe to it. We have season tickets on the front row at Darrell K. Royal–Texas Memorial Stadium, where we get on TV every other game, due largely to our grizzly seatmate to the left, who holds signs like "Bob Stoops drives a minivan" and rings a cowbell after every play. I once turned down a conference because it was during the Red River Shootout. I love football like most girls love shopping. *[2010 Jen? Sydney is going to be a Texas Longhorn in ten years. All your dreams come true. She will never understand football unfortunately, as she says the games "feel crowded," but the Eyes of Texas Are upon Her and in addition to paying for those season tickets for another decade, you will also one day send UT tuition. Take all our money!]*

So I owned my temporary insanity, blaming my faux pas on the Nikes and the stress they caused me. I promised to drive like Danica Patrick to get back on time. Midway through my second delivery, I called and told them to take the other car to practice; I wouldn't make it unless my car turned into a flying DeLorean.

And the one-car family became two.

You could argue that peewee football practice wasn't a sufficient reason to breach *Simple & Free,* but I'd like you to come down here and say that to our faces. Do you think Vince Young's mom made him late for practice while he finished his English homework? Clearly she did not. And the whole state is grateful. Some things are more important than others. When my son is employed by the NFL as a tight end, anchoring the strong side and developing a sturdier pocket, he will point back to his upbringing, extolling the factors that led to his success, and among them will be this:

"My mom made sure I was never late for practice."

DAY 15

I realize the novelty of recycling wore off around 1992, but since I am somewhat late to the party, please indulge my enthusiasm. We decided to recycle every possible item this month: glass, tin, cardboard, plastic, batteries, ink cartridges, paper, and cans. Even our food scraps are recycled into compost, and leftover water goes to Lady's bowl. I have bins for every category just inside the garage door. Breaking news:

We have like zero trash.

We used to roll our trash bin out with the lid propped halfway open, thanks to eight bags of waste crammed inside. Our family was keeping the landfill business in top working order. That big trash swirl in the ocean Oprah did a show on? I think I recognized the cereal boxes I cut Box Tops out of before promoting them to their second career as pollution.

But after the spaghetti boxes and jelly jars and coffee tins and detergent bottles relocate to the recycling bins, there is almost nothing left. We put out one small trash bag for the whole week.

This has become an obsession for me. I inspect the trash can every day to see if something can be rescued for recycling. Every time I find a plastic container or cardboard box, the family gets another rendition of "Why This Does Not Go into the Trash Anymore," which they *love*. I study my recycling bins once a day, marveling at how much trash we generate. I will *not* do the math on how much we've tossed that could've been repurposed.

Speaking of, the United States has 3,091 active landfills and more than 10,000 old municipal landfills. The environmental issues these generate run the gamut from hazardous waste through toxic gas emissions and low-level radioactive waste to leakage into ground and surface water. The health hazards posed cause much protestation and controversy.

Then there is the issue of volume, which even the most sophisticated system can handle for only so long. Americans generate trash at an astonishing rate of 4.6 pounds per day per person, 251 million tons per year.[6] This is twice as much trash per person as most other developed countries. Trash production in the United States has almost tripled since 1960, thanks to the onslaught of prepackaged everything-under-the-sun.

Trash in a landfill will stay there, as is, for a superlong time. Trash is dumped in sections (called "cells"), compacted, and covered with dirt before the next round. With little oxygen and moisture, trash does not decompose rapidly; landfills aren't meant to break down trash, only bury it. When a landfill closes—because no site can bury trash indefinitely—it must be monitored for thirty years because of the contamination threat.

This is an unprecedented problem as ours is the first society to generate disposable material by the millions of tons annually. Plastic bottles, containers and packaging, technology waste . . . these are the by-products of "modern progress." Cheese didn't always come packaged in plastic with paper dividers; people used to just make their own and then eat it.

Twenty-five years ago you'd have been hard-pressed to find a bottle of water for sale, but thanks to a clever industry who repackaged basic tap water and sold it to a society of convenience as a superior option, as if they collected it from the runoff of the Colorado Rockies, we now consume 8.6 million gallons of bottled water a year, at only a wee cost increase of 240 to 10,000 times the price of tap water.[7] Then into the trash, la-di-da. For the bargain price of a dollar, I receive sixteen ounces of tap water and contribute to the waste crisis.

But just when I was feeling tickled pink about recycling, I read this:

> The most effective way to stop this trend is by preventing waste in the first place. . . . Waste is not just created when consumers throw items away. Throughout the life cycle of a product, from extraction of raw materials to transportation to processing and manufacturing facilities to manufacture and use, waste is generated. Reusing items or making them with less material decreases waste dramatically. Ultimately, less materials will need to be recycled or sent to landfills or waste combustion facilities.[8]

In other words, by the time I put my glass in the recycling bin, it has already caused the lion's share of damage via processing and shipping. I'm not sure we should throw a party over a recycled wine bottle that was commercially mold-blown in a factory with its little friends, and then burned up 11,884 nautical miles getting from the processing plant in Brazil to Italy then to my pantry. Recycling at that point is like ordering a super-sized Big Mac Value Meal, then adding, "With a Diet Coke, please." Nice try, sister.

True reform involves purchasing fewer disposable materials in the first place, which you can do by buying bulk products, produce from the farmers' market, and secondhand goods that have already shed their packaging. Best practices include reusing containers over and over, lowering the consumption of single-use materials. Recycling is probably a third-tier tactic toward genuinely reducing waste for maximum impact.

Society was much kinder to the planet before this century. Granted, earth gave society minor problems like the plague and smallpox, but we got the last laugh with deforestation and global warming. Can we unlearn our destructive habits and reimagine a way to live lighter on this earth? What if we changed our label from "consumers" to "stewards"? Would it change the way we shop? The way we think?

My luxuries come at the expense of some of God's best handiwork: forests, petroleum, clean air, healthy ecosystems. We also ravage the lands of vulnerable countries, stripping their resources for consumption. The wealthy world has a sordid history of colonization, ruling by force over indigenous people, and profiting from their natural resources and local labor. Yes, Africa, we'll take your diamonds, gold, and oil, but you can keep your crushing poverty and disease.

What does it mean to be a godly consumer? What if God's creation is more than just a commodity? If we acknowledged the sacredness of creation, I suspect it would alter the way we treated it. I agree with Tracey Bianchi, author of *Green Mama*:

> There are a limited number of resources in this world, and when we take more than we need, simply put, we are stealing from others. By pillaging the earth for more than our share, we break the eighth commandment.... To my dismay, I realized that even in my own, sort-of-green world, I was stealing from people, present and future. Turns out I constantly steal from my kids (and yours). I'm snatching up goodies like clean air and water while millions of families clamor for a drink and struggle with disease. I'm throwing

away excess paper and packaging while rain forests disappear. I'm a kleptomaniac. But I am determined to address my failings.[9]

I am too.

DAY 17

The following account by Molly is true. I've seen the recovered bottles lined up by her trash can, and I literally have a picture of her hubby, Chris, wading through their flooded street to retrieve the recycling box as it floated away like Noah's ark. Perhaps media month made her feel violent, but Molly is the Queen of Green.

It all started four years ago, when my daughter was two and my son was a couple of months old. We were the most consumption-driven family in America. The teeny tiny two-hundred-gallon trash can the city gave us wasn't enough to hold all the diaper boxes, baby toy packaging, wine bottles (clearly the neighbors were sneaking those in), soda cans, junk, and whatever else we just used up and tossed.

I was sneaking our trash into the can next door when I realized those people had a small green bin for their plastic, glass, cardboard, and cans. If I got rid of that stuff from my microscopic trash can, I would have tons of room! That's when I found our city-issued green bin in the garage holding a busted water hose and some garden lights. I cleaned it out and started our Family Recycling Initiative of 2006.

I needed more room for trash, so I started to recycle.

Fast-forward four years. My husband has weekly poker games for which everyone brings their own drinks. At the end of every poker night, I dig through the trash for rogue bottles or cans that were tossed instead of placed neatly on the counter to be recycled. A couple of weeks ago, I crept to my new neighbor's curb, took some huge boxes out of their trash can, and broke them down for my recycling bin. I think I may have a problem at this point.

It started as a selfish act and has turned into a way of life. I can't stand to watch someone throw anything away that belongs in my green bin. I take my own bags to the grocery store, I rarely use a disposable baggie in my kids' lunches, and I helped plant a huge garden this spring. I grew up in a house always set at sixty-seven degrees; we leave ours on seventy-three. I know that's still cool, but I'm making progress. Maybe next year I can stand seventy-four.

There are areas we can improve upon, but those small changes have our families calling us "hippies." I wonder where we got our disregard for the earth?

DAY 18

Good news, everyone.

My melons grew.

Sydney, our resident gardening enthusiast, came running inside breathless, dragging me out to inspect our late bloomer. As I live and breathe, we had six preadolescent fruits exhibiting the firm, round blossoming of youth. Oh sure, they're only a handful right now, but those babies haven't seen the end of their girth. I told you, Watermelon Vine. Mama knew your buds would grow. (Who's laughing now, Tomato?)

As her rite of passage, we outfitted WV with wires and string to hold up her new developments. She perked right up, thrilled with her admission into the fruit club.

Watermelon was the last of our garden babies to sprout. We have green beans, yellow squash, zucchini, peppers, tomatoes, two different kinds of melons, and enough basil to supply the greater Austin area. Our garden is producing despite our profound ignorance. It's a miracle. Treat the earth with care, and it will give you food.

Sydney deserves the credit for the general maintenance of our little plot. She has become a ten-year-old farmer, inspecting her plants and reporting their progress. She plucks the day's ripened produce, exclaiming over every vegetable with the same manic enthusiasm her peers direct at Justin Bieber. Sydney and Steven—our KP partner—are totally in cahoots. ("Steven taught me how to detect squash bores." "Steven says to cut basil at least five segments from the top." "Steven says the cherry tomatoes are ready when they are bright orange.")

The KP team harvests once a week, and we've delightedly worked alongside the volunteers and formerly homeless. The residents who benefit from the KP Project live in an RV community in east Austin, relocated through an initiative called Community First!, which works with chronically homeless men and women, providing recreational vehicle and/or tiny housing and empowering them with support, community, and income.

The KP Project is an arm of Community First!; the residents have several community gardens in the RV park in addition to the backyard gardens they help maintain. They enjoy "Stone Soup Breakfast" every Friday morning at the community trailer in the RV park, bringing fresh produce from their gardens and cooking together. KP partners and residents meet once a month for dinner, supplied by our own produce. Steven and Jen, the oh-so-passionate innovators of the KP Project, moved into the park themselves, making that rare transition from *advocates* to *neighbors*.

The KP Project has kinks to work out, of course. As in any start-up, some things are just trial and error. But I'm so grateful to be a part of its inaugural year. I've learned so much—

about soil, about produce, about loving my neighbor. There is something so healthy about working the ground together, moving beyond the cultural boundaries that normally divide us. Bearing good fruit has many facets—in agriculture, in hearts, in the community. It's as much about the human being as it is about the zucchini.

Some of us were on the streets three months ago, some of us have master's degrees, lots of us are battling addictions, and all of us have failed, but the ground is leveled when together we turn the soil, plant the seeds, cut back the leaves, pluck a perfectly gorgeous tomato, each learning the same ancient practices that have sustained humanity since Eden. The earth brings us together. It is common ground that is becoming holy ground.

DAY 22

When I was ten, I watched *Sybil* at a sleepover and didn't tell my parents. That movie was certainly prohibited, but my friend had HBO *and* MTV, two forbidden fruits I devoured with reckless abandon since we had one console television with manual knobs to flip through all four channels. Oh, Cable, you elusive siren!

Sybil freaked me out. This was the true story of a woman who developed multiple personalities to deal with psychological trauma inflicted by her schizophrenic mom, who abused her in ways that made zero sense to my fourth-grade mind. The emergence of Sybil's sixteen different selves caused me no end of grief.

For months I feared my alternate personalities were preparing to assert themselves. I inspected my brain daily, watching for signs of a split or clues of impending pathology. If my preadolescence succumbed to a moment of hysteria, I'd sit cross-legged on my floor and chant a mantra: "Sybil, you cannot take me over." (I merged the concepts of "multiple personality disorder" and "demon possession." I was a Southern Baptist loyalist who watched HBO. Thank you for understanding.) Anytime a renegade thought passed through, I wondered: *Is that me? Or my alter ego Savannah?*

Friends, my fear of dissociative disorder appears to be manifesting now that I am comfortably in my thirties. And it was triggered not by abuse but by *Simple & Free,* a creation of my own making. After five months of retraining my thoughts, I now have competing voices in my head, struggling for domination as I attempt to shop like a responsible human.

Sometimes my organic personality, Sage Moonjava, emerges, and my top priority is to buy real food with wholesome ingredients. Sage Moonjava doesn't blink at spending $11.99 per pound for bulk organic cashews, because they were harvested responsibly and not doused in partially hydrogenated oil. Grocery chains are the bane of Sage Moonjava's existence; their produce is covered in vegetable oil, beeswax, and lac resin; the aisles contain ten thousand combinations of high fructose corn syrup, refined grains, and chemicals; and the meats are genetically modified and pumped full of antibiotics. I've abandoned a half-filled cart and walked out in utter defeat.

But at other times my "buy local" personality, Ryvre, materializes. Attempting to support the local economy and diminish the high ecological impact of importing goods, this seems like the winning approach. Buying from corporate chains is paying the Man; I like the little guy, the mom-and-pop store, the imaginative small business owner. I'd rather subsidize local vendors who retain creative ownership and feed back into our local economy. Ryvre is into "Live here, give here," and shopping at Walmart solidifies my place in the flock, contributing to a questionable supply chain and putting thousands of locally owned stores out of business every year.

However, my third alter ego, Freedom Shakra, whom you'll get to know more next month, is trying to unhook from the consumer machine, and all this buying is not helping. Freedom Shakra is just trying to spend less, *way* less. This is a numbers game, and the winners are off-brands, generic products, knockoffs, and used goods. F. Shakra understands that name brands and chic labels are the marketing brainchildren of the People Who Sell Us Stuff We Don't Need. There is no good reason to buy designer water, overpriced spaghetti, or two sprigs of basil for $3.99 when it enjoys prolific growth in my own backyard from a $0.25 cut. Addressing our embarrassing overconsumption is practically the whole point of *Simple & Free,* and Freedom Shakra is knocking the budget down by purchasing cheaper things, fewer things, smaller things.

Here's the rub.

Ryvre spots an adorable chocolate brown wrap sweater at a local boutique, the Red Door, right here in our little town. Talk about spending local! It's five minutes away in historic downtown Buda, and the owner lives up the street. Adios, Mall. No Gap for Ryvre! She's supporting the local gal.

But Freedom Shakra emerges and says, "Wait just a minute, Ryvre!" (And she rolls her eyes and pronounces *Ryvre* sarcastically to make it clear she is mentally spelling it "River.") Because that wrap sweater is forty-five dollars, and my bank account couldn't care less whether that money goes to the Red Door or straight into the pocket of Sam Walton. All Freedom Shakra knows is she's down fifty large for a sweater with a two-year shelf life, and I don't care where it came from, that's lame. Buying local is often synonymous with *overspending.*

FS is winning the day, so off she goes to the grocery store, where she spies a dozen eggs for $0.99. Hooray! At a little over eight cents per egg, that is a purchasing victory for this Thrifty Mama. Add the $2.99 package of bacon and $1.69 can of biscuits, and we're talking about breakfast for five for under $6.00. Beat that, Dave Ramsey!

But out pops Sage Moonjava, who gravely reads the biscuit ingredients. All twenty-nine of them. She recalls the dreadful farming practices that produced those hormone-injected, antibiotic-laden eggs. SMJ scolds Freedom Shakra for skipping after this processed, additive-packed bacon like it was the Pied Piper:

> *Fiddle-dee-dee I sing,*
> *Cheap processed food is king!*
> *Who needs organic?*
> *Such ridiculous panic!*
> *GMO products ain't nothing but a thing . . .*

Sage Moonjava would buy the $3.50 eggs from grass-fed, free-roaming chickens, the $5.99 organic bacon from responsibly raised pigs; and the day she feeds canned processed biscuits to her family is the day she turns herself over to the local authorities.

Sprouts is an organic grocery store, but it's not local.

Central Market is a local gourmet grocery store, but it's not economical.

H-E-B is the most economical grocery store, but it's not organic.

So Ryvre is horrified by Freedom Shakra's priority to buy cheap, and Freedom Shakra outright mocks Sage Moonjava and Ryvre for spending more on "local" and "organic" (she uses finger air quotes when she says this). The competing voices confuse me, and I'm not sure which personality should dominate. This leaves me in a mess half the time, and I manage to feel guilty one way or another, no matter which purchasing priority wins the day. I've either spent too much, bought cheap processed junk, or subsidized the sweatshop industry. Evidently simplifying can be complicated. *Gah!*

Sybil, you cannot take me over!

DAY 23

This month of *Simple & Free* has really gotten into my bloodstream. I think about my choices constantly, rescuing recyclable items and second-guessing pretty much everything we consume. All my default habits are up for debate.

The latest matter to enjoy an awkward solo dance in the spotlight of Month Five is school lunches. As school just started, I'm confronted with my dependence on plastic baggies and prepackaged food, two thorns in the flesh of green living. These cause me at least one rock-and-a-hard-place moment every morning. Susana may have discovered the solution:

> Never mind the frozen, sodium-filled, processed garbage the school lunch system is feeding our kids. It turns out even those of us feeding our kids the good stuff are doing some serious environmental damage. Between the organic juice and the individual edamame packs with SpongeBob on the front, not to mention the plastic bags filled with carrot sticks and almonds (I know! Yay me!), my three kids are discarding about two hundred pounds of packaging waste per year. (Oh, wait. Boo me.)
>
> Great, now I have guilt.
>
> So, like I overhauled their lunch menu from sugar water and Cheetos to the current healthy choices, this year I decided to overhaul the packaging situation.

First step, no more zipper bags. I went through these things like water. I vowed a zipper-bag-free school year for my kids. I took a twenty-dollar plunge at the Container Store and bought three supercool lunch boxes with what my freakish six-year-old calls "a center protective barrier" and what I call "a flappy-thingie," which allows for three separate compartments you can fill with food without any intermingling. The whole thing snaps shut nearly airtight and—get this—is dishwasher safe. Sold. Even Adrian Monk would approve.

The next step: prepackaged foods. I'm a sucker for string cheese and juice boxes. As it happens, my kids like Colby-Jack just as much as mozzarella. So now I buy the two-pound block, whip out the cheese cutter, and voilà! Problem solved. I'm still working on the juice box problem. I just like juice boxes so much. (It's a childhood deprivation issue. Don't ask.) It's silly, because my kids got BPA-free water bottles with their lunch boxes, so really all I need to do is fill them. Okay, fine. I'll do it. And then, the final step . . . cloth napkins. Yeah. Ahem. So . . . I hate laundry. We'll just have to see about this last one.

The bonus is, this system is way cheaper. Buying in bulk is saving my family money. Big food corporations are making a killing off lunch-sized packaging. Individually wrapped string cheese averages $9.00 a pound and I get my Colby-Jack for about $4.00 a pound. A no-brainer. Juice boxes are about fifty to seventy-five cents each, and water is—oh yeah—free. Seems to be adding up quite nicely.

If waste-free school lunches were a hassle, as some environmentally friendly things can be, I might complain. But this is pretty easy. It is also a lesson I'm passing to my kids, the future generation. And that might be the most important part of this equation.

DAY 25

Okeydokey.

I need to hem and haw a bit before I say what I need to say. Sooo, hey, everyone! Thank you for making it this far with me. Wow! Five months of this business. Um. My kids are back in school, so if my writing seems more coherent lately, that's why. If not, disregard the previous sentence. What else? Oh! This is actually relevant. We just submitted our dossier to Ethiopia! Hooray! We are officially in line for our referral now, and I've started dreaming about our African kids like I did during pregnancy. Last week I dreamed we brought our baby (?) back from Ethiopia, but we had to pick her up at baggage claim. Another mama was waiting for her baby, too, and I was petrified she was going to take mine, so I kept edging her out. Finally my baby came around the carousel, and she had a giant afro. I named her Kyla.

We bought a used Suburban during green month.

Okay, there. I've said it, but better news is coming, so keep reading. You might remember we drove only one car this month, which was not as challenging as expected. However, we are now on official adoption notice, meaning shortly we will have five children. This will require a big vehicle. The end. I've pulled my hair out, wrung my hands, and shaken my head from side to side, but there is no getting around it. A family of seven doesn't *arrive* at their destinations so much as they *invade*.

We looked at minivans.

We looked at hybrids.

We looked at conversion vans.

We looked at station wagons.

Activating my multiple personalities, we juggled competing priorities: space, price, gas mileage, fuel consumption, and emissions. Prioritizing fuel consumption cancels out space. Choosing emissions can utterly inflate the price. Selecting price can wreck gas mileage. Since space was nonnegotiable for our family, I would have loved a big hybrid Tahoe, but if we'd spent $45,000 on a car, Freedom Shakra would've killed me in my sleep.

We did the math.

We crunched the numbers.

We googled our hearts out.

We bought an eight-year-old Suburban that runs on . . . flex fuel!

Comfortably priced in four digits, it was the best option to appease all the voices. Let me condense the alternative fuel research for you: Rather than running on straight gasoline, flexible fuel vehicles (FFVs) are powered by an 85 percent ethanol—15 percent gasoline blend, which is considered an alternative fuel by the Environmental Protection Agency. Ethanol is produced domestically from corn, reducing our dependence on foreign oil and producing less greenhouse gas emissions.[10] Yay for alternative fuel! We're getting closer to Doc's DeLorean from the future.

Downside: FFVs get fewer miles to the gallon. Upside: Flex fuel is about thirty cents cheaper per gallon, so cost per mile isn't a massive increase. It will cost an additional four hundred dollars a year to run our Suburban on flex fuel. Ouch. Freedom Shakra is not too happy, but Ryvre and Sage Moonjava are thrilled because at 85 percent ethanol it uses a fraction of the gasoline, and we will conserve roughly 735 gallons of gas a year, seventeen fewer barrels. Comparing a regular Suburban to our FFV, the carbon footprint (which measures a vehicle's impact on climate change in tons of carbon dioxide emitted annually) drops from 13.3 to 9.6; greenhouse gases *not* emitted = 4,820 pounds a year.[11]

It's no Prius to be sure, but using only 15 percent of the gas otherwise required is quite an improvement. Like this FFV Suburban owner calculated: "The price of [85 percent ethanol] in my area doesn't justify E85 on price alone, but lowering dependence on oil and cleaner air does justify it for me. Look at the mileage for gasoline consumption alone: At 360 miles per tank using only 4.8 gallons of gasoline (85 percent ethanol and 15 percent gasoline), my gasoline mileage is greater than 75 mpg. That's better than the hybrids."[12]

Following all these numbers? Here's what it boils down to: a little pricier to run but remarkably better for the earth. It's a start, people. And how is this for providence? Austin has only *three* ethanol filling stations: one is just south of us in Kyle, 6.7 miles doorstep to doorstep, and another is in my zip code in Buda, 3.8 miles from my driveway. When God shuts a door, He opens a window. Or something.

Bad sound bite: Jen bought a Suburban during green month.

Good sound bite: It uses less gas than an economy car.

[Reader, I have one tiny victory to share related to our cars: Our kids drive small economy cars, and now that only one child rides with me on the regular, I have downsized my car for the first time in fifteen years. I have exited the world of SUVs. I never thought I'd see this day come. I am in charge of my own self in my own vehicle! I can listen to Hamilton *as much as I want in my little car!]*

DAY 27

Hey? How fun is www.Groupon.com for local buying? You enter your zip code, and Groupon sends a daily e-mail coupon for some local service or restaurant or product. You have to purchase (not use) the Groupon that day, but I just got twenty dollars' worth of food from Mama Fu's for ten dollars. That's free money from a local restaurant I patronize once a week anyway.

Groupon takes the sting out of some pricier local shopping options:

- $12 for $25 worth of food from Hyde Park Grill (their French fries and "special sauce" will change your life)
- $8 for a $24 one-year subscription to *Austin Monthly*
- $69 for four-week unlimited workouts at Boot Camp 512, valued at $150 (I'll pass on this one and eat the fries from Hyde Park Grill instead, thank you)
- $65 for a one-hour photo session and image DVD from Silver Bee Photography, normally $320

This is a great way to keep your money local while not busting the bank. We couldn't eat at a Pizza Hut for less than twelve dollars, but thanks to Groupon, we get a highbrow date night on a fast-food budget. And believe me, we're highbrow people. I call as my witness the cutoff sweatpants and "Beach Week 2002" T-shirt I'm wearing. Which I also wore yesterday. And to bed.

DAY 28

I drove by a neighbor's house on trash day today. I do not know these people. I saw a huge cardboard diaper box sticking out of their bin. I stopped. I reversed. I pulled it out of their trash can, broke it down, and put it in our recycling bin. It might be the creepiest thing I have ever done.

DAY 29

In many ways, I'm more like a dude than a chick. Oh sure, I straighten my hair and wear scarves and earrings, but I don't want to talk about it when I'm mad. I'm a terrible gift giver, and I love stupid humor and dumb movies.

Also excluded from my not-so-feminine DNA is the shopping gene. I would rather have my saliva permanently transmuted to urine than spend extended time at the mall. I just don't like to shop. It's fun for like zero seconds. This is why my clothes come from Target; I'm there for Sharpies, so I guess I'll buy this shirt facing the aisle. If it doesn't fit I'll return it never.

So for this month of *Simple & Free,* "buy only local or thrift" wasn't as hard as it might have been for a real girl. Not going to Express or Kohl's or wherever is a tenet not so much for *Simple & Free* as it is for my entire life. Well, it *is* challenging when we legitimately need something not readily available through local and thrift outlets, but as you might recall, we busted straight through that boundary for tennis shoes. Fine, and backpacks. (My girlfriend: "You could've sewed their backpacks out of reclaimed sweatshirts." Me: "What do you mean, *sew*? I don't understand the words coming out of your mouth.")

That said, I strolled through Goodwill to honor green month. I'm not an accomplished thrift shopper, meaning I never thrift-shop. I'm easily overwhelmed in a *regular* store organized by genre, color, and price point, so throw a little chaos and fifty crammed racks together, and I might start maniacally humming and hitting myself in the head.

Here was my assessment of Goodwill: In the category of organization, I give it a 90 percent approval rating. (The other 10 percent was its consequence for still being a store.) Items were even grouped by color, which is helpful for an antishop-per like me. Sizing had taken a fairly severe hit by entropy, but still. Shoes on the back wall. Furniture to the right. All very clean and orderly. Kudos, Goodwill.

Thanks to the color and genre subcategories, even a skeptic like me scored. My sophisticated thought process went something like this:

Too many things.

Can't breathe!

(Trying not to make hysterical monkey sounds!)

Breathe.

I like shirts.

I like brown.

I like yellow.

Here are brown shirts.

Here are yellow shirts.

I bought a cable-knit brown sweater and a buttery yellow V-neck tee that will make the perfect backdrop for my long Africa necklace. Both styles hit the scene just this year; I saw them everywhere, and by everywhere I mean on commercials. $8.45 out the door.

Plus the staff at Goodwill has a nice, laid-back, *whatevah* attitude I'm totally into. No perky sweater folders, no annoying "I'm on commission" sales reps, no judgmental cashiers following me around because my outfit communicates "I put things in my purse." In fact, as I approached the register with my two little treasures mined from the masses, the cashiers finished up a good fifteen seconds of their conversation before attending to my purchase:

"He a fool."

"I told you."

"His mama didn't raise him like that."

"He stopped going to church five years ago. Thatta tell you somethin'."

"He ain't going back to church unless they get a smoking section."

"Just leave him. Rhonda can have your sorry leftovers."

[Noticing me.]

"Oh hey, sugar. Sorry about that. We're just talking 'bout how men are dogs."

Me: "No please, by all means, carry on. Any man who quits church is up to no good. One day he stops going to church, the next day he's glued to the BarcaLounger barking for a beer."

"Girl, you ain't never told a lie. Come a little earlier next time, sugar. You can sit on the counter and enjoy *all* our gossip."

I just might.

DAY 30

Oh my stars, has this month ever lodged deep!

I keep thinking about our obsession with health. Our kids have been immunized, checked, prodded, measured, tested, and examined since the day they were born. Cuts get antibacterial crème and Band-Aids. Twisted ankles get ice. Strep throats get antibiotics. We fuel our bodies with good food, drinking enough water and milk to keep the wheels on. I make sure my parents get annual checkups, and we visit the dentist twice a year. I'm watching for tricky moles and checking for lumps. I inspect my kids' lymph nodes and keep us all sunscreened. We have a cabinet of pills in case something veers off course, and I can pick up a prescription one hour after a diagnosis.

Why?

Because God gave us spectacular bodies, and we value them.

But as certainly as God created man in His image, He first

created the earth. With the same care that He designed sixty thousand miles of blood vessels in the human body, He also crafted hydrangeas and freshwater rapids and humming-birds. He balanced healthy ecosystems with precision and established climates and beauty. He integrated colors and smells and sounds that would astound humanity. The details He included while designing the earth are so extraordinary, it is no wonder He spent four of the six days of creation on it.

So why don't we care for the earth to anywhere near the degree we do our bodies? Why don't we fuss and examine and steward creation with the same tenacity? Why aren't we re-fusing complicity in the ravaging of our planet? Why aren't we determined to stop pillaging the earth's resources like sav-ages? Why do we mock environmentalists and undermine their passion for conservation? Do we think ourselves so su-perior to the rest of creation that we are willing to deplete the earth to supply our luxuries? If so, we may very well be the last generation who gets that prerogative.

"There is not always more," explained Steven Bouma-Prediger in *For the Beauty of the Earth.* "Except for our en-ergy income from the sun, the world is finite. Numbers of individual organisms may seem limitless, but they are not. Species may appear to be beyond counting, but they are finite in number. Our life support systems may seem beyond abuse, but there are limits to what they can bear. Like it or not, we are finite creatures living in a finite world."[13]

I've been gobbling up the goodies, making a huge mess and assuming someone else would clean it up and foot the bill. But let me tell you, this month put the brakes on that. I cannot believe how God has captured me for creation care. All of it: recycling, using less, gardening, composting, conserving, buying local, repurposing instead of replacing; I'm in. From the nearly empty garbage bin to the lower electric bill, even the immediate effects of a greener lifestyle are obvious.

My land, do we have far to go! My hypocrisies are too numerous to count, but this month birthed something unmistakable: I'm done separating ecology from theology, pretending they don't originate from the same source.

> *The earth is the Lord's, and everything in it, the world, and*
> *   all who live in it;*
> *for he founded it upon the seas and established it upon the*
> *   waters. (Ps. 24:1–2)*

A friend said, "I don't know why you're trying. It won't matter. No one else cares." To that, I'll close with this bit of wisdom by Steven Bouma-Prediger:

> If God is really at the center of things and God's good future is the most certain reality, then the truly realistic course of action is to buck the dominant consequentialist ethic of our age—which says that we should act only if our action will most likely bring about good consequences— and simply, because we are people who embody the virtue of hope, do the right thing. If we believe it is part of our task as earthkeepers to recycle, then we ought to recycle, whether or not it will change the world. Do the right thing. If we think it part and parcel of our ecological obedience to drive less and walk more, then that is what we ought to do. Do the right thing. We should fulfill our calling to be caretakers of the earth regardless of whether global warming is real or there are holes in the ozone layer or three nonhuman species become extinct each day. Our vocation is not contingent on results or the state of the planet. Our calling simply depends on our identity as God's response-able human image-bearers.[14]

Let's do the right thing.

[At this original writing, Greta Thunberg was seven years old in Sweden and had never provoked mockery from the president of the United States for climate change advocacy. (Greta! You will be named Time's Person of the Year in 2019. Enjoy third grade. Your life gets crazy soon.) As I mentioned earlier, climate change and conservation are now subjects of a front-and-center global conversation.

"The world is about one degree Celsius warmer than before widespread industrialization," the World Meteorological Organization (WMO) says. "The 20 warmest years on record all occurred in the past 22 years, with 2015–18 making up the top four. Across the globe, the average sea level increased by 3.6 mm per year between 2005 and 2015.

"The change in the global surface temperature between 1850 and the end of the twenty-first century is likely to exceed 1.5 degrees Celsius, most simulations suggest. The WMO says that if the current warming trend continues, temperatures could rise 3 to 5 degrees Celsius by the end of this century. Temperature rises of 2 degrees Celsius had long been regarded as the gateway to dangerous warming. More recently, scientists and policymakers have argued that limiting temperature rises to 1.5 degrees Celsius is safer. An Intergovernmental Panel on Climate Change report in 2018 suggested that keeping to the 1.5-degree Celsius target would require rapid, far-reaching, and unprecedented changes in all aspects of society."[15]

It is all so real. I am recommitting to doing the right thing. I am examining it all: our meat consumption, carbon footprint, waste, single-use products, travel, sourcing. I want to have an answer for my grandchildren when they ask what I did to reverse global warming. It is not too late. But this will be our generation's legacy . . . one way or another.]

SPENDING

Once upon a time, a girl averaged how many different places per month her little family spent money. She tallied bank statements for the previous year, and they averaged sixty-six vendors a month, not counting repeat expenditures. She wanted to throw up. The end.

When Brandon and I married in college, our joint income was $11,270. We were so poor, people on welfare gave *us* cheese and peanut butter. *[Hey, 2010 Jen? This is not kind. You are trying to be funny, but you wouldn't say this a decade from now. As it turns out, poverty isn't a punch line.]* This trend continued through the early days of youth ministry and into the lean days of one income, babies, and toddlers. I remember Brandon handing me a twenty-dollar bill to feed us for a week. The refrigerator and pantry were empty, I had a preschooler at the table, a toddler on my leg, and a baby on my hip. I sat in the middle of our kitchen and bawled my eyes out.

Back then we didn't just watch each penny; we scrutinized, counted, shuffled, and squeezed every last one. Sonic was an outrageous extravagance. Staying true to our generation, we dug a deep, dark debt hole to purchase the lifestyle we couldn't afford but for some reason felt entitled to. Unwilling to live within our means, we lived paycheck to paycheck, floating checks and nodding politely as the wealthy people at church talked about their vacations and new cars, wondering who we had to make out with to acquire these luxuries (Chase and Capital One were happy to oblige).

Fast-forward a few years and here we are. I no longer fill my gas tank half full or feed my tribe on twenty dollars a week. We've conquered that debt and—brace yourself—we even have a savings account. I assure you, we don't wipe our behinds with Benjamins or anything. "Rich Christian author" is an oxymoron, trust me. Ditto for my hubby's income as "senior pastor." SPs are like farmers—only a few are heavily subsidized into obscene wealth while the little organic guys are just praying for a harvest and trying to keep the lights on.

Anyhow, once I finally quit panicking my debit card would be declined (which took *years* in the black to overcome), the pendulum swung to the other side. Now I am completely careless. And clueless. Anyone who spends money in sixty-six places a month is the most heinous kind of consumer. Had you asked me to estimate, I would've guessed less than half of what we actually fritter away.

I am the consumer the poor world and the responsible world and the world itself can't stand or sustain any longer. How will I answer for my choices when God confronts me with them one day? With this much expendable income funding restaurants, shoe stores, and movie theaters, I doubt Jesus will accept my excuses for neglecting the poor on account of cash flow.

Speaking of cash flow, we're spending money in only seven places this month—a slight decrease in consuming (sarcasm): 89 percent fewer vendors in a month, for the love of Moses. These are the vendors getting our dough:

- Sunset Valley Farmers' Market
- H-E-B gas station (flex fuel!)
- Online bill pay
- Kids' school
- Limited travel fund
- Emergency medical
- Target

Target is the all-purpose back on my roster because there is a (slight) chance the weather will turn and my kids' jeans will neither button nor cover their shins. And for the dozen other glitches (like toilet paper and detergent), Target is there for me, ensuring I don't send my son to a birthday party with kale from the farmers' market. However, we'll attempt to meet our needs any other way before traipsing off to Target, as I could sustain our entire life there without missing a step.

This means no restaurants, movie theaters, Chick-fil-A, no Coke and nachos at the UT/UCLA game (or parking), no Kindle/Barnes & Noble/amazon.com/Borders/Half Price Books to feed my habit, no lunch out after church, no Hays High School football games unless my mom the principal scores us free tickets, no hunting paraphernalia (Brandon), Call of Duty 4 (Gavin), iTunes (Sydney), fishing worms (Caleb), and Mama Fu's spicy Mongolian beef over brown rice with a beef curry roll (moi).

The Council is giving me the proverbial "we'll see" (or its Christian cousin, "Let me pray about it") when I ask about their participation. Let's face it: Month Six bites. Boiling down even moderate spending to seven options is so very un-American. Becky summed it up nicely in this e-mail:

> I thought about this while sitting in the Chick-fil-A parking lot eating dinner by myself. I'd gotten off work early, and

I was only going home. But I thought, "Do I really want to partake in whatever nachos-and-applesauce dinner Marcus made for the girls?" No. "Do I want to cook dinner just for myself?" No. Spending money unnecessarily is fun and I like it. I'm just sorry.

She's *really* going to be sorry if she mentions Chick-fil-A to me again this month.

DAY 2

Let me begin with a caveat since I already spent nonapproved money.

Ahem.

So let's make a distinction between *spending* and *giving*. The beast we are battling is consumerism, defined as "the fact or practice of an increasing consumption of goods."[1] We are severely limiting the purchase of goods or services for ourselves. The stuff *we* eat, *we* buy, *we* use, *we* like. This consumerism has become ordinary to the point of being imperceptible.

Giving, however, floats down a separate river. We're still sponsoring Arun and Aruna, orphans in India; we're still sponsoring Givemore, a fifteen-year-old orphan in Zimbabwe, and we're still tithing, without labeling these as reform worthy. We're hedging with the spirit of the law instead of the letter here. This prompted the "giving clause" via The Council, which exempted charitable spending.

Okay? So I happily funded two events this week: a grill-out for the homeless with our Restore Group, and a fundraiser for our church ABBA Fund for adoption. This is Jesus-approved spending, people. The recipients are not just my belly, my feet, or my indulged life but the ones Jesus told us to care for. Like ten thousand times.

If you don't like us spending on the poor this month, take it up with Jesus Christ and His dad, God.

DAY 2

Molly let herself into my house and left a tub of Central Market pimento cheese in my refrigerator. If I ever say another sarcastic word about her three DVRs or TV-watching spreadsheet organized by network and day with twenty-four weekly color-coded shows and room for additional midseason premieres, may a pox fall upon my house.

DAY 3

Molly offered to bring over a *free chicken biscuit* from Chick-fil-A. (Our new CFA is giving away free breakfast every Wednesday morning this month.) If this is a campaign to become Top Friend, she is clearly winning. *Clearly.*

DAY 5

I have two outlets for shopping at the farmers' market: Saturday mornings on-site and my weekly CSA box from Johnson's Backyard Garden, a seventy-acre organic farm five miles east of Austin. Buying this produce makes me deliriously happy. It is so solidly out of the industrialized food system and so deliciously local I put the smudged, unpackaged produce to my nose and deeply breathe its delightfulness every week.

CSA? Community-supported agriculture, a popular way for consumers to buy local, seasonal food directly from a farmer. Basically, a farmer offers "shares" for a monthly, weekly, or yearly fee. The share is a box of produce picked that week, and you get what you get. This sends me to the interwebbings to scrounge recipes for eggplant, bok choy, Swiss chard, and other delectable veggies I never bought because I didn't know what they were. My box includes a dozen eggs from their happy chickens and a pound of organic, free-trade coffee.

Johnson's Backyard Garden literally started as a backyard garden in urban Austin, supplying thirty families with weekly organic produce. Then it became a backyard, side-yard, and front-yard garden, thanks to word of mouth from thrilled customers. With growing community support, the Johnsons bought twenty, then forty, then another ten acres just east of Austin, and they now run a thousand-member CSA operation. I actually know my farmers' names. People, their kids are running behind the tractor on the website. I mean, come on.

I cannot explain how happy I am to direct my consumer dollar to this food supply. Yes, it is more expensive than inferior grocery store produce. No, it isn't conveniently available 24/7. Yes, my kids complain we don't have any food. Yes, I get produce I might not buy otherwise, but I'm down with this food adventure! CSA members post recipes online, and we've discovered some treasures (I'm looking at you, kabocha squash and beef coconut curry).

We have less food, but what we have is nutritious and local and marvelous and perfect. I sent the kids to school today with homemade soup in their thermoses, English cucumbers, the last of the Texas peaches, and the most scrumptious yellow peppers you have ever eaten in the history of the world. There is a big empty pantry shelf where the individual servings of Pringles and hundred-calorie packs used to be, but let's call that a good step, no matter what my kids have told you.

As Michael Pollan explained, I'm voting three times a day with my fork for a wholesome food supply. I know my dollar is a spit in the wind, but if enough of us start spitting, the Suits that control our food supply will listen—not because they care about our health, but they certainly care about money. Big Food Business will follow the dollar, enticed by a burgeoning organic market that netted $26.6 billion last year, up 5.3 percent from the previous year.[2]

And when I get a teeny bit discouraged that my little rage against the machine is silly, I remember that I'm making healthier choices for my family and rediscovering the farm-to-table system God created, and that counts. When I look at our earth's resources and all the humans it needs to sustain, I have to adopt an "as for me and my house" perspective on responsibility.

Stewardship is like that. I won't answer for the way another Christian managed money. I won't be charged with another person's irresponsible consumption. Nor will I get credit for how another faith community shared or sacrificed luxuries for the marginalized.

I'll answer for my choices.

It won't work to say, "But the church . . ." or "But they . . ." or "What about them . . ." for how we managed our money, our share of the earth. The "my vote doesn't really count so why bother?" attitude our generation loves won't fly when it's all said and done.

Common sense has my back, too. Let's think about it: spray-can cheese and avocado-free "guacamole dip" versus carrots and potatoes pulled out of the ground yesterday; do we need to ask WJWD? (Hey, Jesus! What about the mound of pork slime we developed called Spam? Who wouldn't want a mouthful of meat-flavored Jell-O?)

As for me and my house, we will try to stop buying Oreos.

DAY 8

"Just because I can have it doesn't mean I should."

I heard this recently and it stuck. The counterattack to this perspective involves a list of objections easily accessible to the standard American consumer:

- It's no big deal.
- I can afford this.
- I've worked hard for my money, so I can spend it how I want.
- I want this, back off.
- I deserve this.
- Other people spend way more.*
- I still have money in the bank.

    (*Jen's excuse of choice)

So we spend, spend; amass, amass; indulge, indulge item by item, growing increasingly deaf to Jesus, who described a simple life marked by generosity and underconsumption. Over time a new compartment develops for our spending habits, safely distanced from the other drawers like "discipleship" and "stewardship" (which has been helpfully reduced to *tithing*).

And listen, I am first in line. Don't imagine my life has been characterized by financial simplicity. I wish I had back so many indulgent purchases; specific ones grieve me endlessly. The irresponsible and selfish and vain spending I've endorsed is so staggering, I hope never to know the actual number lest I sink under it. I am in this right now, neck deep. This isn't a sage's manifesto but a sinner's repentance.

I used to say, "But we tithe, and that money goes to stuff Jesus was all into." Except many churches use it for marble floors and shiny buildings and cool videos and expensive mailers and pretty landscaping and fancy sound equipment and, in one recent case, an awesome multimillion-dollar jet.

Journey with me on a quick sidebar for a moment: How have we let the church deteriorate like this? How is this okay? How can we endorse these expenditures? When did this become standard protocol for the Bride of Christ? We've engineered an elaborate two-step to justify this egregious spending *on ourselves*. We are far from Jesus' original vision; the whole enterprise would be unrecognizable to our early church fathers. The earth is groaning, and we're putting coffee bars in our $35 million sanctuaries. Just because we can have it doesn't mean we should. I marvel at how out of place simple, humble Jesus would be in today's American churches.

But for now, let's discuss our share in this, since you don't control your church's checkbook (although you *do* get to choose a church stewarding tithe money for the greatest good, but there I go again). Let's address that original objection: "But I tithe." This basic obedience exempts the rest of our spending, assuaging our consciences and checking the stewardship box. With that drawer comfortably shut, the others can be opened at our leisure.

But you know Jesus, with the quick retort:

When he finished that talk, a Pharisee asked him to dinner. He entered his house and sat right down at the table. The Pharisee was shocked and somewhat offended when he saw that Jesus didn't wash up before the meal. But the Master said to him, "I know you Pharisees burnish the surface of your cups and plates so they sparkle in the sun, but I also know your insides are maggoty with greed and secret evil. Stupid Pharisees! Didn't the One who made the outside also make the inside? Turn both your pockets and your hearts inside out and give generously to the poor; then your *lives* will be clean, not just your dishes and your hands.

I've had it with you! You're hopeless, you Pharisees! Frauds! You keep meticulous account books, tithing on every nickel and dime you get, but manage to find loopholes for getting around basic matters of justice and God's love. Careful bookkeeping is commendable, but the basics are required." (Luke 11:37–42, The Message)

I like this Message version, with the "kick you in the teeth" quality Jesus always nailed. "I know your insides are maggoty with greed" is the very un-PC way Jesus basically put it. And He hammered that "but I tithe" excuse, too. As He pointed out to the Pharisees, they never, ever missed a penny of tithing but shamelessly neglected justice and totally missed the point. The outside was shiny while their insides were a hot mess, but lucky for them, Jesus had the remedy: "Give what is inside the dish to the poor, and everything will be clean for you."

Crickets.

I'm starting to wonder if Jesus actually meant that. Was He serious about sanctification through extreme generosity? Is He really advocating redistribution? I don't know if He knows this, but this would mean completely retooling the way we live and spend.

News flash, Jesus: Almost zero people I know live like this. I feel safer with the prosperity groupthink than with Jesus' ridiculous plan. The justification of the Christian community is happy to oblige me. (A recent statement following an exposé of a massive luxury purchase with church funds: "We operate in a manner that is worthy of the calling of Christ and have no apologies." Oh, Jesus endorses this? Carry on then.)

What if we're buying a bag of tricks? What if wealth and

indulgence are creating a polished people rotting from the inside out, without even knowing it? Is there a reason Jesus called the rich blind, deaf, unseeing, unhearing, and foolish? Jesus never utters a positive word about the wealthy, only tons of parables with us as the punch line and this observation: It is terribly hard for us to receive His kingdom, harder than shoving a camel through the eye of a needle. *That's really hard.* If this is true, then more than fearing poverty or simplicity, we should fear prosperity.

Shall we stop imagining these sad, sorry rich people belong to a different demographic? A brave believer admits, "He's talking about me." Look at our houses, cars, closets, our luxuries; if we are not rich, then no one is. If we aren't swept up in entitlement, indulgence, and extravagance, then Jesus is a fool, and let's get back to living. If tithing the minimum and consuming the rest is okay, then we can dismiss Jesus' ideas and act obsessed about other stuff He said.

But what if?

What if we are actually called to a radical life? What if Jesus knew our Christian culture would design a lovely life template complete with all the privileges and exemptions we want, but even with that widespread approval, He still expected radical simplicity, radical generosity, radical obedience from those with ears to hear, eyes to see?

What if we are camels, on this side of the needle, dangerously content with our fake gospel and avoiding the actual Christian life described in Scripture? What if the number of Christ followers is a fraction of those who claim to be? What if only some have ears to hear and eyes to see, and Jesus was not exaggerating when He predicted few would choose this narrow path and folks will be shocked on judgment day?

I'm exhausted thinking about this. Jesus' brother James had some similar ideas, but I'm too freaked out to unpack them. Literal obedience would require such a radical overhaul, my head is pounding. The ramifications are overwhelming. Today is a good day to steer clear of David Platt or Mother Teresa or Francis Chan or Martin Luther King Jr. And anything Jesus ever said. And the prophets. And the disciples. Or God.

[This entry still rattles my cages. Since this original writing, the American evangelical community has become unrecognizable to me. What we once tucked away quietly—the protection and prosperity of our own privileged lives—has now become the out-and-proud mantra. The working poor, immigrants and refugees, victims of systematic injustice and racism, desperate families—the majority of white evangelicals use their voting power and influence to further disenfranchise these groups. They are mischaracterized and dehumanized all in the name of God. We are on the wrong side of the needle.

This has been the greatest heartbreak.

To say nothing of the indictment this passage still represents for me personally. We have more now than we had then, and although we give so much away and live pretty modestly, I am still not sure we are doing this right. When the richest 0.1% of Americans take in 196 times as much as the bottom 90% combined, what the hell is going on? Where do I fit into this income gap tragedy? Everything is weird and upside down.]

DAY 10

Austin New Church is less encapsulated on Sundays and mostly represented through Restore Groups. Ninety-five percent of attenders are in Restore Groups, because otherwise, they'd be like, "What does this church even do?" since we are superlight on programs (pretty much none) or Sunday pizzazz (pretty much none). We have some churchwide stuff like Serve Austin Sunday and, um, Sunday church, but nearly all projects and Bible studies happen through Restore Groups.

Our own group morphed from one troop into four, thanks to a solid neighborhood domination strategy, executed through the novel concept of "being a good neighbor." (Thanks for the idea, Jesus!) So three groups band together once a month, take our grills downtown, and feed the homeless under the bridge at I-35 and Seventh Street.

There are hilarious nuggets to share about these evenings, including the absolute normalcy this is to all our kids. Like today, Molly's four- and six-year-olds skipped around, jumping over a sleeping man on a cardboard box over and over, oblivious to social boundaries or fear. They are surrounded by dirty men who swear and sing, under a bridge ripe with urine, and you'd think they were frolicking at Sea-World. The kids are so eager to help (handing out napkins, granola bars, bananas, water), we have to physically hold them back so they don't gang-rush our homeless friends. We broke up three fights because the kids were elbowing for position.

This is precious, of course. Proximity is transforming our children. Unaffected by social conventions, they neatly sidestep the thousand reasons we adults bypass this involvement. They pass out full hugs, conversations, and endless handshakes with such unself-consciousness, they'll lick their hands the next second and wonder why the moms are batting their fingers out of their mouths. *[2010 Jen, does this sound nice to you? Does this sentence feel dignified? Are you joking about a lack of clean water and facilities? Kid, you had a ways to go still.]* A homeless man clarified this once: "You know? We've lost so many things: dignity, security, our marriages, our jobs. But one thing we all miss is kids." A tighter safety net exists around homeless children; society won't stand for their vagrancy, so they are whisked into foster care, leaving parents on the streets. "But you guys always bring your kids down here, and it makes us happy. It's a bright spot in our dark lives."

Children bring joy to the homeless for the same reasons they bring joy to us. There is something so dear about a little voice singing or the cutest little bow in the cutest little ponytail or watching kids play football in utter innocence, breaking into dances and making everyone laugh. Plus, our kids aren't repelled by poverty, which is a welcome change from the disgust and apathy the homeless endure daily.

I told my kids, "You being here is a wonderful gift. The greatest offering is your presence—your sweet, funny, adorable presence." Yes, we've had to explain why that man is talking to himself or why that woman is crying out. Our kids are getting a street education, but they are also developing a heart for people and even getting bossy about it. For instance, here's a recent comment from Sydney: "Mom? These hot dogs are cheap calories! We say we care, but we are serving unhealthy food! We need to bring homemade food next time." *Someone* has been brainwashed.

So after our time together, when the men headed to Salvation Army to get in line for a bed, our band of families planned dinner together, like we always do. As everyone piled into cars and hollered out directions, I pulled the kids aside and reminded them we weren't spending money on restaurants. My girlfriends—conditioned as I am *never* to allow our kids to miss out—all offered to pay, but this was a teaching moment, important to *Simple & Free.*

If a fast doesn't include any sacrifices, then it's not a fast. The discomfort is where the magic happens. Life zips along, unchecked and automatic. We default to our lifestyle, enjoying our privileges, but a fast interrupts that rote trajectory. Jesus gets a fresh platform in the empty space where indulgence resided. It's like jeans you wear every day without thinking, but take them off and walk outside, and you'll become terribly aware of their absence. I bet you won't be able to forget you are pants-less, so conspicuous will this omission feel. While that metaphor is in shaky theological territory, that is basically the result of a fast. It makes us hyperaware, supersensitive to the Spirit.

So while our friends went to dinner, the kids and I drove home, talking about *Simple & Free* and struggling through the concept of self-denial. My kids' generation has never been told "no." This is a hard sell. Not quite old enough to grasp obedience to Jesus in a self-serving culture, the kids listed the tangible results of *Simple & Free* so far, including:

- We are eating 100 percent healthier.
- We gave a ton of stuff to people who needed it.
- We maintained several reforms from media month.
- Our carbon footprint is cut in half.
- We learned to garden, and we love it.
- We've pared down our rooms, our drawers, our closets, our stuff.
- We're thinking about, praying for, sharing with, and spending time with hurting people.
- We sponsored a new child through Help End Local Poverty with money we reallocated.
- Lots of our friends have joined us.
- Our prayers are changing.

We came up with this list and then some, culling lessons out of *Simple & Free* thus far. We talked about how fasting helps us think differently. We remembered the lifestyle of our Ethiopian kids, which centers us immediately. I validated their sadness at missing dinner, telling them my hardest *Simple & Free* moments, too.

As usual, Sydney was most engaged, my spiritually sensitive, bleeding-heart child. She will live in Haiti or adopt ten children or translate the Bible into an obscure language one day. She carries her emotions close, and they leak out at the slightest provocation. She thinks deeply. She cares sincerely. She worries about homeless people on cold nights. She cries over dead squirrels (well, he should have looked both ways).

Then there are my boys. I desperately worry they'll have to provide for families someday. Where thoughts on Scripture and life aspirations reside in Sydney's brain, there is a black hole for the boys, crowded out by football and Nintendo and whatever is shiny in front of their faces. I can hold them in deep territory for about forty-three seconds.

After a twenty-minute discussion on fasting, I noticed all three kids staring pensively out the windows, thinking their thoughts. I decided to mine their conclusions to show my readers how well I parented through this experiment. "Hey, guys? Whatcha thinking?"

SYDNEY: You know? We only missed one dinner out with friends. Big deal. Think how many meals the homeless people miss, Mom. Instead of feeling sorry for myself, I'm going to think about them tonight. At least we have a home to go to and food in our kitchen to eat.

CALEB: Mom? If I had to pick a superpower, I would teleport.

Awesome.

DAY 13

Phone call from my girlfriend Stephanie:

STEPH: You want to meet for lunch at Torchy's Tacos?

JEN: I can't this month. *Simple & Free.*

STEPH: Oh yeah. I'm paying.

JEN: See you at noon.

DAY 17

The Karpophoreō Project, our gardening partners through Community First!, launched the concept of "Family Dinner," a gathering of residents (formerly homeless) and KP volunteers once a month for a big meal. Ideally using fresh produce from our gardens, backyard garden hosts cook a meal in the RV park community trailer to share with the residents.

For the first Family Dinner, I volunteered to souschef alongside my girlfriends Amy and Lynde. We assembled a menu of minestrone (thank you, Pioneer Woman!), crusty French bread, green salad chock-full of goodies, and homemade raspberry cobbler. We gathered our produce bounty and drove to the RV community, approximately four inches from the airport, where planes just *insist* on taking off and landing constantly.

The community center is a jazzed-up FEMA trailer with a beautiful three-hundred-square-foot deck built by my adorable, tall, supercute brother, Drew. As we chopped and cooked and baked and roasted, the residents chatted us up with glasses of sweet tea because that is what we drink in Texas, amen.

Most of the residents have worked in our backyard gardens, so we've been in each other's lives for a year. This was a gathering of friends: Gordy, Brooke and Robin, Ms. Rosa, Jimmy, Kenneth and James, Gary, Avon.

And then there was Ben.

Ben has what we call "a little alcohol problem." On this evening Ben had indeed consumed a little alcohol, enough to tranquilize an elephant. After he'd shown my kids the broken-finger magic trick twelve times, I noticed their strained laughter and rescued them. Which is to say I became Ben's new target. The bone of contention he picked was my ridiculous plan to adopt.

JEN: We're adopting two children from Ethiopia.

BEN: Excuse me, ma'am. Excuse me, with all due respect, did you say you're adopting? *Adopting?*

JEN: Yes, Ben.

BEN: Excuse me, ma'am, ma'am, with all due respect, are you *#@!-ing crazy? You're going to adopt kids who are not like you and bring them into your home? Now I'm about to be the dumbest guy in the world, but this is the worst idea I've ever heard. Do you know what you're doing? *Do you?* I'm Puerto Rican! [I don't know how this is relevant, but he included it often.]

JEN: They're in an orphanage, Ben. We're going to be their family.

BEN: Excuse me, ma'am, with all due respect, but you are an idiot! That's like adopting *me.* Do you understand that? Like bringing *me* into your home and expecting that to work!

JEN: It would be exactly like that, Ben, if we were adopting a middle-aged Puerto Rican alcoholic, but these are kindergartners.

BEN: Ma'am, with all due respect, and I'm about to be the dumbest guy in the world, but you're about to *#@! up your life.

After a half hour of this dialogue, Ben was escorted (read: strong-armed) to his trailer to sleep it off. Upon a stern scolding the next morning, Ben couldn't remember a thing, but he was extremely embarrassed and remorseful, which is something I want you to know. Ben is human, capable of regular emotions and reform, just like the rest of us. I, too, have woken up the next day and thought, *My gosh, did I really say that?* His social misstep was no different from any regrets I've suffered from poor choices or flawed discernment. Ben sent his deepest apologies, the most noble response to failure. He messed up, then he asked forgiveness—it's the oldest song of humanity, one we've all sung.

Jen and Steven, the KP directors, declared Family Dinner a colossal failure. (Jen's e-mail to me: "I was mortified. I felt like my children were misbehaving. I have no idea how to play the role of mother at the ripe young age of twenty-six to the residents.")

Failure? I totally disagree.

First of all, "Family Dinner" *implies* some dysfunction. I call as my witness thousands of American Thanksgivings, full of drama and infighting, barely held together by a roasted turkey. Families fly their freak flags with one another; it's what families do. We *expect* Uncle Albert to drink too many rum and Cokes and start telling whacked-out stories. Families circle the wagons around this behavior, balancing concession and reprimand. Oh, Uncle Albert! You did *not* invent Facebook, you crazy old loon! Stop telling that to people! Gah, I love Uncle Albert.

Community First! teaches chronically homeless people damaged by the streets how to live respectfully and responsibly together. Pragmatically, they are being parented again through manners, fiscal stability, recovery, home ownership, and healthy habits. This is a long, messy process that requires grace and patience. If parents gave up on their kids after the first failure, no child would make it past fifteen months old.

Because the community wouldn't tolerate this behavior, Ben learned a lesson; he lost out on Family Dinner. By next year, who knows how consistent modeling and boundaries will affect Ben's addiction? He is a member of a healthy community for the first time in his adult life; we'll be patient while God works on his transformation.

The other residents were absolutely lovely. Dinner discussion was perfectly delightful on the other end of the table. They were thankful and gracious, complimenting the chefs and protecting the spirit of community. My kids sat outside with the smokers, entertaining the men and cautioning them against the dangers of nicotine. (They are a true credit to their public school Red Ribbon Campaign.) Gordy, who has the mental capacity of a nine-year-old, enjoyed a long lament with Caleb, discussing their moms' *annoying rules*; just two brothers under maternal oppression, trying to get by. Ms. Rosa marveled at Sydney's Bible knowledge, holding an impromptu Sunday School class. Gimme that old-time religion; it's good enough for me.

The kids ran around the street climbing trees, their laughter drifting in the window, the men patted their full bellies and retired to the deck with cobbler, while the women packed up leftovers and cleaned the kitchen, and I thought, *Family dinner indeed.*

DAY 18

Simple & Free caused the worst trauma in memory today. It started with a problem called "My oldest son needs a haircut because he looks like a stoner." His blond, shaggy hair had taken over his head. Brandon, as if scales fell from his eyes like Saul, stared at Gavin, tossed his book down, and said, "That's it. Get in the car. You're getting a haircut."

Wait a minute.

Supercuts isn't an approved line item. As Keeper of the Tenets of *Simple & Free,* I put the brakes on this excursion, but Brandon was on a mission. He came downstairs with clippers, positive he could knock this out himself. According to Brandon, this need not be left to the professionals. No money? No problem. Gavin resisted, of course, but with pressure from Brandon, they headed to the driveway for a shaving.

Ten minutes later all good feelings were gone.

Forty times shorter than he wanted and fairly wonkety, Gavin went from shaggy soccer cool to boot camp special. I can't possibly overstate how upset he was. He ran around screaming, assuring us that not with every ounce of our power, nor threat of dismemberment, nor brute force would we get him to school the next day. We coaxed him inside, but he didn't speak to us for three hours. The look on his face was as brutal as a sack of dead kittens.

While he hunkered in the backyard, we threatened our other children's very lives if they said one word about his hair; nay, if they made the slightest face, we would drive them to the local jail. I texted my friend taking Gavin to football practice later to feign blindness, as if she couldn't see his haircut but could miraculously see only to drive.

This was an epic fail; a bad haircut to a seventh grader feels like the end of the world. Gavin is certain everyone is thinking about him 72 percent of the day anyway. I explained this to Brandon, who has no patience for drama, especially since Gavin's hair looked fine; it was just too short for his liking. There is no reasoning with a preadolescent in a tailspin. Just let him pull out on his own.

And he did. Unprompted, Gavin apologized to Brandon for acting like a psychopath (paraphrased). I laid out hair products, cool hats, pictures of short-haired studs like David Beckham and Ashton Kutcher and George Clooney. ("Mom! He's like a grandpa!" You shut your mouth, kid.) We cooed and cajoled and tested to see if we could joke about it yet (no). He forgave, but trust me, he won't forget. He plays for keeps.

So Gavin will probably reduce *Simple & Free* to one sound bite: "My parents wouldn't pay for a haircut, and Dad sheared me like a sheep."

DAY 20

Wow. We spend a lot of money. Combing through a year of bank statements, I see that we are not big-ticket-item buyers; we nickel-and-dime ourselves to death. We spend almost everything we make, and honestly, I can barely account for half of it.

This is why spending has flown under my radar; it is subtle, incremental, seemingly inconsequential. Just this little thing here, and that small thing there. I don't feel like cooking; let's just get this. Individually, nothing too egregious, but together our spending amounts to a startling number.

Big deal, right? Do I really need to care about this high-end lipstick? Does it actually hurt someone if I buy these jeans or help someone if I don't? Let's say I cut spending down and work toward less consumption. So what? Is there even a chance my choices would matter?

I think they might.

Let's imagine a whole group of us, maybe thousands or even millions, decided to challenge an unjust economic system with these sorts of discrepancies:

Annual U.S. spending on cosmetics: $8 billion

Basic education for all global children: $6 billion

Annual U.S. and European spending on perfume: $12 billion

Clean water for all global citizens: $9 billion

Annual U.S. and European spending on pet food: $17 billion

Reproductive health for all women: $12 billion[3]

Consider this report from the United Nations:

> Today's consumption is undermining the environmental resource base. It is exacerbating inequalities. And the dynamics of the consumption-poverty-inequality-environment nexus are accelerating. If the trends continue without change—not redistributing from high-income to low-income consumers, not shifting from polluting to cleaner goods and production technologies, not promoting goods that empower poor producers, not shifting priority from consumption for conspicuous display to meeting basic needs—today's problems of consumption and human development will worsen.
>
> The real issue is not consumption itself but its patterns and effects. Inequalities in consumption are stark. Globally, the 20 percent of the world's people in the highest-income countries account for 86 percent of total private consumption expenditures—the poorest 20 percent a minuscule 1.3 percent.[4]

That's us: that 20 percent at the top buying 86 percent of the stuff. So no, maybe one person pulling out wouldn't matter. But if hundreds and thousands, then millions of us challenged the paradigm, let's say we said "no" for every two times we said "yes," if we acknowledged the power of our consumer dollars—to either battle inequality or reinforce it— then our generation could turn the ship around.

I see three easy shifts we could make, starting today.

One, consume less.

This is the simplest and hardest. It takes true courage to rage against this machine. Could we be countercultural enough to say, "We're not buying that. We don't need that. We'll make do with what we have. We'll use the stuff we already own." If this causes anxiety, I'm with you, trust me. Because who else does that? Who curbs their appetites anymore? Who uses old stuff when they could buy new stuff? Who sews patches on jeans or uses last year's backpacks? Who says "no" when they can afford to say "yes"?

We could. We could wisely discern needs from wants, and frankly, at least half of those line items are misfiled. Let's take advice from Matthew Sleeth in *Serve God, Save the Planet*: "My grandmother has hundreds of axioms. One of them was 'If you think you want something, wait a month.' One of three things will happen if you follow this sage advice. One: You will forget. Two: You will no longer need it. Or three: You will need it more. Most often, numbers one and two will happen."[5]

We can simply stop spending so much, use what we have, borrow what we need, repurpose possessions instead of replacing them, and—the kicker—live with less. Like Benjamin Barber noted in *Consumed*, "The challenge is to demonstrate that as consumers we can know what we want and want only what we need; and that, with the rest of our lives we intend to live as lovers or artists or learners or citizens in a plethora of life worlds in which consumption need play no role."[6]

Two, redirect all that money saved.

Humor me: What if we lived on 75 percent of our income and gave the rest away strategically? Or what if we downsized to 50 percent, bringing fresh meaning to Jesus' command to "love our neighbor as ourselves." Pulling out of a lopsided market is one thing; redistributing wealth to the world's vulnerable is a whole 'nother level. Global microlending, anyone? Go to www.kiva.org to learn about microfinancing for small businesses, for as little as twenty-five dollars. There is a 98 percent repayment rate. Astonishing. Empowering indigenous people to transform their own communities is the most effective weapon against global poverty.

Your giving can effect extraordinary change. Pick a need, country, people group, an organization focused on empowerment and sustainable independence. You could be an answer to countless prayers. The poor don't lack ambition, imagination, or intelligence; most simply lack resources. We have what they require and more than we need. We could share.

Three, become wiser consumers.

We get to choose our vendors. It's simple to find out if products are made with integrity or on the backs of slaves and children. With watchdog groups like Not For Sale, Free-2Work, Change.org, and others now that consumers are denouncing human trafficking and slave labor, there is no excuse for ignorantly supporting a corrupt supply chain. The reason a shirt is four dollars is because a worker was paid ten cents to make it; insistence on the cheapest prices is at the expense of freedom or living wages for workers.

Boycotting vendors who refuse public accountability and conceal their supply-chain records is a demand-side tool of responsible citizenship. This civic consumerism involves thoughtful shoppers who use consumer clout to shape what is sold and how it is sold. Joining watchdog groups, signing online petitions, making twenty-second calls to your senators, buying from responsible producers . . . these are simple steps with potential for massive reform. Exercised strategically, this demand-side power will eventually affect the supply-side manufacturers, insisting on "corporate responsibility in which the producers wear civic caps while captaining their corporate vessels, steering companies away from obvious abuses and profiteering selfishness of the Enron variety toward responsible decisions that benefit society as well as shareholders."[7]

On the positive side, there are marvelous companies who guarantee not only a slave-free product but economic leverage for some of the most vulnerable workers. Free-trade organizations, living-wage employers, Third World suppliers, companies with a conscience—your dollar can accomplish more than making the rich richer.

While it is easy to become paralyzed by the world's suffering and the inequalities created by corruption and greed, we actually hold immense power for change, simply by virtue of our wealth and economic independence. Because we decide where our dollars go. Never has so much wealth been so concentrated; our prosperity is unprecedented. If enough of us decided to share, we would unleash a torrent of justice to sweep away disparity, extreme poverty, and hopelessness.

The world is waiting. Our kids are watching. Time is wasting.

Are we willing?

[In 2015, Brandon and I founded Legacy Collective with the idea that a bunch of normal people could combine modest amounts of money monthly, put it all in a big pool, and fund grants all over the world together—sustainable solutions to systemic problems. Folks give as little as $35 a month and

as much as $250, and altogether, we have invested over $3 million in world-changing initiatives. The truth is, when we divert money toward trustworthy, vetted organizations, it changes lives. This matters and counts.

Not sure what to do? Where to start? Who to trust? Come join the Legacy Collective! It is the greatest thing we have ever put our hands to. Find out more at legacycollective.org.]

DAY 25

I am a word girl. I'm English/language arts/creative writing/ history. I am fully right-brained; the left is a dormant holding cell for the Pythagorean theorem and something about isotopes I forgot twenty years ago, three seconds after I learned it. I correct misspelled words when I text. When the Power-Point has a grammatical error during worship, I have to close my eyes to avoid this language failure. If I lost access to a thesaurus, I would undoubtedly quit writing.

Consequently, words move me. God and I do our best business in the Bible, and stories have changed my life. One well-crafted sentence can sustain me for weeks. Like this one we sang Sunday at ANC:

God, may we be focused on the least,
a people balancing the fasting and the feast.

I almost came undone.

That statement sums up all my tension and hopes for the American Christ follower, the American church, the American me. With good intentions but misguided theology, the church spends most of our time, energy, resources, prayer words, programs, sermons, conferences, Bible studies, and attention on the feast, our feast to be exact.

Now certainly, there is a feast, and thank you, God, for it. Where brokenness and starvation once consumed us, God sets us at a new table:

Your love, O Lord, reaches to the heavens,
  your faithfulness to the skies.
Your righteousness is like the mighty mountains,
  your justice like the great deep.
O Lord, you preserve both man and beast.
  How priceless is your unfailing love!
Both high and low among men
  find refuge in the shadow of your wings.
They feast on the abundance of your house;
  you give them drink from your river of delights.
For with you is the fountain of life;
  in your light we see light. (Ps. 36:5–9)

This is the feast of the redeemed; Jesus made it possible for the wretched to dine with the Most High, neither offending His holiness nor compromising His justice. For those adopted by grace and faith, He no longer sees our failures or omissions; He only sees the righteousness Jesus covered us with. We stand safely behind Christ, made white-as-snow perfect from His substitution on the cross.

The currency of salvation includes blessings, redemption, fulfillment, peace, healing, sustenance, forgiveness, and hope. It's a spiritual jackpot. For those salvaged from the gutter by Jesus, these are new mercies every morning. We are easily overwhelmed by the goodness of God, which knows no bounds. The gospel is so liberating; it is worthy of adoration every single second of every single hour of every single day forever. We will never be the same. This is indeed the feast, and to celebrate it is utterly Christian.

But the feast has a partner in the rhythm of the gospel: the fast.

Its practice is unmistakable in Scripture. Hundreds of times we see reduction, pouring out, abstinence, restraint. We find our Bible heroes fasting from food—David, Esther, Nehemiah, Jesus. We see the Philippian church fasting from self-preservation, sending Paul money in spite of their own poverty, a true sacrifice. John the Baptist says if we have two coats, one belongs to the poor. The early church sold their possessions and lived communally, caring for one another and the broken people in their cities. We see God explain His idea of a fast: justice, freedom, food for the hungry, clothes for the naked. This balance is a given in Scripture.

If we ignored the current framework of the church and instead opened the Bible for a definition, we'd find Christ followers adopting the fast simultaneously with feast. We don't see the New Testament church hoarding the feast for themselves, gorging, getting fatter and fatter and asking for more; more Bible studies, more sermons, more programs, classes, training, conferences, information, more feasting for us.

At some point, the church stopped living the Bible and decided just to study it, culling the feast parts and whitewashing the fast parts. We are addicted to the buffet, skillfully discarding the costly discipleship required after consuming. *The feast is supposed to sustain the fast,* but we go back for seconds and thirds and fourths, stuffed to the brim and fat with inactivity. All this is for me. My goodness, my blessings, my privileges, my happiness, my success. Just one more plate.

Not so with the early church, who stunned their Roman neighbors and leaders with generosity, curbing their own appetites for the mission of Jesus. They constantly practiced self-denial to alleviate human misery. In the Shepherd of Hermas, a well-respected Christian literary work from the early 100s, believers were instructed to fast one day a week:

Having fulfilled what is written, in the day on which you fast you will taste nothing but bread and water; and having reckoned up the price of the dishes of that day which you intended to have eaten, you will give it to a widow, or an orphan, or to some person in want, and thus you will exhibit humility of mind, so that he who has received benefit from your humility may fill his own soul, and pray for you to the Lord.

In the early 200s, Tertullian reported that Christians had a voluntary common fund they contributed to monthly. That fund was used to support widows, the disabled, orphans, the sick, the elderly, shipwrecked sailors, prisoners, teachers, burials for the poor, and even the release of slaves.[8]

The difference between Romans and Christians on charity was widely recognized by unbelievers. The pagan satirist Lucian (130–200 C.E.) mocked Christian kindness: "The earnestness with which the people of this religion help one another in their needs is incredible. They spare themselves nothing for this end. Their first lawgiver put it into their heads that they were all brethren."

These Christians did not limit their assistance to members of their own subculture either. The Emperor Julian, who attempted to lead the Roman Empire back to paganism, was frustrated by the superior compassion shown by the Christians, especially when it came to intervention for the suffering. He famously declared: "The impious Galileans relieve both their own poor and ours. . . . It is shameful that ours should be so destitute of our assistance."[9]

What would members of the early church think if they walked into some of our buildings today, looked through our church websites, talked to an average attender? Would they be so confused? Would they wonder why we all had empty bedrooms and uneaten food in our trash cans? Would they regard our hoarded wealth with shock? Would they observe orphan statistics with disbelief since Christians outnumber orphans seven to one? Would they be stunned that most of us don't feed the hungry, visit the prisoner, care for the sick, or protect the widow? Would they see the spending on church buildings and ourselves as extravagantly wasteful while twenty-five thousand people die every day from starvation?

I think they'd barely recognize us as brothers and sisters. If we told them church is on Sundays and we have an awesome band, this would be perplexing. I believe we'd receive dumbfounded stares if we discussed "church shopping" because enough people don't say hello when we walk in the lobby one hour a week. If they found out one-sixth of the earth's population claimed to be Christians, I'm not sure they could reconcile the suffering happening on our watch while we're living in excess. They'd wonder if we had read the Bible or worry it had been tampered with since their time.

But listen, Early Church, we have a monthly event called Mocha Chicks. We have choir practice every Wednesday. We organize retreats with door prizes. We're raising $3 million for an outdoor amphitheater. We have catchy T-shirts. We don't smoke or say the F word. We go to Bible study every semester. (*"And then what, American Church?"*) Well, we go to another one. We're learning so much.

I think the early church would cover their heads with ashes and grieve over the dilution of Jesus' beautiful church vision. We've taken His Plan A for mercy to an injured, lost planet and neutered it to clever sermon series and Stitch-and-Chat in the Fellowship Hall, serving the saved. If the modern church held to its biblical definition, we would become the answer to all that ails society. We wouldn't have to baby-talk and cajole and coax people into our sanctuaries through witty mailers and strategic ads; they'd be running to us. The local church would be the heartbeat of the city, undeniable by our staunchest critics.

Instead, the American church is dying. We are losing ground in epic proportions. Our country is a graveyard of dead and vanishing churches. We made it acceptable for people to do nothing and still call themselves Christians, and that anemic vision isn't holding. Last year, 94 percent of evangelical churches reported loss or no growth in their communities. Almost four thousand churches are closing each year. We are losing 3 million people annually, flooding out the back door and never returning. The next generation downright refuses to come.

Ironically, this is the result of a church that primarily feasts.

When the fast, the death, the sacrifice of the gospel is omitted from the Christian life, then it isn't Christian at all. Not only that, it's boring. If I just want to feel good or get self-help, I'll buy a twelve-dollar book from Borders and join a gym. The church the Bible described is exciting and adventurous and fraught with sacrifice. It cost believers everything, *and they still came*. It was good news to the poor and stumped its enemies. The church was patterned after a Savior who had no place to lay His head and voluntarily died a brutal death, even knowing we would reduce the gospel to a self-serving personal improvement program where people were encouraged to make a truce with their Maker and stop sinning and join the church, when in fact the gospel calls not for a truce but for a complete surrender.

Jesus said the kingdom was like a treasure hidden in a field, and once someone truly finds it, he will happily sell everything he owns to possess that field, a perfect description of the fasting and the feast. It will cost everything, but it is a treasure and an unfathomable joy. This is the balance of the kingdom; to live we must die, to be lifted we bow, to gain we must lose. There is no alternative definition, no path of least resistance, no treasure in the field without the sacrifice of everything else.

O Lord, may we be focused on the least, a people balancing the fasting and the feast.

DAY 30

This. Month. Was. *Hard*. But good. It's one of those. A good hard.

Vast consumption is so ordinary that its absence was shocking. I didn't realize how casually I "grab lunch," or "run through the bookstore," or "pick up that little scarf." I admit: I have a compulsion to buy something somewhere. My craving is nonspecific; it just involves being in a store or restaurant and handing my debit card over and getting something back.

Specifically, I have never cooked so much. With zero restaurants on the list, I've spent forty thousand hours in my kitchen this month, and I'm a little sick of it. That's right, the girl who loves fresh ingredients and cookbooks and sauté pans wants Chick-fil-A sauce on a fried sandwich. I want to *not* figure out what to do with collard greens. I want to call Pizza Hut. I want to sit on the deck at Serranos with my girlfriends and soak up this delicious weather over a massive intake of chips and salsa.

I'm missing the convenience of consumption, but I missed the camaraderie more. I've created conjoined twins out of *buying* and *connecting*. Time with another human meant eating at a restaurant or buying a four-dollar latte. My friends and I habitually bond over meals at our favorite haunts. Food brings us together with ease.

For the first week I holed up in my house, turning down invitations like a neurotic recluse. It didn't dawn on me to suggest an alternative connecting point. (I am slow.) Finally, I recognized *time together* was the real prize, not the $5.99 lunch special. Enter the rest of the month:

- Breakfast at Jenny's with four of my girlfriends.
- Lunch with my friend Stevie Jo. I pulled a sandwich right out of my purse.
- Amy, Lynde, and Alissa over for brunch.
- Long walks after hours with Jenny and Shonna. (We are "training" for a half marathon. It's next weekend. I don't want to talk about it.)
- Tuesday Night *Glee* Fest at Molly's. You know she has it recorded.
- Reciprocal brunch at Amy's with Lynde and Alissa. I invited us over.
- National Night Out with my neighbors.
- Potluck dinner with my oh-so-beloved Restore Group.
- Family four square tournaments. ("Someone" is a cheater, and his name rhymes with *Paleb*.)
- Longhorn football party on our deck. We're polishing up the phrase "rebuilding year."

So yes, eating is still a starting player, but being in each other's homes, cooking and sharing food together is delightful. Eating a meal in a restaurant is one thing, but friends padding around barefoot in your kitchen and chopping carrots for your soup and sipping their coffee on your deck is another creature altogether. This exits the expediency of consumerism and enters the realm of hospitality.

There is something so nourishing about sharing your living space with people when they see your junk mail pile on the table and peewee football schedule on the fridge and pile of shoes by the front door. Opening your home says, "You are welcome into my real life." This square footage is where we laugh and hold family meetings and make homemade corn dogs and work through meltdowns. Here is the railing our kids pulled out of the wall. This is the toilet paper we prefer. These are the pictures we frame, the books we're reading, the projects we're undertaking—the raw material of our family. It's unsanitized and truthful. We invite you into this intimate place, saturated with our family character.

Maybe this is why hospitality was big to the early church. Living life together in the sacred spaces of our homes is so unifying. When our Christian forerunners were persecuted and misunderstood, when belief in Jesus was dangerous and isolating, they had one another. They had dinner around the table. They had Sabbath together. They had soft places to fall when they traveled. Safe in the home of a fellow Christ follower, they could breathe, pray, rest. What a gift.

So here at the end of the month, I have some sweet memories, mostly in my own and my friends' spaces. There were hilarious stories confessed around my table, which I shall go to the grave with under threat of beheading. I let my girlfriends inspect all my closets one morning, which is like going to work naked. People rummaged in my pantry and used my chopping board. I examined Amy's garden and lounged on her couch over five cups of coffee, enjoying our XM Radio Coffee House channel obsession. I've dropped seven pounds, thanks to the absence of restaurant food and walks with my girlfriends. My little tribe enjoyed double the evenings around the dinner table, laughing through High/Low. (Caleb: My low is that my feet really stink right now.) We put a chunk of money into adoption savings and gave a few hundred away, because guess what? When you don't spend money, you have more at the end of the month. This financial wizardry is brought to you free of charge.

I've discovered reduced consumption doesn't equal reduced community or reduced contentment. There is something liberating about unplugging the machine to discover the heartbeat of life still thumping. Maybe we don't need all those wires after all. Maybe we're healthier unhooked from the life support of consumerism than we imagined. Is there a less-traveled path through our me-first culture that is more adventurous and fulfilling than the one so heavily trod? One that sacrifices none of the good parts of the story but inspires us to reimagine the sections that are bleeding us all dry?

I think maybe there is.

It is no accident that despite the fact that bazillions of dollars are spent telling us we are just consumers, and that's all the story we could ever need, people by the thousands and sometimes even millions are frustrated and looking for a better story. And it is here. Is it any wonder, if you live your life like a baby bird with your mouth open, that what gets dropped into it every time is a worm? People will attempt to reshape your worm and convince you that it is extra-yummy this time, but it is still a worm. And the story of consumers is still boring.

If we are going to get better than that, we're going to have to participate, and go out and seek new sources and resources and options, we're going to have to replace much of our consumption with rituals of nonconsumption. We're going to have to write a good and compelling story with our lives. The good news is that it is a lot more fun to be a citizen than to be a consumer, and rituals of nonconsumption are just as satisfying as retail therapy. The good news is that there are better stories out there for the claiming and the living, and events are conspiring to keep our times interesting. The good news is that we can do better than worms.[10]

[Of all the months, this one was the hardest by a mile. Inside the confines of Simple & Free, *we basically didn't spend any money outside of necessities. What strikes me as I recall it is this: I wasn't even ordering everything online yet. Amazon was a fraction of its current ubiquity. Most grocery stores and restaurants were not delivering yet. Subscriptions were in their infancy. As I write this, I can get literally anything delivered. And do. If I thought this month was challenging in 2010, it would be downright shocking today.*

When 7 was first released, folks wrote to me and said: "We canceled cable, Jen Hatmaker! How dare you!" First of all, I never asked you to. Lord knows we didn't. But second of all, I get the outrage, because this section is hurting my own feelings ten years later. "Don't mess with my delivery services, Jen Hatmaker!" I am actually making the conscious choice to not research the carbon footprint of delivery services right now; I am uninterested in the additional impact of drivers, trucks, gas, packaging, transport, and waste. Tra la la. It is probably the same.

Ugh.]

STRESS

- Conferences and retreats
- Airports
- Conference calls
- Radio interviews
- Meet the teacher
- *Jersey Boys*
- Coffee (tons)
- Lunch dates (gobs)
- Brunches (lots)
- Fifth-grade parent meeting
- KP garden maintenance schedule
- Restore Group Tuesdays
- Meals delivered to sick/new baby/ grieving friends
- Paint the Hays County Food Bank
- Garlic Creek Game Night
- Middle School Wyldlife meetings
- Peewee football practice/pictures/ games
- Seventh-grade flag football league
- Elm Grove Open House
- Adoption dinner party
- Grill-outs for the homeless
- Marathon "training"
- CSA pickup on Fridays

- Birthday parties
- Neighborhood National Night Out
- ANC Girls' Night In
- Dinner parties
- Carb-load spaghetti supper for the marathon team
- Shabbat with friends
- Half marathon
- College friends in for the weekend
- Orthodontist appointments
- Ninja Club (don't ask)
- Youth group
- Pumpkin patch visitation
- Ten thousand hours of correspondence

I inspected my calendar for the last two months and compiled this list. I counted five blank squares in eight weeks. This doesn't include the daily labor that keeps our children from flunking out, like Sydney's character sketch of Mother Teresa with handmade costume and biography bag or Gavin's report on the history of American coins (yawn). Also not listed is marriage maintenance to keep the hubs from turning into a roommate, because honestly? A little heat is mandatory so he is okay with making concessions for my impulsive, "oops-I-forgot" approach to life, and in exchange I'll act graciously when our DVR is filled with seventy episodes of *The Unit* and *River Monsters*.

Add leading a church.

Add *Simple & Free*.

Add Brandon's first book, due next Monday.

Add this manuscript, due in five weeks.

Add a daughter whose love language is quality time.

Add sons who need supervision so they don't die.

Add midnight bedtimes and 6:00 A.M. wake-up calls.

We are the center attraction at the Freak Show Circus. Ladies and gentlemen, boys and girls, step right up! Be amazed by the family juggling flaming batons while riding a unicycle on a tightrope with their heads stuck in a lion's mouth! No net! Duh, duh, da-da-da-da, duh duh da-duh!

For the love of Barnum & Bailey, we have too much going on. We are short fused, stressed out, overextended, and unrested. This pace is not sustainable. I don't want it to be. This season of life is passing me by, accelerated by a lack of boundaries. Most days I just try to keep the wheels on, not living in the moment at all; I'm just getting it done while thinking about what's left. My kids and husband get half answers, and eye contact is a crapshoot. Every day I could take a two-hour nap, so exhausted do I feel at 1:00 P.M. I have considered abandoning my career over the volume of e-mails.

Such is the ridiculous American life. Every one of my friends has a similar story. None of us are happy about it, yet we keep filling the calendars. Yes, I'm in; we'll sign up; I'll do it. We race from one activity to another, teaching our children to max out and stress out. Nice legacy.

This biblical concept of rest is whispering to me, "You're ignoring me." And I am. Not only do I *not* take God's command for rest seriously, but I act like it's not in the Bible. Ah, Sabbath. How cute and archaic. It's adorable how the Hebrews obeyed that. Good for them.

Clearly I believe my labor is more encompassing than that of the ancients, what with their little cultivating the land and harvesting their own food and making their supplies and raising gobs of children and traveling to festivals and worshipping at the temple and dodging enemies and getting captured and released and whatnot. Oh, you Israelites don't even know busy! I have thirty-one unanswered e-mails from yesterday! Perhaps you managed *rest* between the spring harvest and impending war, but I have to write three thousand words today *and* meet someone for lunch. I don't mean to be condescending, but God expected more from you because of your lack of discipline and little idolatry problem.

Ahem.

There are six days when you may work, but the seventh day is a Sabbath of rest, a day of sacred assembly. You are not to do any work; wherever you live it is a Sabbath to the Lord. (Lev. 23:3)

Well, that's Old Testament. That law doesn't apply to us. Or something.

There remains, then, a Sabbath-rest for the people of God; for anyone who enters God's rest also rests from his own work, just as God did from his. Let us, therefore, make every effort to enter that rest, so that no one will fall by following their example of disobedience. (Heb. 4:9–11)

Oh. But hey! Jesus was always breaking the Sabbath with healings and such!

JESUS: The Son of Man is Lord of the Sabbath. (Matt. 12:8)

JEN: Um, so?

JESUS: Are you Lord of the Sabbath, Jen?

JEN: I'm not sure.

JESUS: You're not.

JEN: Okay, then.

Evidently, this thing still stands. And maybe for good reason. Maybe this isn't just another spiritual task to wear us out. Perhaps God designed this as a gift, not an obligation. What if God understood our tendency to overwork and underrest, so He made it mandatory for believers to *breathe . . . pause . . . pray . . . relax* every week? Maybe Jesus meant it when He said, "The

Sabbath was made for man, not man for the Sabbath" (Mark 2:27). God ordained the Sabbath *for* us, not as just another requirement *from* us.

After six months of *Simple & Free,* I am ready to tackle resting and prayer. On the seventh day God rested, and in the seventh month we will too. The kids are thrilled, instinctively understanding that fasting from a fast life has "marvelous" written all over it. Plus, it won't mess with their Game Boys or access to Double Dave's Pizzaworks for the Wednesday buffet.

We will follow the ancients, the monastics, and the contemplatives into the practice of honoring the hours through seven prayer pauses every day: midnight, dawn, midmorning, noon, midafternoon, twilight, and night. Those humble enough to pause and touch the grace of the hour have hallowed these rhythms for centuries. Some of these come from traditions and even language outside the typical evangelical experience, but they are most definitely characterized by the practice of resting before God, which is rarely cultivated by the evangelical writers and speakers of our day. These hours, echoed in Scripture, have been revised and expanded in many ways, known by several names: the canonical hours, the Divine Office, the Prayer of the Hours, the Divine Hours, the Liturgy of the Hours.

For Month Seven, our guide will be *Seven Sacred Pauses,* written by Macrina Wiederkehr, member of the monastic community St. Scholastica, whose wisdom is so profound, I underlined nearly every sentence in the book. She quotes Pius Parsch, who describes the pauses as "breathing spells for the soul," oases to remember the sacredness of life, who we are, how to offer God the incredible gift of our lives, and learn to *be* in the midst of so much *doing*.[1] We will pause and pray seven times a day:

The Night Watch (midnight)

The Awakening Hour (dawn)

The Blessing Hour (midmorning)

The Hour of Illumination (noon)

The Wisdom Hour (midafternoon)

The Twilight Hour (early evening)

The Great Silence (bedtime)

Each pause has a focus, and like Wiederkehr explains, "Each day we are summoned to be creators of the present moment. Artists know the value of white space. . . . Perhaps you are being called to the spiritual practice of bringing a little of the white space—of *nada*—into your workday. There in that white space you will find your soul waiting for you. Allow the anointing rhythm of the hours to touch and teach you each day."[2]

In addition to these daily pauses, the Hatmakers will observe the Sabbath from sundown on Saturday to sundown on Sunday. Traditionally, Sabbath begins on Friday evening, but we are adhering to the spirit of the day, which calls for corporate worship and family rest, and for us that is Sunday (unless the country would like to move church services to Saturday and push all games, tournaments, birthday parties, and community events to Sunday). Additionally, Saturday is sometimes a workday in our family, as ministry requires. We have a weird life. For us the day of rest is Sunday, when we gather with the saints, pack up the week's work, and claim the treasure of the Sabbath.

We're shutting down the circus, people. For this month, rather than Barnum & Bailey, we'll be the low-budget sideshow carnies without a big production and with a fraction of the star power. We've been a sorry bunch of clowns, running around like idiots, cramming into cars, driving in circles and getting nowhere. We're exhausted (and we suspect the elephants are plotting a coup). It's time to breathe and pray and learn to be still and rest. Now *that* sounds like the Greatest Show on Earth.

[I am so happy to have good news to report. This month really stuck. Ten years later, we are still very proactive about honoring the Sabbath. I am hard-pressed to think of many exceptions. We circle the wagons come Saturday night and Sundays are downright off-limits. Remy Hatmaker would tell you that I nap virtually every Sunday afternoon, and we gather with our best friends on the porch almost every weekend in what we call "Sunday Night Church." I loved what this month taught us. My absolute favorite of them all.]

DAY 1

O PILGRIM OF THE HOURS

Each morning
night's curtain
opens on a new day.
You are invited
to join the great opening.
Receive the gift
of seven sacred pauses.
Practice waking up
seven times a day.
　　—Macrina Wiederkehr[3]

I'm going to admit something to you: I'm not a good prayer, okay? I never have been. I love the Word; I connect naturally to that medium. I like words on paper. I like a tangible
passage. I like actual language to focus on. I process through
writing. Scripture is how I know God and feel known by
Him.

Prayer is harder for me. Whether it's a communication
weakness or an undisciplined mind, I don't know; but I have
to work hard at consistent, focused prayer. My prayers include
rogue parenthetical thoughts: (I'm so hungry.) (I forgot to
order books for my event.) (Why do these pants feel so tight?)
(When did I go to the dentist last?) I'm a concrete thinker, so
ordering my thoughts without an anchor is a struggle. This
final month of *Simple & Free* is necessary for me.

The structure of *Seven Sacred Pauses* is perfect for a wan-
dering mind like mine. Every prayer has a rhythm, a focus,
and—three cheers!—written prayers and psalms and readings. The language will tutor me. Here are the basics of each
prayer pause:

The Night Watch

My eyes are awake before each watch of the night,
that I may meditate on your promise. (Ps. 119:148, NRSV)

Also called Vigils, *which I love,* this pause is around midnight. "Like Jesus, keeping watch the night before he died, I
keep vigil with those who wait alone."[4] This is a deep, even
dark prayer of waiting and interceding, keeping vigil with
Christ, who never sleeps and guards us in our darkest hours
(Isa. 40:28). The Night Watch advocates for others in a dark
night of the soul: the suffering, abandoned, oppressed,
lonely. "Perhaps some night when you get up to pray, something will turn over in someone's heart and find its voice all

because of your small prayer. . . . Perhaps our very waiting in the darkness gives some struggling unknown pilgrim of the hours hope."[5] Sometimes vigils are for waiting, when your struggle has been voiced and God's hand hasn't moved. The Night Watch is a time to say, "I will wait for you, Jesus."

Although there are beautiful prayers and psalms to use, this pause is also powerful when observed silently—a simple, quiet connection with Jesus, staying awake together to shoulder the suffering that plagues this planet and our hearts. "For God alone my soul waits in silence" (Ps. 62:1). It's like sitting silently together in the waiting room while a loved one is hanging on by a thread in the ER—words aren't necessary, but there is something powerful about your presence, your attention, the vigil you and Jesus are keeping.

READINGS

Psalm 42

Psalm 63

Psalm 119:145–152

The Awakening Hour

Satisfy us in the morning with your steadfast love;
so that we may rejoice and be glad all our days. (Ps. 90:14)

At dawn it's time to begin our day in glory, remembering God's goodness. Even after the darkest night, the sun will rise. The Awakening Hour includes thankfulness for a new day, a fresh slate. It's the moment to pray for resurrection: What needs to rise in us today? Do we need to awaken to joy? Forgiveness? Should we pray for the resurrection of love in our hearts for our spouse or children? Ask for a dawning in our own soul:

Even in darkness light dawns for the upright,
for those who are gracious and compassionate and righteous.
   (Ps. 112:4)

We enter a new day, where our lives can become a living praise. Our desire to live this day well, for Jesus' glory, is an offering. After the Night Watch this moment celebrates God's intervention, His redemption. We never have to look far to see what He has repaired and whom He has transformed. Vigils are for waiting and interceding; the Awakening Hour is for praising and celebrating. "This day is Yours, Jesus. Awaken Hour love in my heart so that I am a vessel of light today."

READINGS

Psalm 19

Psalm 95

Psalm 147

The Blessing Hour

Let your loveliness shine on us, and bless the work we do,
bless the work of our hands. (Ps. 90:17)

This midmorning pause has two emphases: The first is mindfulness of the Spirit's abiding presence. When the early church first commemorated the coming of the Spirit, it was the midmorning hour of terce, or "third hour," which became a fixed time of prayer in almost all Christian liturgies.

At this hour the opportunities are still endless, making it the perfect time to invite the Spirit to stir our souls. This pause can redirect our morning trajectory from "efficient" to "inspired." We invite the Holy Spirit deeply in before the day gets away from us.

Second, the Blessing Hour is about the sacredness of our hands and work. Whatever our work looks like—an office, raising children, working from home, a classroom, ministry— we ask the Spirit to bless us with creativity, composure, inspiration, love. Kahlil Gibran said, "Work is love made visible"; what if we approached our work as an opportunity to show love? To our coworkers, those we serve, our children, to our students . . . visible love is possible if we work mindfully, as carriers of the sweet Spirit of Christ.

What a lovely moment to share over a fresh cup of coffee with a Christian coworker or a midmorning snack with our kids. Together, we ask Jesus to bless our hands and reveal the sacredness of our work, inviting the Spirit to breathe fresh wind into our tasks. We turn our affections to the Spirit, receiving the affection He feels for us.

READINGS

Psalm 67

Psalm 84

Psalm 121

The Hour of Illumination

You are the salt of the earth. . . . You are the light of the world. (Matt. 5:13–14)

When we greet the middle of the day, we pause to consider the moment when Jesus embraced the cross. We consider how we are called to the same act: to give our lives away. In this great act of sacrifice, Jesus demonstrates his power and leadership through servanthood. In the spirit of the hour, we pledge to shine brightly, becoming hope to the hopeless and light in the darkness.

During the Hour of Illumination, we ask Jesus to send light into our hearts so intensely that they break wide open, so we can make the decisions that lead to peace—from death to life, deception to truth, despair to hope, hate to love. We self-inspect our hearts for violence we are choosing to harbor—toward ourselves, spouses or family members, co-workers, community, those who are different, toward any part of creation. We ask God's love to illuminate the parts of our souls darkened with bitterness or anger or unforgiveness or apathy.

By all means enjoy this pause outside with your face turned toward the sun. We pray to be sons and daughters of the light, bringing joy to a dark world. We pray against the darkness that consumes and steals and ruins. We offer our hands and words as agents of change and justice. Like Gandhi said, "Be the change you hope to see in the world." This midday prayer is our pledge to pour out our lives, just like Jesus did at great cost.

READINGS

Psalm 24

Psalm 33

Psalm 34

The Wisdom Hour

For to me, to live is Christ and to die is gain. (Phil. 1:21)

At midafternoon the Wisdom Hour embraces the themes of surrender, forgiveness, and wisdom, and the impermanence of this life—including aging, maturing, and death. It is the hour Jesus died and gave up His spirit (Mark 15:34). This prayer acknowledges all things are passing, not in a macabre way but in the spirit of wisdom, which knows this life is temporary, and we should live like we believed that. Frankly, who would like this day to never end? This season to never pass? For greater things to never be realized?

This hour is the prayer for wisdom to help us live like we were dying, which we are. Imagine the fearlessness we'd embrace with this understanding! Imagine the risks we would take, the love we would share, the forgiveness we would not withhold, the dreams we would chase. Envision the bitterness we would release, the hang-ups we would let go of, the beauty we would create.

With evening approaching, we pray for *perspective* on this short, fleeting day, this short, fleeting life, and accordingly, we hold out forgiveness, release our grudges, and offer our gifts to the world, understanding we have only a few years to share them or they will be wasted.

READINGS

Psalm 71

Psalm 90

Psalm 138

The Twilight Hour

Also called Vespers, this is the much loved evening prayer, prayed for centuries at the end of the workday, as dusk approaches. The main themes are gratitude and serenity as the evening lamps are lit. We invite God's peace as we leave work and transition to dinner, family, home, rest. Training our minds toward tranquility, Wiederkehr poses some questions we can ask: What is the greatest blessing of this day? What specifically can I smile over? What is unfinished that I can gently lay down until tomorrow? Is there anyone I need to make peace with? The Twilight Hour is for exhaling, calming our minds, and transitioning into the evening.

A major theme of Vespers is gratitude. No matter the chaos of the day, Wiederkehr reminds us, "If you search out reasons to be grateful, you may be amazed to discover that your gratitude room is overflowing."[6] We practice being thankful for the gifts of the day, the loveliness of the season we are in. Even with disorder at this hour, we say "thank you" for employment, for children and home, for our gifts. We say "thank you" for tomorrow, a perfect landing spot for unfinished tasks. We say "thank you" for hands to labor and love with and ask for grace for the work of the approaching evening.

READINGS

Psalm 34

Psalm 139

Psalm 145

The Great Silence

By day the Lord directs his love,
at night his song is with me—
a prayer to the God of my life. (Ps. 42:8)

This prayer concludes the day; a beautiful time to pray with children as we tuck them in or with a spouse or friend before we sleep. Also called Compline, from the Latin word for *completion*, it begins with a gentle evaluation of the day. The focus is on awareness, and we include not just weaknesses but the strengths and accomplishments of the day. The Great Silence teaches us to be healthy sinners, living in neither denial of our sin nor despair because of it. God reminds us we are loved sinners. We learn to live with more integrity and obedience than we did the day before, as together in prayer we examine the day.

The second theme is darkness—protection from some forms and acceptance of other forms. We ask the Spirit to guard against our enemy, protecting our zeal and innocence in Christ. We pray our children are sheltered under God's wings. As sin is a darkness that envelops from within, we confess and repent from the tentacles that bind us. We intervene for those seized by darkness: suffering, sickness, death, disease. We pray for our brothers and sisters who need our intervention desperately.

On the other hand, we welcome the soft darkness that is exquisitely beautiful and healing. God dims the lights on our weary bodies, making the way for sleep, allowing us to see the stars. There is a beauty to the darkness, the natural rhythm of the earth that invites us to be still and rest. It is time to let go of the day and enter the Great Silence.

READINGS

Psalm 23

Psalm 91

Psalm 134

Here we go.

DAY 2

I met Jenny and Christi for lunch at Fire Bowl Cafe. After yammering about whatever we yammer about, I slipped my Bible out of my purse. The table went silent.

JENNY: Are we about to get rebuked?

CHRISTI: Are we having devotions?

JENNY: Is this an intervention?

CHRISTI: Am I in trouble?

JENNY: Are you about to admit something bad?

CHRISTI: Is this a Bible drill?

I reminded them about the Hour of Illumination (Christi: "Geez-o-pete, *Simple & Free* is still going on?"), and I read excerpts from *Seven Sacred Pauses* and opened Psalm 24. We let those beautiful words energize our midday while we passed Christi's teeny baby around, and the girls were thrilled we were just praying together, not holding an intervention.

Yay, me! I have friends I can do this with. I've prayed and studied so many times with these two. I know everything about their spiritual lives, and they know all the gory details of mine. We've wrestled through every issue imaginable and prayed through our best and worst times. Christi was so smitten that my phone rang two hours later with a call from our friend Laura:

"Christi told me all about the pauses. Tell me everything. I have a baby, a toddler, and a preschooler. My sharp mind has turned to cornmeal and I think I've developed an anxiety disorder. My hair is dirty. I've forgotten how to spell. I haven't gone to the bathroom alone in four years. I need God forty-nine times a day, but I'll settle for seven. Spill it."

Thus continues the cannibalization of my friends by *Simple & Free*.

DAY 6

I sent an SOS e-mail to The Council, admitting I'm having trouble observing all seven pauses each day, particularly the Night Watch, which is spectacularly meaningful but, um, at midnight.

Jenny to the rescue: "I am doing the Night Watch for you tonight. Just go to sleep and I'll take it." She sent me this the next day:

I read all the psalms for today: 42, 65, and 119. They were all awesome. I felt so excited about this after reading them! This time is not about me, but interceding for the forgotten:

PSALM 42:9–10, THE MESSAGE
Sometimes I ask God, my rock-solid God,
(Hear their cry, sweet Jesus)
"Why did you let me down?
(Why are you letting the orphan, oppressed, poor, and lonely down?)
Why am I walking around in tears
(Why are they all in tears?)
harassed by enemies?"
They're out for the kill,
these tormentors with their obscenities,
taunting day after day, (Lord, protect them from being tormented by the enemy)
"Where is this God of yours?"
(God, this question makes me feel so desperate for these people. And so sad that they probably ask this.)

PSALM 42:11
Put your hope in God,
for I will yet praise him,
my Savior and my God.

(Thanks for being hope! God, I want to be hope too. And I pray these forgotten, lonely, and abandoned people will not give up hope.)

Tonight I'm praying for

The women and children beaten by their husbands/ boyfriends or parents

The women and children being raped

The people thinking about ending their lives b/c of hopelessness

The children who just lost their only living parent

The children dying from lack of food and water and lack of medicine and those still alive with aching bellies b/c we don't care enough

The 27 million slaves and those driving the demand for them

The teenagers and adults addicted to drugs and alcohol

The lonely parents who have lost a child, and those sitting next to a child who is near death

The abandoned children who are scared and alone

The widow or widower who just lost their best friend

The homeless who feel unloved and forgotten

The 147 million orphans

Those who are feeling so dark and desperate

The children being held captive/kidnapped

The prisoners

The sick

This is *not* my writing for your book, stupid! But I loved these verses and wanted to share. Plus, I wanted you to know I was serious about taking your Night Watch!

How precious. Jenny kept vigil for millions suffering a dark night of the soul. She sat with Jesus, remembering them, interceding, naming their suffering and begging for justice. Her intervention has integrity because she is learning to shop "slave-free," is active in the foster system, sponsors orphans and supports widows, and loves wayward teenagers her kids befriend.

You participate sincerely in the Night Watch when your daytime hours maintain the same intervention. Like James said, "Suppose a brother or sister is without clothes and daily food. If one of you says to him, 'Go, I wish you well; keep warm and well fed,' but does nothing about his physical needs, what good is it? In the same way, faith by itself, if it is not accompanied by action, is dead. But someone will say, 'You have faith; I have deeds.' Show me your faith without deeds, and I will show you my faith by what I do" (James 2:15–18).

Note to future friends: If I ask you to participate in a social experiment, and you send me material and say it is "not writing for the book," I will ignore this and copy and paste it exactly as is, with complete disregard for your feelings.

DAY 7

I haven't observed all seven pauses in a day yet. For crying out loud! Stopping in midstream is way harder than it sounds. It's not that I don't want to; I can't remember to. You would think since this concept is not only a spiritual exercise but book fodder, I would stay on it, but you would be wrong. I blink, and it's lunch. I blink again, and I'm cleaning dinner dishes. Seven pauses is kicking my butt and taking names.

Plus—*bleh*—it is making me feel superguilty. At the end of every day, I count how many I missed and scold myself for prayer failure. I'm not the highest heel in the closet, but I think I'm missing the point. If prayer and rest equal guilt and frustration, then I'm doing something wrong. I can practically see God rubbing His temples.

Today I remembered something from *Seven Sacred Pauses*: "One of the things I have learned is the importance of the bell. The bell calls us to the Prayer of the Hours. The bell is annoying. The bell is good. . . . When I hear the bell, I pray for the grace to put aside the work I am doing. In listening to the bell I am actually listening to an invitation for union with the Beloved. In answering the bell I am proclaiming by my actions that there is an even greater Love than the loving service I am performing."[7]

I need the bell! (Read: iPhone alarm.) Done. Alarms set.

While we're discussing failures, our first Sabbath was a hot mess. It started with me flying home at 8:30 P.M. on Saturday night. Kids were heading to bed. Dinner was over, meaning the chips my children ate while Brandon was sequestered upstairs to finish his book due Monday. Even if we'd tried to observe Shabbat around the dinner table, we couldn't have, since we sold the table in the ABBA Fund Garage Sale. It seated only five and we're about to ratchet that up by two, so we have a rug with a light fixture over it.

Sunday morning Brandon dashed out earlier and zanier than usual, as the heater broke at church and the thermostat read 57 degrees. The kids and I came four hours later for the second service. Then we zipped to my mom's for lunch, finished our last bite, and raced Gavin to his flag football doubleheader, which I bailed on for training at church, where I'm leading a new initiative in which I have no idea what I'm doing. I got home at 7:30, and the kids asked, "What's for dinner? We're starving. No one fed us." So I dumped frozen soup in a pot, served it to everyone on the rug, and sent the kids to bed.

Sabbath fail.

Between the travel, football, the book deadline, and the training, this day was unsalvageable. Our redemption: That was my last event of the year, Gavin's final game, and the Internet will mercifully whisk the book away from our home tomorrow; thus Sabbath potential increased 100 percent for the rest of this month.

Gentle reader, I shall shake the dust off my feet from this first week of malfunctions and try again, starting fresh tomorrow.

I have seven daily alarms set.

I have a clear weekend calendar.

However, three to five pauses a day was better than none, and some were very, very sweet. (Jettison the guilt, Jen. You abandoned that response with its partners in crime: traveling revival evangelists and awkward attempts to clap in church.) These are not a yoke of bondage, but breathing spells for the soul. Remember the point. Don't miss the forest for the trees, even if the trees come in rapid succession all day, making them impossible to keep up with; then they conspire against you on the Sabbath like a haunted forest.

DAY 8

Like Zack and Kelly and Screech and Slater, I'm saved by the bell! I set seven repeating alarms on my phone with text reminders on the themes, and we hit six out of seven (sorry, Night Watch, but you're so late). The monks have that bell thingy down; I should've listened.

Four of the seven prayers happen while the kids are home. Yesterday during the Wisdom Hour (right after school), Sydney prayed about forgiving a classmate, who has been *mean as the devil* to her. I don't know why I didn't pray first, what with my gift of discernment. I previously considered (1) whispering to this kid that I'm sending psychotic fairies into her room at night to eat her legs off, or (2) just barely nicking her with my car, not enough to sustain a serious injury but enough to send a message (minor injury? gray area).

Evidently prayer was a better option.

Sydney came home today and said, "Mom! You won't believe this! Out of nowhere, Jill said, 'I'm really sorry I've been so mean to you. I don't even know why I acted that way. I really want to be your friend if you'll forgive me.'" The day after Sydney released her from this debt in prayer, she repented on her own.

What happens in the spiritual realm when we pray? It's such a mystery. What words prompt the Spirit to move? What goodness do we join Him in when we pray for peace? How powerful are our prayer words? They are catalysts for miracles, the impetus for healing. Does God wait for us to pray in His will, primed to move for righteousness? How many relationships is He waiting to mend? How much turmoil is He poised to soothe? How much peace is He ready to administer? Are we withholding the necessary words to trigger God's intervention?

Perhaps this is why He urges us to forgive, release, lay down, let go, trust, offer, submit, and obey; these are the keys that turn the locks that bind. Like Jesus promised:

> I will give you the keys of the kingdom of heaven; whatever you bind on earth will be bound in heaven, and whatever you loose on earth will be loosed in heaven. (Matt. 16:19)

Maybe after we say, "I'll forgive," He inspires repentance in the offender. Perhaps when we say, "I'll finally trust you," He delivers. Is He waiting to hear "I'll do it" before clearing the path? If we can bind and loose things in the spiritual

realm, why are we squandering prayer words on football vic-
tories and temporary luxuries? What a waste! We could be
binding evil, injustice, and hatred while releasing freedom,
recovery, and healing—partners in mercy, not just consumers
of it.

God is inviting me into this spiritual clout seven times a
day—seven times the power, seven times the influence, seven
times the effect. I'm frustrated I ruined the first week with
legalism, missing the exquisite opportunity to join God in the
work of redemption. I *knew* Jesus was offering something
wonderful, but my drift into legalistic entropy is strong, people.

And good news! Now I won't be named in a personal injury
suit against a minor.

---

*[Good reader, I just wrapped up my fifth and final journey
through middle school with my children, and the people that
said, "You will miss this" are damn liars. No, I will not. I said
on the final round, "We're not going to make it through this
one. This is where it ends for us." God bless and keep middle
schoolers and their poor mangled little minds, and Jesus be
near to their teachers. Please accept them all straight into
heaven, Lord, because they deserve eternity in glory.]*

DAY 13

Sweet, sweet Sabbath. People, please enjoy this sacred practice with your little families. There is such beauty to it, a spiritual rhythm. It is different from just another dinner at home.
There is something supernatural in this form of worship.

Beginning around 5:00 Saturday evening, Brandon and I
joined forces in the kitchen, preparing dough and toppings

for pizza plus a fig and goat cheese salad with toasted almonds and fig vinaigrette tossed with butter lettuce *from our own garden*. I would be remiss if I didn't mention this is the best lettuce we've ever tasted. Ever. More delicious lettuce has never been grown. May I also brag on our carrots, snow peas, spinach, and potatoes? Please act impressed over our first winter garden, because we are morons and still managed to grow a bunch of our own food.

Everyone gathered to top their pizzas, layering goodies over a brilliant homemade sauce, which I've included for your eating pleasure:

Sauté three garlic cloves and 1 tsp of red pepper flakes in ¼ cup of good olive oil for 3 to 4 minutes. Add 1 28-oz. can of Muir Glen organic crushed tomatoes—please trust me, this brand matters and it *must* be "crushed tomatoes" or you will regret it the rest of your life. Add 2 T of sugar and whisk until it is all incorporated. Simmer for as long as you want, add salt and pepper and a bunch of chopped fresh basil, put on your pizza, and die of happiness. Set leftover sauce out for everyone to dunk their crusts or bread in. Now you're a hero. Everyone loves you.

The pizzas smelled up the house like heaven. We set out the "nice" dishes, poured wine and grape juice, positioned the candles, laid Shabbat readings on each place setting, situated challah bread in the middle, and the family assembled around our new lovely table, which now seats eight. Oh yes, we will soon have two little new faces at this gathering.

A mood accompanies the Sabbath dinner. It is festive and affectionate, expectant and joyful. My littles had happy faces; Sydney asked to do this every week forever. Relief surrounds the evening; the meal is special, the mood is light, and the next twenty-four hours are wrestled from the grip of stress and frenzy.

Brandon led us through the readings as I lit two candles representing *remembrance* (of creation and deliverance) and *observation* (of rest and Sabbath). We drank our wine and juice; we ate the bread. Communion belongs in the home as certainly as it belongs in the church. We prayed. We closed with "Shabbat shalom! Shabbat shalom!" Peace on the Sabbath.

Then commenced movie night with popcorn and hot chocolate. The rest of Sabbath involved our beloved church, lunch with friends, then home for naps. Brilliant. We wrapped up Sabbath at my parents' house for dinner Sunday, feasting on homemade fried chicken and mashed potatoes for my brother-in-law's birthday.

Delicious food, family, church, friends, rest, worship . . . thank you, God. You're smart.

DAY 14

During the first week of October, I suffered inexplicable sadness for our Ethiopian kids, yet unknown to us. I couldn't quit crying. I couldn't stop worrying. I felt heavy and dark without knowing why. With tears burning at the slightest provocation, I threw my emotions into the Facebook ring for some backup. From adopting friends a common thread rose up:

"God is prompting you to pray for them for some reason. You don't know them yet, but He knows them. Intercede for them this week; then write these dates down. Once you receive your referral, check their paperwork, and you might discover divine timing." A slew of similar experiences were posted.

So Brandon and I prayed desperately for them. Were they losing a parent? Were they suffering? Were they tender and lonely? Were they especially hopeless? Their need was unknown, but the ache was acute. So I cried the tears I just knew they were crying, and I begged Jesus to be so near, so gentle in their young lives while they waited.

Sensitive to their fragility, I spent that week checking (obsessing over) the Waiting Children's List on our adoption agency's website. I've been drawn to these kids since the beginning of our adoption journey. These children have not been requested or matched, unwanted even within the adoption community. Their crimes: (1) too old—meaning over five; (2) too sick—HIV, TB, birth defects; or (3) too many—siblings.

This very week a new little face hit the WCL: a darling, bright and shiny seven-year-old boy. I instantly loved his personality. He looked like Gavin in an African way. He seemed ornery, which I adore. So I pulled him up every day. Every day. Every day. I sent the link to family. I sent the link to friends. I checked back in. I watched other WCL kids move from "available" to "file under review" while his smiling face remained "available." On a Wednesday I sent this to our family coordinator:

Hi Caitlin!

Sweet adorable Beniam is a healthy seven-year-old on the WCL. He totally falls within our approved range; and since he's on there, I'm assuming there are no other requests for a seven-year-old boy. Would AWAA consider placing him with an unrelated younger girl and allowing us to consider them together?

We would be so happy to apply for unrelated kiddos if this is a possibility.

Thoughts?

Jen Hatmaker

For a week we e-mailed back and forth about unrelated kids (sweet, precious Caitlin—extra jewels in her crown for fielding my relentless e-mails). I cannot explain how drawn to him we were. Every time we looked at him, he became more beautiful, more precious, more dear. Our social worker needed to approve us for an unrelated placement, as we were approved for siblings. That, friends, *sounded* like a formality, so we got our ducks in a row to speed that process up.

Exactly one week after that e-mail, the following Wednesday, my phone rang with that heart-attack-inducing-breath-stealing caller ID: "AWAA—Caitlin" (America World Adoption agency). Adopting parents with submitted dossiers wait for that call with such anxiety and anticipation, that should we be on a conference call with the president of the United States, we would scream in his ear, *"I GOTTA GO!!!!!"* and click over. Parents call their agencies 10 billion times; they call us never, but when they do, this is what they say:

"Jen? It's Caitlin. Sit down . . . this is your referral call."

The world stopped spinning.

Time froze.

Nothing else existed.

"Shut up!!!" is how I responded as a mature, emotionally controlled girl. Our dossier had been submitted forty-eight days ago; this referral was fast. I couldn't think straight. The referral call includes sitting at your computer while your family coordinator sends the highly anticipated e-mail file, including pictures.

We discovered our referral was one gorgeous, unbelievably perfect five-year-old girl. She was beautiful in every way. With her little Chiclet teeth and her shy smile, it seemed we might finally have a "gentle child," which required adoption since our gene pool squashed that characteristic.

But besides "adopting" and "Ethiopia," the other crystal-clear detail was "two children." Back in December, when

adopting from Ethiopia was imminent, Brandon kept bringing up *two kids*. Normally the bleeding heart, I was reluctant
(could also be defiant, obstinate, terrified) to consider two,
knowing we are already a circus and doubting my ability to
parent five kids. But he couldn't shake it; so we spent a week
praying and fasting about one versus two.

On the final day of our fast, unknown to anyone but us, one
of my dearest friends called: "Jen? I've been praying about
your adoption. If this is irrelevant, just forget it; but every
time I pray, I get the feeling you and Brandon are considering
siblings . . ."

Jen stops breathing.

". . . I don't know why I keep getting this message. But if
you are, we've prayed about it, and we want to pay for the increase. Whatever the cost hike is for adopting two instead of
one, we'll cover the entire amount."

Jen bawls eyes out.

Without question we knew God had two kids in mind, so
this referral for just one was terribly confusing. We were
starved for clarity, staring at each other like one of us had an
explanation, the key to unlocking this baffling development.
Our strategy has been "Go back to what you know for sure.
What was the last thing you heard?" So I went three weeks
back to those dark days full of prayer and sorrow. I confirmed
the dates, then searched this beautiful girl's file:

It was the week she was brought to the orphanage.

Shipped twelve hours north of her village, her people, everything she knew, to a crowded orphanage with children and
workers who spoke a different language—it must've been devastating. She must've felt so alone. At age five. Except Jesus
never leaves His little ones, His most vulnerable. He was there.
And He made sure we were there in spirit, too.

She was the "younger unrelated girl." It all locked into

place. Within hours of the call, we asked to adopt Beniam too. For four agonizing days, we fought for his referral, this bright, shiny boy who'd seen hundreds of babies and toddlers come and go while he waited. For four days we pleaded our case against staunch resistance. For four days prayers and e-mails and calls flooded in as our Christian community rallied for this boy.

Enter the Great Silence, Compline, the prayer of completion. Every Sunday night at 9:00 P.M., the parents adopting through our agency join in prayer all over the world. We pray for our children, their families, the nannies, our paperwork, referrals, court dates, traveling mercies, approvals, and grace. I asked my adoption community: "Please pray for our expanded referral."

From nearly every state and several other countries, we prayed at 9:00 P.M. We interceded for one another and begged God to move. We voiced our impossible circumstances and trusted Him to work the common, everyday miracles that surround adoption. We prayed for completion. Hesitantly, timidly, I said, "I trust you, God." *At 9:27 p.m.,* our social worker sent this:

"I am going to approve this referral."

No words can describe the rejoicing.

We've been invited into a beautiful story. God captured an entire community with love for two children whose names were on our lips. As selfish plans fail daily, and greedy dreams burn out when God removes His hand from endeavors we are using His name to endorse, Jesus gently placed two children in the center of a faith community with the tenderest of care.

I want you to know their names.

Our Beniam is seven, and we'll call him Ben, the son we fought for. Our daughter's name is Matawi, which means "Remembrance." We will call her Remy because she was never forgotten—not by her Creator, not by her Savior, and not by us. God walked with our children; their lives were ever before Him. God never forgot, never slept, never stopped working.

He remembered them.

> For the Lord comforts his people
> and will have compassion on his afflicted ones.
> But Zion said, "The Lord has forsaken me,
> the Lord has forgotten me."
> Can a mother forget the baby at her breast
> and have no compassion on the child she has borne?
> Though she may forget,
> I will not forget you!
> See, I have engraved you on the palms of my hands;
> your walls are ever before me. . . .
> See, I will beckon to the nations,
> I will lift up my banner to the peoples;
> they will bring your sons in their arms
> and carry your daughters on their hips.
> Kings will be your foster fathers,
> and their queens your nursing mothers.
> They will bow down before you with their faces to the ground;
> they will lick the dust at your feet. Then you will know that I
>   am the Lord;
> those who hope in me will not be disappointed.
> Can plunder be taken from warriors,
> or captives be rescued from the fierce?
> But this is what the Lord says:
> "Yes, captives will be taken from warriors,
> and plunder retrieved from the fierce;
> I will contend with those who contend with you,
> and your children I will save." (Isa. 49:13–16, 22–25)

[This entry made me sob. For more than one reason. It is hard to even remember this version of me, the one who knew the kids only on paper. It is crushing to recall that season for them. We know and love them so entirely now. Ben and Remy are everything to this family. They are such delightful kids and good siblings. I can barely summon any memories before them.

And of course now I know their living parents. We've been back so many times; we took Ben back to see his mother and Remy is up next to see her father. We love them too. *It is all more complex than I understood. Their first families had so few options. It wasn't fair. Their loss was our gain, and that is unjust. Desmond Tutu once said, "There comes a point when we need to stop just pulling people out of the river. We need to go upstream and find out why they are falling in." Our work through Legacy Collective is to go upstream. Adoption is an answer to a tragedy that has already happened, but what if kids no longer fell in the river because their parents were empowered to flourish? Economic development is orphan prevention, and we see this as our life's work.]*

DAY 16

Yucky post ahead

You've been warned.

You know what's lame? Jealousy in a grown woman. I work in a weird industry-ministry hybrid. The subject is God, but it involves contracts, marketing budgets, cover designers, PR directors, publishers, and some hype. It takes fussing to

get a book into your hands. Like me, most writers are neurotic and paranoid about this, certain everyone else is getting
a better contract, better everything. They are probably all
having secret dinners without me. I'm already self-conscious
about my work, so add the success of other writers and perceived slights, and I'm like a melodramatic character on the
CW. (I'm grossed out by myself, too. It's not just you.)

Around 11:00 A.M., I heard about a friend's massively wonderful book deal. It involves a team of committed experts and
a lot of zeros. The word "synergy" was used and I threw up in
my mouth. I became instantly furious with everyone who
ever collaborated on my contracts. Publishers, editors, PR directors, my agent . . . they are all in on it. With complete certainty I knew they'd been at the secret dinners conspiring
against me. Not only do they not believe in me, but now I
know they despise me. They actually wish harm to me since
none of my contracts ever matched this synergetic one.

I may have pulled up my Amazon reviews, which confirmed the free fall.

Icky ick ick. Oh, ego, you ridiculously fragile ballast! I
thought I'd banished you by now. I hate when you show up all
insecure, trying to garnish credit and edge into the limelight.
You ruin things. You steal honor and joy that rightfully belong
to others. You turn beautiful tasks into garbage, and you
wrestle glory from Jesus' hands. I hate you. I mean, I really
hate you. I wish you were dead. But you're so hard to kill.

And the bell tolled at noon—the Hour of Illumination. Uh-
oh. Written by Jen Hatmaker twenty-two days ago:

> During the Hour of Illumination, we ask Jesus to send light
> into our hearts so intensely that they break wide open, so we
> can make the decisions that lead to peace—from death to
> life, deception to truth, despair to hope, hate to love. We
> self-inspect our hearts for violence we are choosing to

harbor—toward ourselves, spouses or family members, co-workers, community, those who are different, toward any part of creation. We ask God's love to illuminate the parts of our souls darkened with bitterness or anger or unforgiveness or apathy.

I walked outside with Lady Bird and turned my face to the sun, marveling at the ugly war that rages in me and God's unfathomable patience with it all. I thought about Jesus, who never angled for credit, ever. In fact, He had the most perplexing habit of telling people *not* to talk about His awesomeness, how He healed and saved. Jesus always deferred glory, redirecting people to one another and toward His Father and Spirit, who was to come. What Jesus didn't do was complain the other rabbis got more temple time or had better synergy.

I am commissioned to be a light, but I can't illuminate this world while competing with the lights of others. I mean, really? It isn't possible to miss the point any worse. Together we are a city on a hill. When one of us shines, it is a community victory. If we all lived radiantly, we simply couldn't be hidden any longer. This is not about individual wattage; our power is communal, or it is meaningless. "How good and pleasant it is when God's people live together in unity!" (Ps. 133:1).

God, this is the story you've given me to live. Write it with beauty and light. Banish the dark pockets of selfishness and jealousy with truth. Forgive me for choosing envy when I should have been thrilled your name will become even more famous. My gosh, I am a mess. Teach me peace in a violent world, already riddled with competition and greed. Give me a heart of flesh that contends for your glory through anyone, everyone, anywhere, everywhere. Reign over me until there is only you.

I am so grateful for this pause today because without it I would've continued the downward spiral, uninterrupted. I'm sure of it. I was four seconds away from googling myself. This simple prayer stopped the hemorrhaging before I lost a whole day (week/weeks) nurturing my jealousy like a little pet. Maybe that's one reason Paul told us to "pray continually" (1 Thess. 5:17). Constant prayer interrupts our ego trips and disrupts our toxic trajectories. It says, "Whoa, missy, stop right there. Really? You're going to keep feeding this beast? Let's count to ten and rethink this. You know, Jesus always said . . ."

Who can argue with that? It's like seventh grade when Mom let my sister get her ears pierced two years earlier than I did and extended her bedtime *that same week,* and when I was simply showing her the error of her parenting by yelling in her face about the injustice I lived with and the favoritism she was clearly showing Lindsay because obviously I was the most unloved yet high-achieving daughter in the house and maybe I should just go live with Gran . . . *Slap!* Right across the face. Stunned us into silence until we both burst out crying.

That's how the Hour of Illumination was today. A nice slap in the face to shock me out of an old-fashioned hissy fit. Good medicine. Think of all the damage I wouldn't inflict if I prayed in the middle of all my episodes! Perhaps I'll keep these alarms set past this month. And maybe I'll delete this confrontational e-mail I drafted to my agent about a pending contract. Sorry. The devil made me do it.

DAY 18

I marvel at the company I keep. My friends would be intimidating if they weren't so fun and occasionally naughty. My comrades are adopting, serving, raising money, raising awareness, sacrificing, advocating, giving away, sharing, fostering, sponsoring, fighting, dreaming. This planet is brighter for their presence. They are good people. (Do not believe what you have heard about them. Unless you've seen pictorial evidence, which may or may not exist.)

I have friends, including Council Member Trina, seized for the plight of refugees in Austin. Refugees were forced from their homelands by war, civil conflict, political strife, and/or gross human rights abuses. These survivors were persecuted—often tortured and brutalized, their families murdered—and ultimately displaced because of their race, religion, nationality, tribe, or social group and are unable to return home. Approximately 14 million refugees have sought sanctuary in other countries, and roughly three thousand settle in Austin each year.

While they've escaped the violence and instability of their homelands, they face daunting obstacles in America. Refugees receive a small stipend, less than unemployment, for four months. In this amount of time, on an income below poverty level, they are expected to become self-sustaining. It is clearly impossible, and the odds are stacked against them heavily. With fragmented English and no context for American culture (computer skills, banking, enrolling kids in school, employment, junk mail versus real mail, shopping, bus routes, homework, this list goes on forever), refugees get stuck in minimum-wage jobs with no tools to escape, and the cycle of poverty continues.

Keep in mind these are incredibly smart and resourceful people who've overcome unfathomable evils and lived to tell. Their station has nothing to do with work ethic or capabilities and everything to do with language barriers and cultural displacement. They simply need advocates to mentor them toward a stable place in the American economy.

Which brings me back to my friends who dreamed up a social enterprise called Open Arms Studio, a for-profit business employing refugee women in Austin at a living wage, a company with a conscience. Using donated T-shirts, Open Arms repurposes them into beautiful scarves, pillows, purses, bags, rugs, and more—a metaphor for the women who craft them. Additionally, Open Arms provides on-site seminars (computer skills, language, banking, budgeting), plus childcare and early intervention for their young kids, breaking another link in the poverty chain.

Their debut is this weekend at the illustrious Christmas Affair, a ginormous four-day market organized by the Junior League with more than two hundred merchants and attendance north of thirty thousand people. Granted a coveted booth, Open Arms needs five hundred pieces to sell, and everyone is working their little fingers to the bone to make it. My friend Leslie, the engine behind Open Arms, wouldn't even let *the team* take a scarf in advance to start wearing, *not even if they paid for it*. She counted every day. That girl runs a tight ship.

Jenny, Shonna, our friend Larkin, and I volunteered all morning, three days before the Christmas Affair. We received our task: take T-shirt scraps of scraps (*nothing* wasted!), cut them into 11 x ¼-inch strips, tie them through each Open Arms tag, and pin tags on every item ready for sale. While the international women hummed at their sewing machines doing the skilled work, we chattered and giggled and pinned the ever-lovin' business out of those tags.

At 10:00 A.M. sharp, my trusty bell rang, reminding me to pause for the Blessing Hour, including wonderful themes for our morning at Open Arms: an invitation to the Spirit, acknowledging His presence and recommitting the day to His glory, and a simple prayer to bless the work of our hands, all of our hands.

With my heart in my throat, we all paused together and prayed God's Spirit displayed in every scarf, each bag, that He become famous for His redemptive work in the lives of these women. I asked God to bless the work of the hands in the room: Sudanese hands, Burmese hands, Congolese hands, Ugandan hands, American hands. I asked God to remember these women who have seen so much violence yet still work cheerfully, humbly. I petitioned the future work of their hands: raising children, creating beauty, embracing healing. I prayed blessings over this beautiful business of reclaiming, reimagining, repurposing shirts and lives. I thanked the Spirit for planting this dream in Leslie's heart then fanning the flames to others committed to living out His mission. (Tears? Maybe a few.)

Then back to work as our friend Lacey had thrown down the gauntlet earlier in her sweet, sweet voice: "We were hoping maybe everything could be tagged and boxed by 11:30 . . ." That sounded like a challenge packaged in sugar, and we took the bait. 11:30? Oh, we'll see your 11:30 and raise you "boxes loaded in cars."

Now reader, go to www.openarmsstudio.org and buy something, or I will never speak to you again for the rest of my life.

DAY 20

Leave it to the Hatmakers to dumb down something as sacred as Sabbath dinner. People, I just play the hand that is dealt me, okay? Brandon was out of town until midnight, so it was just the four of us, and we were leaving Sunday morning for eight glorious days off.

Gentle reader, if you are not a mother, here is the translation:

When transporting your family away from your quarters for longer than one solar period, you engage in a marathon of preparations that make you question the decision to go anywhere the rest of your life. The list is exhaustive, and you will discover not one human on the planet who feels like being helpful. This is on you, Mom. You'll answer for every omission while getting zero credit for performing the duties of a packing mule for your crew. It goes something like this:

"Get down your suitcase. We're packing for eight days, everyone. Remember, it's cold in the mornings and warm in the afternoons. Did you get your suitcases down? Everyone come get their clean clothes and put them away! We are coming home to a clean house, do you hear me? Where are your boots? Where is your toothbrush? What do you mean, it's been missing 'for a while'? What have you been brushing your teeth with? Don't answer that. Why are you playing Xbox right now? Pack socks! Pack underwear! Why is your suitcase not down? Bring books to read. Yes you will. Because I'll make you. Where is Lady's leash? Why is it connecting your bikes? What is 'slingshot riding'? Pick out movies to bring! No, we are not bringing *Cats & Dogs: The Revenge of Kitty Galore*. Because it makes my brain shrink. So help me, are you *still on the Xbox*? What do you mean you're done packing? I see one pair of jeans and an airsoft gun in here. I'm coming up in five minutes, and I'm giving away everything that is still on your bedroom floor. Oh my stars, is your suitcase *still* not down?"

This tirade continues until the second you pull out of your driveway. It will take your husband ten miles before he is speaking to anyone again, and you declare a moratorium on all talking and sound until lifted by you, the keeper of the details and the packer of the things. Approximately one hour later, your teeth unclench. On the third day of your vacation, you decide that you might possibly, maybe, travel again with your family, but you're not sure yet. It's too soon to tell.

So packing cut into my meal preparations for Sabbath.

However, we still wanted to inaugurate our day (week) of rest, the launch of our little sabbatical.

We still had candles.

We still had the readings; Gavin read the "man" parts.

We still used the nice dishes.

We had, um, chicken strips and macaroni and cheese.

We shared Communion with the last heel of sliced cinnamon bread.

And water, since we drank all our juice before leaving town.

But we put the water in fancy cups.

We got supertickled about all this, and I snapped a picture to commemorate what the kids dubbed "the Mom Sabbath." Amazingly, this jolted me out of drill sergeant mode and restored laughter to the house. We thanked God for the gift of time off, for the family ranch, for thousands of good days behind us and even better days ahead.

Shabbat shalom!

DAY 23

On the last day of school in seventh grade, fifteen of my friends met at Shoney's for breakfast, dominating the restaurant while our moms pretended not to know us. Please try to remember seventh grade, especially if you are a girl. Recall the cruel awkwardness, the certainty you were tipping the scales at 102 pounds, the fear no boy would ever get past your home perm and lack of booby buds, and the feeling you were destined for Dorkville. Population: only you. Remember how all your friends wore Esprit and Guess jeans, and your mom said she'd book a one-way ticket to commie Russia before shelling out fifty dollars for jeans? (I was a tragic twelve-year-old stuck in the lower middle class during the Cold War.)

That fine morning at Shoney's, my friends and I were showing off and making enormous nuisances of ourselves, when *a miracle happened.* Ron Coyle, the finest junior in the history of the world, oldest son of my parents' best friends, came behind me, wrapped his arms around me, and kissed me in front of everyone. My memory swears he got a centimeter of lip. Then he set me back down and walked away.

You could've heard a pin drop. Forks stopped in midair. Girls froze in midbite. A gorgeous high school boy just kissed a member of their prepubescent tribe in front of their faces. I tried to play it cool, but I didn't really have that skill set. Everyone gaped at me, not believing my good fortune while simultaneously wishing I were dead.

It was pretty much the greatest day of my life.

Sometimes the stars align to wrap up a season perfectly; you didn't plan it, but the universe throws you a bone, and everything congeals in perfect harmony. The bow is lovingly tied on top, and the circle of life is completed. You'd like to imagine you are responsible for this, but the truth is, it's dumb luck and coincidence, and you just get to stand in the winner's circle.

Similarly, thus begins the final week of *Simple & Free.*

At my parents' ranch.

For eight days.

During Thanksgiving.

A literal sabbatical, including the first two Sundays off since we started ANC, in 2008.

A planner would've engineered this finale on purpose, finishing a month of rest and prayer with family, sequestered on 350 beautiful acres, happily meal planning for Thursday, when we'll break bread in total thankfulness for this month, this year, this blessed life. But this all just sort of happened to me.

Regardless, I'm happily typing on the porch of the barn as the breeze blows, watching Sydney and Lady leap across hay bales and listening to my boys gun the four-wheeler in the front pasture. My mom and dad are reading books in the afternoon sun, and the boys are setting up mid- and long-range targets for a Hatmaker Shoot Off. We have no cell service. We have no Internet. There is no cable either, but we do have one spotty TV with a VHS player where we watch old movies every night, piled on the couches like puppies. We'll feed cows this week and move hay bales. The guys will hit the deer blinds and attempt to fill our freezers for the winter. (An armadillo already lost its life last night, thanks to Caleb's sharpshooting. It's Texas, people.)

We'll wear the same clothes over and over, and four days from now I'll ask if anyone has taken a shower. The answer will be no. I didn't even bring makeup. At least once we'll head "into town" to eat at the Rockin' J's in Comanche, a converted gas station where 95 percent of the patrons will have on camouflage. We'll order biscuits and gravy because we aren't imbeciles. We've been here less than twenty-four hours, and I've already read a book and a half. The kids brought bones and other treasures from their explorations. By 8:30 A.M., I'd already washed a load of filthy clothes after Caleb and Lady decided to "walk through the creek instead of go aaaaaaaallll the way around it" (fifty additional yards). We'll enjoy coffee in the morning, sweet tea in the afternoon, and a glass of Cabernet Sauvignon on the porch at night, while the sun sets over the coastal fields.

This week will lovingly bookend *Simple & Free,* offering the best space to reflect, gear down, and express gratitude. I'm surrounded by my favorite people at my favorite place during my favorite week on earth. It's the proverbial public kiss, the finest possible ending to this incredible experimental year. I'll gratefully pray through the hours in the pasture, on the four-wheeler, and in the barn; while cooking breakfast for the hunters and dinner for the explorers; with my kids, my husband, and my parents; in the early morning on the porch and as we turn off the lights after movie night.

"Dear Artist of the Universe, Beloved Sculptor, Singer, and Author of my life, born of your image I have made a home in the open fields of your heart. The magnetic tug of your invitation to grow is slowly transforming me into a gift for the world. Mentor me into healthy ways of living. Help me remember to pause."[8]

DAY 26

The rhythm of the ranch is healing to the frantic pace of normal life. It's also a tutor, teaching me the superior tempo of living well. At the ranch there is no hurry. There is no racing from one thing to the next unless you count trying to outpace Lady Bird on the four-wheeler. Thanks to its strategic geography, we aren't distracted by the Internet, TV, or phones (if you stand on a chair in the southwest corner of the barn while holding your phone to the heavens, you get one bar).

Friend, you might be imagining a luxurious, chic, rustic ranch with overstuffed leather furniture and antler chandeliers. Please let me set the record straight. This is a working cattle ranch, no house, just a barn that houses a four-hundred-square-foot office/living room/kitchenette/bathroom. The utility sink, refrigerator, and washer and dryer are out in the barn, so during the winter we fight over who has to brave the frigid barn to fetch jelly from the fridge or—horror—hand-wash the dishes while bundled like an Eskimo.

At night the two couches fold out into beds: voilà, a bedroom. These beds are slightly less comfortable than sleeping on an inverted mat of ball bearings. Add a kid draped all over you, and we basically pray for each night to end. "Why are the lines squiggly at the top of the screen?" the spoiled modern children ask about the ancient TV. They don't know about tracking, a cross we children of the eighties had to bear. The pipes freeze at the first sign of a cool breeze, so we keep milk jugs of water in the bathroom so we can fill the tank up and flush. It's all very glamorous.

So believe me, the ranch life is a simple one, devoid of all the extravagances we're addicted to.

And yet.

None of us could wait to get out here. We've been talking about this week for two months. We love, love, love the ranch and every rustic detail. We crave the outdoor air and dirty farm boots. The boys were on the four-wheeler before we put the car in park. The kids explore for hours. We would have no clue where they were if not for the hilarious walkie-talkie communiqués we eavesdrop on.

The boys experience pure bliss from their hunting endeavors, and why not? We have twelve deer blinds on the ranch, all ironically named: the SpongeBob, the Bishop, Crow's Nest, Alaska Stand, North Creek, Penthouse, the Grove, and, of course, the Bellagio, named for its opulence with its retractable windows, carpeted floor, and heater. (Caleb falls asleep in this deer blind every time.)

As the sun set and the hunters were returning, I started dinner and entered the Twilight Hour, that grateful transition from the activity of the day to the relaxation of the evening. I love gathering my chicks after days like today, when muscles and imaginations were stretched to their limits and flushed cheeks walk in the door competing for space to tell their tales. Hats pulled off and ponytails released, a mountain of ranch boots left by the door. The family assembled with fresh, new memories and an eager anticipation of the next day.

I read Psalm 145 and repeated a beautiful prayer from *Seven Sacred Pauses*:

O You whose face is a thousand colors . . . look upon us in this twilight hour, and color our faces with the radiance of your love. As the light of the sun fades away, light the lamps of our hearts that we may see one another more clearly. Let the incense of our gratitude rise as our hearts become full of music and song. May the work that we bring with us into this hour fall away from our minds as we enter into the mystical grace of the evening hour. Amen.[9]

[Oh, my heart. I love reading these entries. My dad and his brother bought the ranch in 2006, and it is in the final stage of sale as we speak. It is time. Running a working cattle ranch is a monumental task for two seventy-plus-year-old brothers. But it is the location of my children's memories and will forever be precious to me. Lady Bird was only two when I wrote this, and she'd run for eight straight hours at the ranch back then. She is a good old girl now, gray-haired, lying at my feet this very second, the greatest dog that ever lived. We celebrated our final Thanksgiving at the ranch just this year, house packed to the brim with everyone we love. I am so thankful for the ranch season of our lives. Lucky us.]

DAY 30

What a finale to Month Seven! Thanksgiving was epic: We ate our weight in honey ham and fried turkey, jalapeño cranberry relish, and my grandma's carrots, which are legendary and will go down in King family history. We cooked and laughed and napped and ate again. My mom made pumpkin cheesecake and homemade whipped cream. Clearly nothing can top that, so I'll end this food paragraph on that high note.

I'm thankful for the contemplatives who've stirred me: Henri Nouwen, Brother Lawrence, Macrina Wiederkehr, Mother Teresa, Richard Rohr; David, Isaiah, Jesus. Their noble embrace of prayer and stillness has inspired me into deeper communion with God. This mindfulness has been terribly stretching.

I've discovered I can fast from clothes and waste and spending easier than I can fast from busyness. Wear the same outfit six days straight? Sure. Garden and recycle? No problem. Pause seven times a day in the middle of my life? Now that's asking a lot. I found this month very challenging and equally beautiful. Evidently, I don't respond well to interruptions, Spirit-led or otherwise.

But these pauses, plus the Sabbath, plus the sabbatical taught me something: My heart craves a slower life. I want people to stop prefacing their phone calls with this: "I know you're so busy, but if I could just have a second . . ." I want to figure out what this means for our family. We can't live in the barn forever, nor can we pull out of work, ministry, school, community, mission, family, and all the activities that accompany them. But what can we do to cultivate a quiet ranch heart in a noisy urban world?

I know we'll be keeping the Sabbath. Um, hold your applause since we've been instructed to do this from Exodus to Hebrews. As God explained at the inauguration of the Sabbath:

Remember the Sabbath day by keeping it holy. Six days you shall labor and do all your work, but the seventh day is a Sabbath to the Lord your God. On it you shall not do any work, neither you, nor your son or daughter, nor your male or female servant, nor your animals, nor any foreigner residing in your towns. For in six days the Lord made the heavens and the earth, the sea, and all that is in them, but he rested on the seventh day. Therefore the Lord blessed the Sabbath day and made it holy. (Exod. 20:8–11)

Is it coincidental that God named every person included in the rest? Sons and daughters, servers and animals, guests and visitors; we all need this. My neglect of the Sabbath affects not just me but my entire household, my extended community. The pace we keep has jeopardized our health and happiness, our worship and rhythms. We belong to a culture that can't catch its breath; rather, we refuse to catch our breath.

God doesn't pull any punches here: The Sabbath is holy. Not lazy, not selfish, not unproductive; not helpful, not optional, not just a good idea. *Holy.* Like God demonstrated in Exodus 16, He'll provide for daily needs, but on the sixth day He'll rain down a double portion to store up for the Sabbath, covering our needs while we rest. The only day a double collection wouldn't spoil by dawn's light was the Sabbath; God made a way.

He still does. Originally, the Sabbath had to be planned for, food gathered a day in advance. It wasn't handed to the Hebrews on a silver platter. This principle remains. I still have to plan for the Sabbath, tying up loose ends and gathering what we'll need. I still have to prepare the family for rest, enforcing healthy boundaries and protecting our calendar. I still have to set work aside and trust in the wisdom of God's design. "Bear in mind that the Lord has given you the Sabbath" (Exod. 16:29).

My heart feels renewed at the completion of the month. Perhaps the greatest gift is clarity. My mission is concentrated: This matters, this doesn't, this counts, this doesn't. It's actually not that complicated. The Bible is true; no matter how contrary to reality it appears. I've discovered you can press extremely hard on the Word, and it will hold.

It *is* healing to forgive.

You *do* gain your life by losing it.

Love *does* truly conquer evil.

A simple life really *is* liberating.

As I wrap up Month Seven, I'll quote a prayer written by Henri Nouwen, which resonates so deeply, it's as if he stole my thoughts:

Dear Lord, you have sent me into this world to preach your word. So often the problems of the world seem so complex and intricate that your word strikes me as embarrassingly simple. Many times I feel tongue-tied in the company of people who are dealing with the world's social and economic problems.

But you, O Lord, said, "Be clever as serpents and innocent as doves." Let me retain innocence and simplicity in the midst of this complex world. I realize that I have to be informed, that I have to study the many aspects of the problems facing the world, and that I have to try to understand as well as possible the dynamics of our contemporary society. But what really counts is that all this information, knowledge, and insight allow me to speak more clearly and unambiguously your truthful word. Do not allow evil powers to seduce me with the complexities of the world's problems, but give me the strength to think clearly, speak freely, and act boldly in your service. Give me the courage to show the dove in a world so full of serpents.[10]

CONCLUSION

How do I summarize *Simple & Free,* an experiment that has forever altered our lives? My takeaways are so vast, I can't keep an idea still long enough to write about it. New thoughts have so usurped old thoughts, I can't remember what I used to think about. Then there are these ideas we are dreaming about: community development, mixed-income housing, the three Rs (relocation, reconciliation, redistribution), downsizing. Of course, there is the poetic irony of our impending adoption, rounding out our family to *seven.* I'm regretting manuscript omissions already: my book collection eradication, the half marathon I ran for adoption, James 5, the Global Voices summit. There was just too much to tell.

Also swimming in my brain is the huge list of reforms with new habits and practices. Not to mention the crash course I've received on the economy and capitalism and alternative fuels and sustainable farming and neurological processes and industrialized food and local economics and consumer trends and ancient liturgy. I've read precision analogy by global economists and rhythmic prayer poetry by a monastic nun. I've digested articles by farmers, food lobbyists, social activists, missionaries, financial advisers, marketing analysts, pastors, insurgents, doctors, ecologists, waste managers, priests, advocates, nonprofit leaders, documentary makers, politicians, revolutionaries, troublemakers, and dreamers. I've ingested information through a fire hose and find myself sputtering and gasping. However, after curbing my appetites for so long, I've discovered my appetites have changed.

I realize some of you are hoping for a romantic ending here, something with aplomb, a juicy Twitter sound bite (@jenhatmaker moved from the suburbs to a van down by the river with her five kids. Astonishing. #SimpleAndFree #reddit). You're waiting for some surprise radical ending I've been saving to drop on my readers, like becoming missionaries or farmers or the quirky stars of a new "Simple Life" segment on the *Today* show ("Welcome back, Hatmakers!" "Thanks, Matt! Good to be here again!" "Wow! Great dress, Jen!" "Thank you. I sewed it out of discarded plastic bags dredged up from the bottom of polluted lakes." "You are truly amazing." "It's all for Jesus, Matt.")

But that's not where we are. Honestly, we're not sure what's next for the Hatmakers. We know something new is coming; we recognize the winds of change that seem to blow on our little life with regularity. *Simple & Free* allowed us to slowly break up with some of our ideas, our luxuries. It was something of a long good-bye. It's not you, it's us. Well, it *is* you.

This was the beginning of a process, not a complete story by itself. We didn't live out *Simple & Free* and cross the finish line. This adventure was something like being morbidly obese and unable to schedule a lifesaving surgery until losing weight first. We had to shed and cull and purge before God could even remotely begin to deal with the serious issues. This was pre-surgery business, the required fast before the real procedure.

However, even if I had a clear directive, I'm not sure I'd share it here. Whatever God has done or is doing in our family is certainly not a template, and I don't want it to be. We live in a certain city with a certain task, we have specific gifts, and we're horribly deficient in others. Our life looks like it does because we are the Hatmakers, and God is dealing with us the way He's dealing with us. We have history and sin issues and circumstances and geography that God takes into account as He stakes our place in His kingdom.

You have an entirely different set of factors. I have no idea what this might look like in your life, nor do I want that job. Your story is God's to write, not mine. Some of us are going to live in the suburbs, others downtown. I'm going to garden; you're going to take the subway. We're adopting, you're redistributing, they're downsizing. I use words, you use a hammer. There isn't a list here. There is no stencil we can all trace into our lives in perfect unison. Here is our baseline as a faith community:

Love God most. Love your neighbor as yourself. This is everything.

If we say we love God, then we will care about the poor.

This earth is God's and everything in it. We should live like we believe this.

What we treasure reveals what we love.

Money and stuff have the power to ruin us.

Act justly, love mercy, walk humbly with God. This is what is required.

Interestingly, as I write this a few weeks after the completion of *Simple & Free,* I've discovered something surprising. I engaged in a fast with my adoption community last week, and *it wasn't even hard.* I couldn't believe it. I kept waiting to feel desperate, but instead the fast was simple and beautiful and focused on prayer rather than the mechanics. Gone were the screaming voices in my head; gone was the simmering anxiety. It was like putting on a familiar sweatshirt. After saying "no" to things I wanted for nearly a year, I guess I gained some control over my emotions and impulses. God used fasting as a tool to curb my appetites and regulate my reactions. It was a concise realization: *Something in me has deeply changed.*

Perhaps this is why Scripture calls us to the practice of fasting—from food, from greed, from selfishness, from luxuries. It isn't just the experience; it's the discipline. It changes us. Fasting helps us develop mastery over the competing voices in our heads that urge us toward more, toward indulgence, toward emotional volatility. Like consistent discipline eventually shapes our children's behavior, so it is with us. Believe it or not, God can still change us. Not just our habits but our hearts. Say "no" for a year and see for yourself.

Steven, our KP partner, asked me this morning while harvesting carrots and potatoes (!) and lettuce: "Who is your reader?" and that got me thinking about you. I'm going to guess you are probably a middle- to upper-middle-class parent (but love to my nonbreeders!), and mostly your life is terribly blessed. Your world is pretty controlled: kids are in good schools, neighborhood is safe, jobs are fairly secure, wardrobe is impressive enough. These advantages cause you some tension, but you're not sure why or what to do with it.

You're likely a believer, but whether you're a lifer or a recent devotee, I'm not sure. A few of you are teetering on the edge of faith, drawn in by Jesus but repelled by His followers. As for church, you probably go to one, but a bunch of you don't; the elitism and waste and bureaucracy became too much and you left, or you want to leave. Some of you are solid attenders, but you feel like crawling out of your skin sometimes, valuing faith community but worried yours is missing the point. A few of you have found the church of your dreams. Half of you read *Radical,* or *Crazy Love,* or *The Irresistible Revolution,* and since you're reading this, you might've read *Interrupted.* You loved and hated it.

I'm guessing you've cried over orphans or refugees or starvation or child prostitutes, heartbroken by the depravity of this world. It's not okay with you that your kids get school and birthday parties while Third World children get abandoned and trafficked, but you don't know how to fix that. You're wondering if your lifestyle is connected to these discrepancies, and you have a nagging suspicion that less is more, but it's a muddy concept. Everyone has ideas. It's confusing and overwhelming. This creates a sort of war within, and it leaves you raw. Sometimes you're a full-blown mess over it.

Hear this: I don't think God wants you at war with yourself.

He sent the Prince of Peace to soothe those tumultuous waters already. Self-deprecation is a cruel response to Jesus, who died and made us righteous. Guilt is not Jesus' medium. He is battling for global redemption right now; His objective hardly includes huddling in the corner with us, rehashing our shame again. He finished that discussion on the cross. Plus, there's no time for that.

We're so conditioned to being a problem that we've forgotten we're actually the answer. God is not angry at you; how could He possibly be? You are His daughter, His son; you're on the team. Don't imagine He is sitting us all down for a lecture. Rather, He's staging a rally, gathering the troops. The church is rising like a phoenix right now, collecting speed and strength and power.

> I saw heaven standing open and there before me was a white
> horse, whose rider is called Faithful and True. With justice

he judges and wages war. His eyes are like blazing fire, and on his head are many crowns. He has a name written on him that no one knows but he himself. He is dressed in a robe dipped in blood, and his name is the Word of God. (Rev. 19:11–13)

Something marvelous and powerful is happening in the church. The Bride is awakening and the Spirit is rushing. It is everywhere. This movement is not contained within a denomination or demographic, not limited to a region or country. It's sweeping up mothers and pastors and teenagers and whole congregations. A stream became a current, and it is turning into a raging flood. It is daily gathering conspirators and defectors from the American Dream. It is cresting with the language of the gospel: the weak made strong, the poor made rich, the proud made humble.

The body of Christ is mobilizing in unprecedented numbers. Jesus is staging a massive movement to bind up the brokenhearted and proclaim freedom for captives. The trumpet is blowing. We are on the cusp, on the side of the Hero. So while we're mistakenly warring with ourselves, Jesus is waging war on injustice and calling us to join Him.

This is way more fun than self-condemnation, no?

So imagine me linking arms with you, giving you an affectionate Texas squeeze. Guilt might be the first chapter, but it makes for a terrible story. Jesus gave us lots of superior material to work with. If your stuff and spending and waste and stress are causing you tension like mine is, just do the next right thing. Ask some new questions; conversation partners are everywhere (their name is Legion, for they are many). Take a little baby step. Tomorrow, you can take another. Offer yourself the same grace Jesus has given you. We're no good to Him stuck in paralysis.

For most American Christians, this will begin with deconstruction, but the real thrill is in the reconstruction. I don't want to base my life on what I'm against. How boring. That's not inspiring enough motivation. I imagine the sooner we untether from the trap of "more," the clearer this will all become. We're building the scaffolding; the real construction comes next.

I value you desperately, my sisters and brothers in this adventure. I marvel at your gifts; you're so essential to this conversation. I am stunned by the collective goodness of the Bride. As I hear stories of intervention and reduction and courage, I applaud Jesus in selecting you for your tasks. We serve an unruly Savior on a recklessly wild ride; I'm glad you're on it with me. May we embrace unity over infighting, bravery over comfort, *us* over *me,* people over principles, and God's glory over our own. Together, let's become repairers of broken walls and restorers of streets with dwellings.

> *The Lord bless you*
> *and keep you;*
> *the Lord make his face shine on you*
> *and be gracious to you;*
> *the Lord turn his face toward you*
> *and give you peace. (Num. 6:24–26)*

CONCLUSION . . . TEN YEARS LATER

So I was right and wrong.

I was right about the preparation. I didn't have the slightest idea what the next decade was going to look like when I first wrote Simple & Free. I knew we'd have more kids. I knew there was a pressing on my life to lead in a larger, very visible way, but I had no clue what that meant. I knew we'd be launching kids out of this house in short order, and that required some muscle memory I learned during Simple & Free: the release, the open hands, the letting go. I had no idea Simple & Free would teach me how to hold my career loosely, which it did. And good thing, because I put the whole enterprise on the altar of conviction six years later by standing unequivocally with the LGBTQ community. I would lose a great deal, including this exact book you are holding, as it was pulled off every shelf and put out of print by its original publisher.

The irony is not lost on me, nor is the spiritual redemption. I forfeited the whole account; the Simple & Free story was erased from the public eye. My ministry was reduced, my voice silenced, and my belonging revoked. Less, less, less. Could I do it? Could I handle the losses? Could I let go of all I'd built and trust that God was leading me well? Would I be content with whatever was left and steward it well? Could I be faithful?

Yes. Simple & Free taught me how.

I was also wrong. At the original writing, I was still in the bull's-eye of American evangelical subculture. I had a sense of optimism that belongs only to the privileged and naïve. In the middle of the pack, you can't even see who is outside the flock. As I looked to my right and left, the crew I collaborated with—surprise!—looked a lot like me. I hadn't yet placed myself under leaders of color, or queer guides, or feminist scholars. My doctrines hadn't been challenged by liberation theology. I had yet to witness the fragmentation of the 81 percent from the 19 percent in the 2016 election. I was embedded in a small sect of western Christianity and I thought it was the whole world.

I assumed Simple & Free *would cement my advocacy primarily for the poor, but it actually prepared me to wage war against injustice. I learned to see discrepancies, double standards, hypocrisy, greed. I developed eyes to see bad fruit, power differentials, dehumanization, the lure and lie of prosperity. I needed every lesson* Simple & Free *offered me. Reengaging the posture of a student would serve me well; if I thought I learned a great deal during this project, I would become absolutely flattened by new input, new knowledge, and new ideas soon after. It seems like all I've done since is listen and learn, listen and learn. The next decade would require humility and courage, and* Simple & Free *built the scaffolding I'd need.*

This experimental mutiny against excess showed me that God and people matter. That's basically it. Everything else disintegrates when you clutch it too tightly. We have around one minute on this planet before our time is up, and this is our shot to build a more equitable world. It is our responsibility to challenge structures and systems that keep people out and down, locked in suffering while the same few prosper. This is our work. We are able in Jesus. His kingdom will come. His will done. May it be on earth as it is in heaven.

ACKNOWLEDGMENTS

No one lost their lunch on this joyride more than my family, swept up in another one of "my little ideas," as the hubs says. God love them. There are not four people I'd rather eat eighty pounds of avocados and learn how to compost with more than the Hatmaker tribe. Hey? I know! Let's add two more kids and become a full-fledged circus. I love you, family.

The second gaggle of people who invested in *Simple & Free* is The Council. For reasons yet unclear, you joined the fray and kept the wheels on. You ate seven foods and wore seven items of clothing and gave your stuff away and shut down Facebook . . . *and you weren't even getting paid*. Your wisdom and enthusiasm were my fuel. Becky, Molly, Jenny, Shonna, Susana, and Trina: I love you, you crazy, wild, hilarious, inappropriate, loyal girls. Be mine forever.

Our little Austin New Church family has changed my life in such acute ways I can no longer envision my life without you in it. You are adopting, sacrificing, fighting human trafficking, dreaming, fostering, feeding, building wells, building orphanages, building the kingdom. In the context of ANC, *Simple & Free* fit right in. I'm not even a weird girl around you people, and that is really saying something. I love you profoundly.

I want to thank the advocates and visionaries and dreamers and thinkers who guided me through the mazes of *Simple & Free*. I didn't understand demand-side economics. Now I do. I didn't know how sugar snap peas grow. Now I do. I've had so many teachers. Thank you for your books, your articles, your divergent and courageous lives. Keep saying what you're saying. It matters.

NOTES

SIMPLE & FREE: SEVEN YEARS LATER

1. Goodreads, https://www.goodreads.com/quotes/7-it-is-not-the
   -critic-who-counts-not-the-man.

INTRODUCTION

1. See Cru's obituary for Bill Bright, http://www.billbright.com/
   howtofast.

MONTH ONE: FOOD

1. I went to www.nutritiondata.com, but given how the Internet
   changes, a different site might be preferred depending on when
   you're reading this.

2. See "Caffeine Withdrawal Headache Explained," Science Daily,
   May 4, 2009, http://www.sciencedaily.com/releases/2009/05/
   090501162805.htm.

3. See "Ethiopia Rejects Warning of Hunger After Drought," BBC
   News, Dec. 31, 2009, http://news.bbc.co.uk/2/hi/africa/8436534
   .stm.

4. See the United Nations World Food Programme website, Ethiopia, http://www.wfp.org/countries/ethiopia.

5. See W. Travis McMaken, "Types of Theology," *DET,* Oct. 27, 2008, http://derevth.blogspot.com/2008/10/types-of-theology.html.

6. See Hillary Mayell, "As Consumerism Spreads, Earth Suffers, Study Says," NationalGeographic.com, Jan. 12, 2004, https://www.nationalgeographic.com/environment/2004/01/consumerism-earth-suffers/.

7. Michael Pollan, *In Defense of Food: An Eater's Manifesto* (New York: Penguin Books, 2008), 13–14.

8. Ibid., 6–7.

9. Ibid., 10.

10. See Boston Children's Hospital, "Explosion of Child Obesity Predicted to Shorten US Life Expectancy," EurekAlert, Mar. 16, 2005, http://www.eurekalert.org/pub_releases/2005-03/chb-eoc031605.php.

11. Barbara Kingsolver, *Animal Vegetable Miracle: A Year of Food Life* (New York: Harper Perennial: 2007), 126–27.

12. Abigail Abrams, "How Eating Less Meat Could Help Protect the Planet from Climate Change," *Time,* Aug. 8, 2019, https://time.com/5648082/un-climate-report-less-meat/.

13. Ibid.

14. Robert Goodland and Jeff Anhang, "Livestock and Climate Change," *World Watch,* Nov./Dec. 2009, https://awellfedworld.org/wp-content/uploads/Livestock-Climate-Change-Anhang-Goodland.pdf.

15. Alex Preston, review of Jonathan Safran Foer, *We Are the Weather, The Guardian,* Oct. 6, 2019, https://www.theguardian.com/books/2019/oct/06/jonathan-safran-foer-we-are-the-weather-saving-planet-begins-breakfast-review.

16. Tara Stiles, "High Fructose Corn Syrup: A Sweet Surprise for America?," Apr. 7, 2009, https://www.huffpost.com/entry/high-fructose-corn-syrup_b_172545.

17. Pollan, *In Defense of Food,* 150–52.

18. Richard Rohr, *Simplicity* (New York: Crossroad Publishing, 2003), 99–100.

MONTH TWO: CLOTHES

1. Susan Scafidi, *Who Owns Culture?: Appropriation and Authenticity in American Law* (New Brunswick, NJ: Rutgers University Press, 2005) quoted in Gretchen Brown, "Is It Cultural Appropriation?: Why Language Matters," *Rewire,* Nov. 22, 2019, https://www.rewire.org/our-future/cultural-appropriation/.

2. Benjamin R. Barber, *Consumed: How Markets Corrupt Children, Infantilize Adults, and Swallow Citizens Whole* (New York: W. W. Norton, 2007), 9.

3. Ibid., 9–11.

MONTH THREE: POSSESSIONS

1. Shane Claiborne, *The Irresistible Revolution* (Grand Rapids, MI: Zondervan, 2006), 113–14.

2. Per SafePlace.org.

3. Benjamin R. Barber, *Consumed: How Markets Corrupt Children, Infantilize Adults, and Swallow Citizens Whole* (New York: W. W. Norton, 2007), 11, 281.

4. Richard Rohr, *Simplicity* (New York: Crossroad Publishing, 2003), 59–60.

MONTH FOUR: MEDIA

1. See Matt Richtel, "Attached to Technology and Paying a Price," *New York Times,* June 6, 2010, http://www.nytimes.com/2010/06/07/technology/07brain.html?_r=1&pagewanted=all.

2. Ibid.

3. Chelsea Greenwood, "9 Subtle Ways Technology Is Making Humanity Worse," *Business Insider,* Aug 23, 2019, https://www.businessinsider.com/technology-negative-bad-effects-society-2019-8#instant-access-to-information-makes-us-less-self-sufficient-9.

4. Sean Illing, "Technology Isn't Just Changing Society—It's Changing What It Means to Be Human," Vox, Feb. 23, 2018, https://www.vox.com/technology/2018/2/23/16992816/facebook-twitter-tech-artificial-intelligence-crispr.

MONTH FIVE: WASTE

1. Wendell Berry, *What Are People For?* (New York: North Point, 1990), 98.

2. "Who We Are," The Karpophoreō Project, https://kprojectmlf .wordpress.com.

3. Per SustainableTable.org.

4. Judith D. Schwartz, "Buying Local: How It Boosts the Economy," *Time,* June 11, 2009, http://content.time.com/time/business/arti cle/0,8599,1903632,00.html.

5. Per SustainableConnections.org.

6. Craig Freudenrich, Ph.D., "How Landfills Work," HowStuffWorks, https://science.howstuffworks.com/environmental/green -science/landfill.htm.

7. Free Purity website, "Bottled Water vs. Tap Water," https://www .freepurity.com/blogs/resources/what-could-you-do-with-the -saved-money.

8. See "Reduce, Reuse, Recycle," EPA.gov, http://www.epa.gov/epa waste/conserve/rrr/reduce.htm.

9. Tracey Bianchi, *Green Mama* (Grand Rapids, MI: Zondervan, 2010), 18–19.

10. See "Alternative Fuels," FuelEconomy.gov, http://www.fuel economy.gov/feg/current.shtml.

11. See "Hybrids, Diesels, and Alternative Fuel Cars," FuelEconomy .gov, http://www.fueleconomy.gov/feg/byfueltype.htm.

12. See Planet E85, http://e85vehicles.com/e85/index.php?topic =467.0.

13. Steven Bouma-Prediger, *For the Beauty of the Earth: A Christian Vision for Creation Care* (Grand Rapids, MI: Baker Academic, 2010), 20.

14. Ibid., 182.

15. Matt McGrath, "Final Call to Save the World from 'Climate Ca-tastrophe,'" BBC News, Oct. 8, 2018, https://www.bbc.com/news /science-environment-45775309.

MONTH SIX: SPENDING

1. See Dictionary.com, http://dictionary.reference.com/browse/consumerism.

2. See "Organic Market Overview," Organic Trade Association, http://www.ota.com/organic/mt/business.html.

3. "The State of Human Development," United Nations Human Development Report 1998, chapter 1, 37.

4. Human Development Report 1998 Overview, United Nations Development Programme (UNDP).

5. J. Matthew Sleeth, *Serve God, Save the Planet: A Christian Call to Action* (Grand Rapids: Zondervan, 2007), 83.

6. Benjamin R. Barber, *Consumed: How Markets Corrupt Children, Infantilize Adults, and Swallow Citizens Whole* (New York: W. W. Norton, 2007), 292.

7. Ibid., 293–94.

8. See ChristianCadre.org.

9. *Epistles of Julian,* 49.

10. See ScienceBlogs, http://scienceblogs.com/casaubonsbook/2010/04/why_im_not_an_organic_purist.php.

MONTH SEVEN: STRESS

1. Macrina Wiederkehr, *Seven Sacred Pauses* (Notre Dame, IN: Sorin Books, 2008), 13.

2. Ibid., 14.

3. Ibid., 17.

4. Ibid., 29.

5. Ibid., 32.

6. Ibid., 138.

7. Ibid., 8, 26.

8. Ibid., 177.

9. Ibid., 147.

10. Henri Nouwen, *Seeds of Hope* (New York: Doubleday, 1997), 112.

JEN HATMAKER is the author of the *New York Times* bestsellers *For the Love* and *Fierce, Free, and Full of Fire*. She hosts the award-winning *For the Love* podcast, is the delighted curator of the Jen Hatmaker Book Club, and leads a tightly knit online community, reaching millions of people each week. Hatmaker is a cofounder of Legacy Collective, a giving community that grants millions of dollars around the world. She is a mom to five kids and lives happily just outside Austin, Texas, in a 1908 farmhouse with questionable plumbing.